By the Editors of ORGANIC GARDENING

600 Garden Answers

Expert Solutions to Your Gardening and Landscaping Problems.

Rodale Press, Emmaus, Pennsylvania

Contents

Part FOUR: **Beautify Your Home**

Part FIVE: **Keeping the Garden Healthy**

Introduction

You got questions? We got answers!

Hey, it would be tough for us not to have those answers. ORGANIC GARDENING magazine has been answering reader questions for more than 50 years now; questions about compost and sweet corn, raccoons and radicchio, raised bed building and tomato seed saving. In fact, we've got something like 600 issues worth of accurate organic answers under our belt—or is that under our staples?

Whichever, we want you to know that you've turned to the right place for the answers to your garden questions. In fact, you've done so twice and then twice again! How's that, you ask? Well, first of all, we pride ourselves on our relentless research and fanatical fact-checking; we don't give off-the-cuff answers, we call the experts to get it right and then we call them again to double-check those answers to be sure we get it right.

OK, you say, that's *one;* what're the other three? Well, the next reason we're the 'right place to turn' is that all our answers are chemical-free solutions. We not only solve your problems, we solve them safely, so you have a problem-free garden you can really feel good about.

And the 'twice again' explanation? That's easy—you're about to get a double-dose of those accurate organic answers! First you've got this great book just chock full of answers to some of the most common garden questions we encounter. And you've got ORGANIC GARDENING magazine coming, each page of which will be packed with info, inspiration and yes, even more answers to your garden problems—just when you need them the most!

So—any questions?

Didn't think so. Welcome aboard!

Mike McGrath
Editor
ORGANIC GARDENING magazine

Build a Better Garden

Chapter 1

Tips to Plan and Plant a Bountiful Garden

Planning Your Plot

Turn, Turn, Turn

Q. If you fertilize carefully, does it hurt to plant the same vegetable in the same spot each year?

A. Regardless of how well you fertilize, you should rotate garden crops every year. The more you move your crops around, the more diversified the demands placed on the soil and the more varied your cultivation practices will be. By growing one crop in the same space every year, you increase the likelihood of certain insects establishing themselves in the area. As a result, you'll see increasing insect problems in coming years. However, if you practice good rotations, you will be cultivating the same ground at a different time each year, disturbing many insects' life cycles.

Additionally, by rotating legumes with non-legumes, your fertilization requirements will be reduced because the legumes will leave nitrogen in the soil. Another advantage of good rotations is the buildup of minerals near the top layers of the soil by the roots of the different plants. While one plant may accumulate calcium in its roots, another may do the same for manganese; by rotating, you allow the crops that follow to take advantage of the accumulated minerals.

Small-Time Rotation

Q. **As long as I use plenty of compost, is a rotation plan actually worthwhile for a small garden?**

A. The smaller a garden gets, the harder crop rotation becomes. Still, there's no substitute if you want to avoid disease and pest buildup and keep soil nutrients from becoming depleted. Move your crops around the patch as much as possible.

A New Direction

Q. **Should the rows of a garden be planted east to west or north to south?**

A. The best advice is to orient rows and pathways according to the lay of the land. Rows should run across a slope to prevent erosion. If your land allows, however, you can choose either direction, according to your needs.

Concern with row and path orientation centers around the shading that occurs in early morning and late afternoon. During summer, the sun is essentially overhead through most of the day, so row direction has little effect on how much sunlight reaches plants. Early and late in the day, however, tall crops can cast shade on short ones. When rows run east to west, most of the shadow a crop casts falls on its own row members. When rows go north and south, all of the shadow a crop casts falls on the adjacent rows. For that reason, east-to-west planting has been the traditional recommendation. But you can use these shadows to advantage. For example, shade from corn can protect fall cauliflower transplants from the late-afternoon heat.

Battling Bolting

Q. **What is meant by the term *bolting*, and what causes it?**

A. Bolting is a term used by gardeners to describe the flowering of a vegetable. It refers most often to plants grown for their foliage, like lettuce, spinach, and Chinese cabbage, but can also apply to celery stalks, onion bulbs, or broccoli.

While bolting is a natural part of the plant's life cycle, it is undesirable for gardeners because it turns the edible portion of the plant bitter. In the case of onions, it keeps the bulb from developing fully and creates a woody core.

Several environmental factors induce bolting. Hot weather causes lettuce and spinach to bolt, but cold spring weather makes celery flower. Alternating periods of cold and warmth promote bolting in onions and Chinese cabbage. Onions also may bolt if exposed to drought or insect stress. These vegetables are all cool-weather crops, so they tend to do best in spring and fall. To prevent bolting in celery, don't expose the plants to night temperatures below 45°F for an extended period. Generally, careful timing of plantings will help prevent bolting.

A Well-Bred Plant

Q. I have often seen the word _cultivar_ used. Could you define it for me?

A. A cultivar (short for cultivated variety) is a plant that has been selected or hybridized. It probably wouldn't be able to survive for more than a few generations outside the garden. The term was coined by botanists to distinguish cultivated varieties from natural or botanical varieties of species—those that originated and reproduce in the wild. Most garden plants are cultivars, but the term is used interchangeably with variety, horticultural variety, and garden variety in most garden publications.

Seed and Seedling Stumpers

Seed-Storing Savvy

Q. What's the best way to store seeds?

A. It's best to store seeds in a cool, dry place—a closet, for instance. The refrigerator is a good storage place, too, but don't store them in the freezer.

To store seeds in the refrigerator, keep them in a jar tightly covered with a canning lid to seal out moisture. Dehumidify the air inside the jar by covering the bottom with a layer of silica gel (about an inch per gallon jar), available from camera stores, or with 2 heaping tablespoons of powdered milk folded into a pouch of Kleenex or other facial tissue. If you use powdered milk, discard and replace it twice a year. Silica gel can be dried and reused indefinitely. Naturally, it's a good idea to use seeds as soon as possible, because no matter how well you store them, time has a way of draining seed vitality.

Germination on Trial

Q. **I have a lot of seeds left over from last year. How can I tell if they're still good?**

A. Most vegetable seeds will remain capable of germinating for three to five years if stored under cool, dry conditions. But the only way to know for sure if they'll sprout is to run a germination test.

Count out 20 seeds from the same packet. Spread them on three layers of premoistened paper towels, then roll them up carefully in the paper so the seeds stay separated. Tuck the rolled paper towels in a plastic bag and keep the incubating seeds in a warm place. If you're testing more than one batch, be sure to label each roll.

Check the seeds after two or three days, then check them every day thereafter for a week. If a root or cotyledon protrudes through the seed coat, the seed has germinated. Allow three weeks for most varieties to germinate, then calculate the rate of germination. Ten seeds out of 20 means 50 percent germination. Fifteen seeds out of 20 means 75 percent germination. Adjust the number of seeds you plant according to the percentage of seeds that germinated. For instance, if three-fourths of the test seeds germinated, sow one-fourth more of those particular seeds than you would ordinarily plant.

Toss Old Seed

Q. **I got 50 percent germination when I tested my three- to four-year-old lettuce and carrot seed. Is it OK to use the seed, as long as I sow extra thickly, or should I throw it away?**

A. When the germination percentage drops by more than one-third, it's best to throw away or compost the seed, says Dr. Jim Alston, director of research at Park Seed Company. Old seed tends to produce weaker, slower-growing and poor-yielding plants. But even if you use new seed, germination percentages will vary widely. For example, while the minimum official federal germination percentage set by the U.S. Department of Agriculture (USDA) for new lettuce seed is 80 percent, it's only 55 percent for carrot seed. Since the germination of the lettuce seed has dropped by at least one-third, you should probably discard it, but the carrot seed is OK to use.

Saving Hybrid Seed

Q. Would you explain the difference between hybrid and regular seeds? Can you save hybrid seeds for next year's garden?

A. Seeds described as "F-1 hybrids" are produced by crossing two pure strains, usually inbred. Often, these two strains are not particularly striking themselves, but when they are artificially cross-pollinated, the resulting plants may have more vigor and produce better than either parent. If you save seed from these varieties, the hybrid vigor is lost in the second generation, and the result will probably be unlike either of the parents. Seed from "open-pollinated" or "standard" stock, on the other hand, will stay true for generation after generation; so if you save seed, stick to these varieties and avoid hybrids.

Beware Cross-Pollinators?

Q. Can you plant several varieties of the same vegetable (like squash) together and not have the cross-pollination affect their taste and appearance?

A. Cross-pollination has little noticeable effect on the taste and appearance of vegetables. Only the characteristics of the seed are affected. The portion we are after—and generally call the fruit of the plant—is tissue that surrounds the seed. It is part of the mother plant, not the seed, and remains unchanged genetically by cross-pollination.

Squash, for example, cross-pollinates readily. The fruit will be true to the parent plant, while the seeds inside will be changed. Corn is the major exception. It cross-pollinates easily, and the part we eat *is* the seed. Popcorn and sweet corn planted too close together can produce poor-quality crops of both. Some of the new supersweet varieties can lose nearly all their sweetness due to cross-pollination. Peas, dry beans, and limas—because of the mechanics of their blossoms—are almost always self-pollinated.

Colorful Seed Coats

Q. **I've heard that most bean seeds sold in the North are treated by coating them with dangerous fungicides. Tell me why that is so, and where I can order untreated seeds.**

A. Actually, it appears that most of the big seed companies *don't* put fungicides on seed unless the customer requests it. The few that *do* routinely treat bean seed will sell you untreated seed if you ask for it.

The reason large seeds like bean, pea, corn, and sometimes squash, melon, and cucumber are ever treated is to protect the germinating seeds from rot if they are planted in cold, damp soil. The chemical used most frequently is captan, a fungicide that has been linked to birth defects. Seed rot is easily avoided without fungicide. Just wait until the soil has warmed thoroughly. A well-drained, friable soil helps, too.

You should be able to spot coated seed by its powdery surface, which is usually colored blue, pink, or purple. But to make sure you're getting safe, untreated seed, check in the catalog for a note explaining the company's policy. If you can't find a note, beware. Call or write the company if you're not sure.

Let's Seed
Some Identification

Q. **What is meant by** *certified seed*?

A. Certified seed is guaranteed to be true to name and uncontaminated with other varieties. State-run certification programs were begun in the early 1900s to preserve the genetic purity of new varieties, and all subscribe to the standards of the Federal Seed Act, signed into law in 1939. Today, there are about 45 programs, primarily overseeing agricultural crops and grass seed. Vegetable varieties are federally protected by the Plant Variety Protection Office and the Plant Patenting Office.

Seed potatoes (the small potato tubers that are planted instead of true seed) are also certified by state-run programs. However, the objective is to provide disease-free seed to growers. Certified seed potatoes aren't guaranteed to be free of diseases but have been spot-checked by inspectors. Seed cannot be certified if bacterial ring rot or viruses are identified. Small percentages of fungal diseases may be allowed.

Dr. Frank Manza, a potato pathologist at the University of Maine, stresses that home gardeners should always request certified seed potatoes, both to ensure a productive crop of their own and to prevent the spread of disastrous potato diseases to other gardens and commercial fields.

Confusing Calculations

Q. **Being a relatively new gardener, I'd like to ask about a problem I have interpreting the phrase "Safe Planting Dates for Vegetables in the Open." Does this mean that it's safe to plant seed in the ground, or does it mean it's safe to transplant the plant itself into the garden?**

A. Both. Basically, these dates indicate the earliest safe time for sowing seeds outdoors. They also mark the earliest times to put transplants out safely. "Safe planting date" differs from "frost-free date." For weeks after the frost-free date, the soil temperature may remain too low and the daylength too short for many tender plants to survive. Check with your county agent for planting dates in your own area.

Speeding Up Seeds

Q. **If a seed requires a minimum soil temperature of 50°F to germinate, and my soil is 45°F in the morning and 55°F late in the day, how do I know when to plant?**

A. The seed will begin germination as soon as the temperature gets above its 50-degree minimum requirement. Soil temperature affects how quickly germination takes place. In this case, when the soil temperature drops into the forties at night, the process will stop until temperatures get back into the required range.

The best way to decide when to plant is to take soil temperature readings at the planting depth for the seed. Read at sunset for the day's high and early in the morning for the low. You can plant when the daily average matches the seed's minimum requirement.

Taking soil temperatures is very easy to do. The most convenient thermometer for this reading is the long-stemmed dial type, which can be found in scientific supply catalogs. Besides being the surest way of knowing the right time for planting, soil thermometers can be used to show the effects of mulching and irrigation, or to see when the compost pile needs turning.

Give Seeds the Hot Seat

Q. **Is bottom heat necessary for starting vegetable seeds?**

A. It's not essential, but bottom heat is a sure way to keep the soil temperature at a steady 70° to 75°F—the best temperature for germination of most vegetable seeds. Tomato, melon, eggplant, celery, and brassica seeds do best at 70° to 75°F, while lettuce has a range from 65° to 70°F. Soil-heating cables can be used in flats indoors, in greenhouse beds, or outdoors in insulated coldframes. Although these cables maintain ideal temperatures for only pennies a day, you can also use the free heat available on top of your water heater or console television or near a radiator or woodstove. Check the soil temperature in the flat periodically with a soil thermometer. Once the seedlings are established, remove them from the heat.

Scheduling Ins and Outs

Q. **What is the most desirable schedule for sowing my seeds indoors and transplanting my seedlings into the garden?**

A. There is no set time for sowing and transplanting, since so much depends on climate, soil temperature, and seed varieties. You should allow six to eight weeks for germination and seedling growth indoors, so count back that much before the date you'll plant the seedlings outside. For example, cold-sensitive seedlings like tomatoes should be ready for transplanting about one week after the last spring frost date.

Most seeds germinate well at soil temperatures between 70° and 80°F, and most seedlings do best between 60° and 75°F. The temperature of your room affects seedling growth, too. If it is cold, you can expect the plants to take the full eight weeks, and then some, to reach transplanting size. If it's warm, then you can figure on less growing time.

Let There Be Light

Q. How much light do my vegetable seedlings need for a good start indoors?

A. That all depends on whether you grow them by a window, grow them exclusively under fluorescent lights, or use both. In January or February, even a south window may not offer seedlings the full 18 hours of light they require for optimum growth. A rule of thumb is to augment 6 to 8 hours of natural light with 10 to 12 hours under fluorescent tubes. If plants get no outside light, keep them under the fluorescents for the full 18 hours.

You don't need special plant-growth lights, which are designed mainly for year-round indoor houseplants. Standard fluorescent tubes designed for room lighting will produce stocky, thick-stemmed seedlings and cost only pennies a day to run. Never use common incandescent light bulbs, because they produce light chiefly in the red end of the spectrum. Such light makes plants tall and spindly, with pale, thin leaves. Incandescents also give off heat, which dries out the soil surface and the fragile plants growing under them.

A double row of fluorescent tubes provides sufficient light to grow a 16-inch-wide array of plants. One tube will illuminate a 6-inch-wide band. Because seedlings need more intense light than mature plants, keep the light tubes as close as possible to the leaves, short of touching them. Be sure to turn the flats every day to prevent seedlings at the ends of the rows from getting leggy as they stretch for more light. To make sure that seedlings get all the light they need, replace fluorescents when they reach 70 percent of their stated service life. By that time, they'll be delivering about 15 percent less light than when new.

Let It Be Close

Q. How far above my seed flats should I hang fluorescent lights?

A. Lights should be no more than 3 or 4 inches above seedlings for the first three to four weeks after germination, or they'll get leggy. In fact, veteran gardener Nancy Bubel recommends keeping seedlings as close as possible to the fluorescent tubes without letting the foliage touch the glass. As the young plants grow, raise the lights slightly (or lower the flats). For the most even growth, shift the positions of the flats every week or so, since light at the ends of the tubes tends to be somewhat weaker.

No Fungus among Us

Q. **I've had trouble with damping-off disease for several seasons now. Is there any way to prevent this organically? I'd prefer not to bake my potting soil in the oven to sterilize it.**

A. Damping-off is a fungal disease that causes wilting and early death of seedlings. The fungus parasites usually grow near the soil surface and enter the tiny plants at the point where they emerge from the ground.

Crowding of seedlings, high humidity, and lack of sufficient aeration all favor damping-off. If you're sowing seeds outdoors, remedial measures include thinning the seedlings, ensuring proper ventilation, drying the soil in which the seedlings are growing, and sprinkling powdered charcoal or finely pulverized clay on the ground.

To keep damping-off from gaining a foothold indoors, start with a good potting soil. Make fast compost, which heats up to 150°F or more—pasteurizing temperature. When the temperature drops to 110°F, sift the compost and store it in a tightly closed plastic bag until the time comes to mix the potting soil. Blend this compost 50–50 with vermiculite or perlite. These are both created by a high-heat process and are usually sterile. Add a little steamed bonemeal. This potting mix will be free of disease organisms.

When you plant the seeds, you can cover them with "play sand" which has already been sterilized. It is available at most lumberyards. The sand ensures that the neck of the seedling—where damping-off attacks—will be surrounded with a sterile medium that contains no nutrients to support reinfection by disease organisms via the air. Keep the area around the seedlings cool, well lit, and well ventilated. Don't plant them so thickly that they are overcrowded, and don't overwater.

One type of damping-off attacks seedlings before they break through the ground. If there are many blank spaces in your seed-starting flats, this may be your problem. The disease attacks seeds in cold, wet soils. Use bottom heat to get the seedlings up and out of the earth fast.

Hints for Hardening-Off

Q. **What's the safest way to harden-off seedlings?**

A. Start by giving seedlings a cool, dry week without fertilizer. The temperature should be several degrees lower than that at which the seedlings were raised. The result will be a shorter, more fibrous plant that suffers less from the transition to the outdoors.

If the seedlings have been indoors and have never had full sun, expose them to a few hours of *filtered* sun each day—in the shade of a bush, porch railing, lath house, or any improvised shelter. Daytime temperatures should range from 60° to 70°F. Gradually increase the amount of sun the plant receives until, at the end of a week or ten days, the seedling is accustomed to a full day in the sun. To protect the plants from strong and gusty winds, choose a sheltered corner for the plant's first week outdoors. Make sure to keep the soil moist enough to prevent wilting.

Although some gardeners like to soak the planting flat with a liquid fertilizer just before setting the plants in the garden, try leaving them a little on the hungry side. The roots will then put out extensive new growth in search of food when the plant is placed in its permanent home.

Working the Soil

Plowing Preference

Q. **Perhaps you can settle an argument I'm having with my neighbor. I say it's best to plow in the spring. He says it's best to plow in the fall. What do you say?**

A. Spring tilling is best. Some people plow in the fall to "roughen up" their soil to help it hold water and stem erosion, but a thickly sown cover crop of rye is far superior. Laying the soil bare to the elements over winter kills off many beneficial soil organisms in the layer that alternately freezes and thaws. The soil could be recolonized by disease organisms instead of friends. A cover crop with roots that hold the soil together, covered with mulch during the frozen months, is the best way to take the garden through the winter. The mulch and cover crop can be tilled in during the spring, adding lots of decaying organic matter to the soil.

Hop Off Those Clods

Q. **Please clarify the following statement: "Do not work soils when they are wet, especially those with considerable clay. This causes damage to the tilth, or physical structure, of the soil, which may last for a long time."**

A. The structure of topsoil is very easily destroyed, particularly when clayey soils are plowed when too wet or too dry. Wet clay soil becomes sticky and easily molded into various forms under pressure—by tiller or otherwise. The end result is that the turned earth forms hard clods when the soil is allowed to dry.

In clay soils, work around the problem by keeping cultivation to a minimum, especially in wet areas. Sand added to such soils helps. You want the soil to be left with a granular structure that is suitable for seeding yet coarse enough at the surface to resist erosion and the puddling that results from heavy rains.

Ground Work

Q. **Would you elaborate on the expression "as soon as the ground can be worked"? It appears regularly in planting instructions, but no one I've asked has a good explanation of its meaning.**

A. The soil can be "worked" when it thaws and dries enough to be plowed, tilled, or dug without causing serious compaction. In many areas of the country, the ground is saturated with water in the early spring. If turned over before it is sufficiently dry, compaction and loss of soil structure will result. The surface can turn into hard dry lumps, making it difficult for seedlings to emerge. Generally, the higher the clay content of the soil, the longer you have to wait to begin digging. A high amount of organic matter will offset this by improving drainage and aeration. On the other hand, sandy loam soils may never have a problem with excess moisture and can be worked as soon as the weather warms enough.

To see if your soil is ready, place a shovelful in a pot with drainage holes. If water seeps out the bottom, your garden is still too wet and shouldn't be worked. Another rule of thumb is to take a handful of soil and squeeze it. If it forms a ball, there's too much moisture in it. If it crumbles, however, you can get to work.

The Long and Short of It

Q. **Do fast-maturing vegetables use fewer nutrients than longer-season varieties?**

A. Generally, the total plant weight is the primary factor in determining the amount of nutrients removed from the soil. But there's no simple answer. A few varieties of short-season crops may require less fertilizer. If you grow a compact tomato that starts producing early, it may require fewer nutrients than a heavy-yielding, late-maturing variety that produces large vines.

In many cases, you will need to fertilize fast-maturing vegetables more heavily at planting time because they take up minerals at a faster rate than their later-maturing counterparts. Vegetables that begin bearing early in the season and outproduce later varieties definitely need more nutrients than ones that are slower to mature.

Mulch-Gardening

Q. Would you please explain how vegetables grown from seed sprinkled on top of the soil and covered with mulch can obtain sufficient nutrients?

A. This method of gardening is most often used for growing potatoes, as the tubers prefer a moist, cool soil and the mulch provides just that. While the plant's roots grow down into the soil, the tubers are formed in the mulch, not underground, making harvesting easier. In tests at the Rodale Research Center, researchers found that you can expect an increase of 40 percent or more in potato yield by planting in a mulch. The method they used called for tilling the plot and planting the seed potatoes in a small furrow so the eyes were just covered. Then a 6-inch layer of mulch was put on top. No weeding was needed during the growing season, thanks to the mulch.

The traditional method of mulch-planting calls for laying the seed potatoes directly on top of the soil and covering with mulch. In the Rodale test, this was not done because of the possibilities of mice eating the potatoes and of the tubers drying out before they sprouted. In other cases of mulch-gardening, the mulch is scraped away from the soil, the seeds are planted in the soil, and when small seedlings are established, the mulch is pulled up to the seedlings for the remainder of the growing season.

The Safety Factor

Pollution Solution

Q. My garden is near a road. Can auto emissions be washed off my vegetables?

A. Yes, if you use a little vinegar or dishwashing liquid in the wash water. Washing lettuce and other crops with water alone removes only a small amount of lead, the most serious hazard from auto emissions. But washing the vegetables in a dilute vinegar or soap solution removes most of the lead, according to research by plant physiologist Nina Bassuk at Cornell University in New York State. Use a 1 percent solution of vinegar (about 2½ tablespoons to a gallon of water) or half that amount of dishwashing liquid. Vegetables can also absorb heavy metals like lead and cadmium that get into the soil from auto exhaust. You can't wash them away, but a pH above 6.5 will prevent uptake of lead and cadmium. (See pages 26–28 for more information concerning pH.) If you haven't already done so, plant a hedge or erect a solid fence between your garden and the road to help shield the garden from auto emissions.

Skip the Salt

Q. **The border of our property gets saturated with road salt every winter. What can we do to correct or prevent this problem for the garden plants, trees, and shrubs already located there?**

A. Consider erecting a barrier, possibly of wood, to keep the salt spray from covering your garden or trees. If a barrier is impractical, a heavy mulch, such as leaves that will pack down, will provide more protection to plants than no mulch or even a light mulch. (But don't work the salt-covered leaves into your garden in the spring!) You might also bank your garden beds in the fall with a layer of black plastic mulch, sloped away from the garden but held in place by regular mulching materials.

Reoyle Washing-Machine Water?

Q. **I am a gardener in Arizona and wonder about the effects of washing-machine water on the vegetable garden. Does it matter whether I use nonbiodegradable or biodegradable soaps? Water is expensive in this arid climate, and almost daily watering is necessary.**

A. The common problem with soaps and detergents is that they both contain sodium, an element that, in excessive amounts, is harmful to soils (it destroys soil aggregation) as well as to plants (it induces tissue burn). The best strategy is to use as little soap as possible and to choose soap flakes or biodegradable soaps rather than detergents.

Avoid softeners that are rich in sodium-based compounds, minimize or eliminate bleach, and absolutely stay away from boron-based (borax) detergents. Low-phosphate detergents are preferable because they generally contain less sodium.

If you want to recycle your washing-machine water, the key is to direct the water onto the soil via a soaker hose or to run the water out the end of the hose to flood the soil. Do not spray recycled water on leaves! At the end of the hose you may want to attach a cloth bag (cotton or canvas) with a hose clamp to intercept particulates and soap residues.

If at all possible, collect the water in a 55-gallon drum after it is flushed from the washing machine. Make sure the drum has a valve for water to escape. This method enables the higher concentration of soap in the first washing cycle to become diluted by later rinse cycles.

Septic Tank Garden?

Q. Would it be advisable to plant a vegetable garden over our septic field?

A. Because there's a chance of pathogenic organisms in the soil (especially if sewage does find its way to the surface occasionally), it's better to plant food crops in other areas where direct contact with effluent is not possible.

Walnuts at 50 Paces

Q. Last spring we set out our tomato transplants 30 feet from the base of the black walnut tree in our yard. Still, they all died by mid-July. How far away must tomatoes be planted to escape any of the tree's toxic effects?

A. Your tomatoes should be safe if planted at a distance equal to 1½ times the height of the tree. Black, Persian, and Japanese walnut roots release a potent toxin called juglone. So do the roots of butternut, a close relative. The allelopathic effect extends through the area occupied by the tree roots. Peppers, alfalfa, apple trees, peonies, blackberries, mountain laurels, and red pines are all hurt by the toxin. It remains effective for a year after a walnut tree is removed.

Grains and other shallow-rooted plants are not hindered. Kentucky bluegrass and black raspberries actually seem to benefit from being planted near walnuts. As yet, plant pathologists haven't been able to explain why.

On the Lighter Side

Q. To prevent burglaries, many people around here keep their backyards lighted all night. What effect does the constant light have on garden plants and fruit trees?

A. Almost none. Most security lights are either high-pressure or low-pressure sodium lamps. The intensity of light they produce is too low to endanger the fruiting or growth of nearby plants. In addition, many common fruits and vegetables are day-neutral— their growth and fruiting are neither harmed nor helped by longer photoperiods.

Gardening with Tires

Q. Are tires safe to use in the garden? I'd like to use some as coldframes for my melons but am concerned that tires may contain harmful chemicals.

A. Yes, they're safe. In past years, we've recommended not using tires, but new information shows they will not harm plants. While tires contain some iron and zinc from the manufacturing process, these are actually essential plant nutrients, explains agricultural engineer Dr. A. Higgins of Rutgers University, who has studied the use of shredded tires in sludge composting. The amount of lead from car exhaust that may be on the surface would not be enough to cause concern, according to Higgins and USDA lead specialist Dr. Rufus Chaney.

Asbestos Woes

Q. I have a vegetable garden next to an old barn with an asbestos-shingle roof. Could the rainwater running off the roof onto my vegetables cause a health hazard?

A. As long as the shingles are in good condition, the asbestos fibers will remain tightly bonded and the chance of any getting on your vegetables is slight, says Stephen Schanamann, environmental protection specialist with the Environmental Protection Agency's Asbestos Action Program.

If the shingles are showing signs of wear, like breakage, cracking, or cupping, the risk of exposure to fibers is greater. Consider replacing the roof or channeling the runoff to deep drains.

Rubbish to Radishes

Q. If I incorporate kitchen scraps into an area of my garden, how long should I wait before planting vegetables there? Will the scraps attract animals?

A. The best way to compost directly in your garden is to dig a 1-foot-deep trench down the center of a bed or in between two rows. Each time you put kitchen scraps into the trench, cover them with 2 to 4 inches of soil. Vegetables can be planted over the filled-in trench at any time. Animals generally won't bother compost that is covered with soil, but if they do, try burying it a little deeper or cover the spot with several inches of mulch.

The Right Vermiculite

Q. Is it safe to substitute insulation-grade vermiculite for horticultural vermiculite in potting soil?

A. No. Insulation-grade vermiculite contains high amounts of magnesium limestone and can have a pH as high as 9.8. It makes potting soil too alkaline, leading to micronutrient deficiencies. Horticultural vermiculite is mined in Georgia, has a nearly neutral pH (7.0 to 7.5), and doesn't tie up micronutrients.

Plastic Potting Soil

Q. Can polystyrene packing materials be shredded and safely added to potting soil in place of vermiculite?

A. Polystyrene is safe to add—it doesn't biodegrade or release toxic substances into the soil—but it replaces perlite, not vermiculite. Unlike vermiculite, which absorbs large amounts of water, perlite and polystyrene hold water only on their surfaces, promoting fast soil drainage.

Polystyrene beads or flakes are harder to wet and hold less water than perlite, causing the soil to dry faster, according to researchers and commercial growers who have compared the two materials. Polystyrene is also lighter than perlite, making it more difficult to mix with soil and more likely to float to the top with heavy watering.

To make mixing easier, moisten the soil before adding polystyrene, then water from the bottom or gently from the top until plants are established. Because polystyrene melts at high temperatures, it must be added after the soil has been sterilized.

Projects

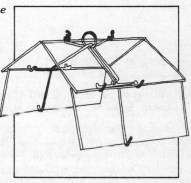

Barn Cloche

Barn Cloches

Q. I'd like to make some barn cloches. Could you please explain how they are constructed? What kind of frame is required?

A. Four pieces of 12-by-24-inch glass are held together by a set of bent heavy-gauge wire. Although single-strength window glass will work, it is better to use thicker glass (at least ⅛ inch) double strength.

Good to the Last Drip

Q. My husband and I are interested in installing a watering system for a vegetable garden and 40 fruit trees. What type do you recommend?

A. A drip-irrigation system has several advantages over sprinkler irrigation and may suit your needs. It uses one-third to one-half less water, reduces weed growth, and eliminates moisture stress.

These systems come as kits with five parts: head, filter, header, laterals, and emitters. The head, with a filter to prevent clogging, is attached to the water source. Then the header, a hose that carries water to the garden, is attached with laterals connected to it that run along beds or rows. The emitters, flexible tubes with a tiny hole in the end of each tube for water to drip out slowly (1 to 4 gallons per hour), extend from the laterals to the base of each plant. (For very closely spaced plants, substitute a drip tube for the emitters. It allows water to seep out along its length.)

To decide how many feet of each part you need, plot your garden's and orchard's dimensions on graph paper and plan the irrigation layout. Since the lines, made from polyethylene or PVC, will degrade in sunlight, they should be covered. The orchard section can be buried, allowing enough slope to drain the water if you live in an area with hard winter freezes. In the garden, cover the hoses with mulch and for longest life, store in a protected place over the winter.

Homemade Capillary Mat

Q. What kind of material should I use to make a capillary mat for watering seed flats and houseplants from below?

A. Use the cheapest acrylic blanket you can buy, advises Tom Seiler, past president of the Philadelphia chapter of the Indoor Light Gardening Society of America. Many light gardeners prefer them to commercial capillary mats, he says. Capillary watering will work only if there is direct contact between the mat and the potting soil, so don't cover drainage holes with crockery. When you place a container on the mat, water it from above the first time to start capillary flow. Thereafter, keep the mat moist.

Compost-Heated Hotbed

Q. How do I build and use a hotbed?

A. First, dig a pit to accommodate 2 feet of compost. Then fill the pit with composting materials and let it sit about a week or until it starts to heat up. Cover the compost with a foot of rich soil and plant your crops in it. In a week to ten days, the soil should be well warmed.

Hot compost below a coldframe can raise soil temperatures ten degrees higher than normal, but after about seven weeks, the hotbeds cool off to soil temperature. Thus, hotbeds are more practical in the spring, providing moderate, steady heat early in the season, while it's coldest outside. (In fall, you can always force the cold-hardy, leafy-green vegetables to mature earlier. Hotbeds are less useful in fall because the compost is working while the weather is warmest. Before the vegetables can mature, the compost will have stopped heating and the weather will have turned cold.)

Chapter 2

Soil and Soil-Building Basics

Secrets of the Soil

Keys to Soil Colors

Q. Could you give me a basic explanation of soil color? I've always been curious about the different colors of the soil and wondered how to interpret them.

A. The changes in soil color that you see from one area to the next usually mean that there was a difference in mineral development sometime along the way. Mineral deposits create characteristic colors and consistencies. Here are a few of the signals:

• Whitish colors usually indicate that a heavier concentration of salts and lime deposits are present in the soil.

• A dark color indicates a high level of organic matter. Black soil can mean good humus content, but it may mean nothing more than manganese-bearing rock particles.

• Reddish soils usually have a high iron content.

• "Spotty" soil that shows different colors, particularly shades of rust, reveals a problem with insufficient aeration. This type of soil goes through periods during the year when it cannot get enough oxygen.

• Blue, gray, or greenish subsoil suffers from periodic waterlogging.

- Tan, light gray, or light bluish-gray usually indicates poor soil, but subsoils of these colors often contain good supplies of minerals.

Indicator Plants

Q. **I'm thinking of buying some property. What can I tell about the soil from the plants that grow there?**

A. Plants can tell you a lot about the soil they grow in. An obvious example is the cattail. Cattails thrive in wet, marshy soil—which is far from ideal for a garden. Other plants that like wet soil include marsh marigold, nutsedge, porcelain vine, skunk cabbage, pin oak, red maple, swamp white oak, sour gum, weeping willow, honeyset, starwort, winterberry, and buttonbush. If you see tiny mosses that give the soil surface a greenish tinge that persists into the summer, this area is also too wet for gardening. But it can be reclaimed for gardening if it is tile-drained.

If you are looking for an ideal spot for your garden, look for burdock, pigweed, lamb's-quarters, and purslane. They flourish in well-drained, fertile soil with lots of organic matter. You'll almost always find good-sized walnut trees on rich ground—often in well-drained river or creek bottom soil. Stay away from areas with sorrel, mayweed, broomsedge, and chamomile, unless you are willing to work to develop the soil. These plants are usually a sign of soil that's lacking in humus and fertility.

Bluegrass and alfalfa thrive on land that is not too acid. Scrub oak, white cedar, huckleberry, hemlock, fir, azalea, blueberry, pine, mountain laurel, rhododendron, white birch, and red cedar are often signs of acid soil. If you find many of these plants on the property you're looking at, it may be more suitable for a woodland garden than a lush lawn.

The Look of Loam

Q. **Gardeners frequently use the phrase "good fertile loam." Just exactly what does that mean?**

A. Good loam soil has lots of silt in it, as well as enough clay and sand particles to give it good texture and structure. It also has plenty of organic matter. The secretions of earthworms, slugs, and snails, plus decayed vegetation, a host of bacteria, and fungi in the soil, all combine to create loam. You can tell good loam by touch. If the soil feels soft and oily when you rub it between your fingers, it's probably fertile loam. Squeeze fertile loam soil and it will hold together for just a minute in a loose lump; however, it will fall as crumbly bits when you drop it back on the ground.

Taming Tough Clay

Q. **My California soil is gray clay. I sink into it up to my ankles in winter, but in summer it gets so dry it develops wide cracks. I tried gardening in raised beds filled with topsoil, but yields were poor. How can I rebuild this soil?**

A. Stick with raised beds. To improve crop yields, it's more important to add organic matter than topsoil. You will need to add lots of it annually. The best approach is a three-part program: compost, mulch, and cover crops.

One *Organic Gardening* contributor from California, John Meeker, has done wonders with heavy clay. To start, he applied three dump truck loads of compost on 800 feet of raised beds, then tilled it in. Timing is critical, says Meeker, since there is only a brief period between wet and dry when clay soils will crumble easily in your fingers. Meeker used mushroom compost, but he recommends substituting the best locally available materials. For fastest results, the materials should be fully composted.

Always keep the soil covered, either with mulch or with cover crops. The mulch keeps soil and compost moist so the plants can make the most of it. As the mulch rots, it adds more organic matter. Cover crops trap the nutrients you have added, and they add more organic matter. Their roots break up heavy soil. Plant a cover crop as soon as a patch of ground has been harvested for the season, then turn it under one week before planting. Meeker uses buckwheat in warm weather and fava beans interplanted with rye when it's cool.

Adobe Gardening

Q. **We will be moving to the Southwest this year and hope to start a garden. Having lived in a relatively moist climate all our lives, we're not sure how to prepare the soil in that dry area. Can you help?**

A. The adobe soils of the Southwest tend to be heavy clay that is often rich in minerals but almost entirely deficient in humus. Sometimes they are a mixture of clay and silt. Of all soil types, adobe is one that benefits most from organic gardening methods. Since it's heavy, it requires aeration. In its natural state, this soil will contain no earthworms, and it will probably be alkaline. The pH will register at 7.5 or above. Because of this, some essential nutrients, such as phosphorus and iron, will be unavailable to your plants.

You can minimize all of these problems by adding humus. Then the soil will become easier to till and will retain moisture. Add earthworms to the humus and they'll flourish. Since humus is a neutralizer, it will bring the alkalinity down to a suitable level for many garden plants. This will free iron and phosphorus for your vegetables. Supplement these nutrients by using ground phosphate rock and acidic organic materials such as peat moss, sawdust, and oak leaves if your soil is still iron-deficient.

Double-Digging Duty

Q. **I have double-dug my garden about 2 feet deep every fall for the past several years. Could I do it every other year without any loss in productivity?**

A. Usually yes, but it depends on the amount of rainfall received, the crops grown (shallow- or deep-rooted), and the soil type, according to Stephen Gliessman, director of the Agroecology Program in Santa Cruz, California. If you grow mostly shallow-rooted crops in clay soil in an area with heavy rainfall, the soil will compact faster, and you might need to double-dig every year. The productivity of your crops is the best indicator. If you've seen no increase in growth or yield after several years of double-digging, try skipping a year. You don't need to redig until you observe a check in top and/or bottom root growth.

Footprint Fiasco

Q. **How can I keep my soil from compacting? Since my whole family has taken an interest in the garden, I worry that the increased foot traffic will cause problems.**

A. The obvious way to prevent soil compaction is by providing paths—either around the beds or between the rows. With growing beds, the number of plants subjected to root zone compaction is greatly reduced, because four or five rows of plants are put into one bed—instead of five rows flanked by six paths. Once you cultivate and mark off the areas you will be growing in, stay off them and limit your movement to established paths.

Salty Soil

Q. Our first year at this house, nothing grew in our garden. A soil test showed toxic levels of salt. We were told the only way to solve the problem was to put down drainage tile and leach out the salt. Can you offer a less expensive solution?

A. Up to 95 percent of the salts in your soil can be leached out with water. Unless the water table under your garden site is very high (less than 4 to 5 feet), drainage tile shouldn't be necessary. If you dig a 5-foot-deep hole and haven't hit water, you're probably OK. To leach your soil, irrigate the garden twice with at least 2 inches of water each time (measure with a rain gauge).

Once the salts (mostly calcium and magnesium) have been washed down below the plants' root zone, it's essential to keep the soil moist. If it dries out, the salts will be carried right back to the surface, and you'll have to start all over again. A thick layer of mulch over the entire garden is important in keeping salinity at bay. Incorporating lots of organic matter will also help your soil stay moist. But if you've got manure, Dr. Jack Goertzen of the U.S. Salinity Laboratory recommends that you compost it first, because it is high in salts. Acidic materials such as pine needles, leaves, and peat moss are preferred because they help to lower the soil's pH, which is often around 8.0 when high salt levels are present. Continue to water the garden during the winter and plant a cover crop like winter rye. As long as you keep a constant vigil on your soil's moisture level, you should be able to garden successfully.

Solarize Your Soil

Q. I've heard I can rid my soil of wilt-causing organisms by heating it. Can I do it right in my garden?

A. Soil solarization kills both fusarium and verticillium wilt-producing fungi, while it greatly reduces nematodes and weeds. During the process, soil is pasteurized by the sun to a depth of 12 to 18 inches. To solarize garden soil, thoroughly soak the plot with water. This soaking increases the soil's ability to conduct heat and is necessary because moist heat kills organisms at lower temperatures than dry heat. Next, cover the plot with clear polyethylene plastic (not black mulching plastic) 1 to 4 mils thick, and bury the edges in a trench dug around the plot. Leave the plastic in place for three to four weeks. Plastic laid during the hot summer months, when the light intensity is greatest, can heat soil to 140°F—high enough to kill pathogens but leave beneficial soil microorganisms unharmed.

Microwaved Soil

Q. Can a microwave oven be used to sterilize potting soil?

A. Yes. Plant pathology researchers at the University of Kentucky use a home microwave oven to sterilize up to 10 pounds of soil at a time. The soil should be moist and crumbly, not squishy—if it's dry enough to work, it's dry enough to microwave, says Dr. R. S. Ferriss, who developed the technique. Place the soil in a plastic bag (polypropylene bags, the kind used for baking, are less likely to break than polyethylene bags) or in a large, loosely covered microwave-safe mixing bowl. Give the top of the bag a twist, but don't seal it or it might explode as steam builds up, cautions Ferriss.

With the oven turned to full power, heating a 2-pound batch of soil for 2½ minutes or a 10-pound batch for 8 minutes will kill most pathogens. If you've had problems with damping-off or other soilborne diseases in the past, you can extend—even double—the heating time without ill effect, says Ferriss. Doubling the treatment time may be necessary to sterilize compost or leaf mold. The high water content and myriad pore spaces of these organic materials are slow heating. After sterilization, let the soil stand uncovered until cool, then store in sealed containers.

pH Posers

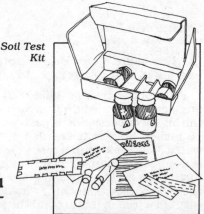

Soil Test Kit

Problems with pH

Q. Last year, my soil tested acid, so I limed it. Is it necessary to test it again this year?

A. You should test your soil again this spring. In fact, one of the best ways to safeguard your garden's productivity is to test it at least *twice* a year—before planting and in the middle of the season. Your soil's acid-alkaline standing (called pH) can change from one planting to the next—and from one place to another in your garden. If pine needles—which have a very low pH—fall on part of your garden, that section will gradually become more acidic. Certain crops will also affect the acidity or alkalinity of the plot on which they grow. Acid rain, a result of industrial pollution, lowers the pH of soil dramatically.

Soil test kits and test meters offer a fairly precise reckoning of soil pH. Test kits use colored papers or solutions to chart changes in soil pH. Meters are compact and fast-acting. All you do is insert the probe in soft, moist soil, wait a minute or two, and read the needle on the gauge. It gives a direct reading on a numerical scale. (A pH of 7.0 is neutral; lower readings, from 6.0 to 1.0, indicate increasing acidity, while higher readings, from 8.0 to 14.0, indicate increasing alkalinity.) For a small fee, state Agricultural Experiment Stations provide a soil analysis service. Although it is the most complete analysis available to home gardeners, a lab soil test is also the most time-consuming and expensive.

Sweet Water Is OK

Q. The well water at our new home has a high pH—8.0 to 8.5. Will it harm our azaleas or vegetable garden if we water with it?

A. No. Even acid-loving plants such as azaleas won't be affected. Soil has a high "buffering capacity." As soon as the alkaline water soaks into the ground, its pH will become the same as that of the soil. Alkaline water can sometimes be a problem when used to irrigate potted plants over a long period of time. With potted plants, include acid humus, peat moss, and leaf mold in the potting mixture and, if possible, use collected rainwater in place of well water.

Aloha Soil

Q. I garden in Hawaii. What can I add to my soil to make it more acidic? The soil has a pH of 7.0 to 7.5, and I'd like to get it down to 6.5.

A. A pH of 7.0 to 7.5 isn't excessively high for most vegetables. Since rainfall in your area is fairly low, the high soil pH is probably due to accumulated salts. (Beans, carrots, onions, peppers, and lettuce are most vulnerable to salt buildup.) Building up the organic matter in the soil with compost, mulch, or leaf mold will help to buffer the effects of your pH. You can also lower the pH with elemental sulfur. University of Hawaii soils extension agent George

Nakasato recommends applying 2.25 pounds of sulfur per 100 square feet. Check the pH annually and apply sulfur as recommended by the test results or your county agent.

Fertilizers,
Soil Builders, and More

Fertilizer Figures

Q. **My county agent recommends a 5:10:10 fertilizer for vegetable gardens. What organic materials can I substitute?**

A. The numbers "5:10:10" mean that the fertilizer contains 5 percent nitrogen (N), 10 percent phosphorus (P), and 10 percent potassium (K). A 100-pound bag would contain 5 pounds of N and 10 each of P and K. The other 75 pounds are mostly fillers. If, for example, you applied 25 pounds of 5:10:10 per 1,000 square feet, you'd actually be applying 1.2 pounds of N, 2.5 pounds of P, and 2.5 pounds of K. With a little figuring, you can substitute almost any organic fertilizer. For instance, suppose chicken manure is the nitrogen source that's easiest for you to get. Although the analysis of chicken manure can vary widely from sample to sample, an NPK rating of 3.63:1.54:2.64 is the amount found in several samples of broiler litter.

How much fertilizer does your 1,000 square feet need to get 1.2 pounds of N? Simply divide 1.2 (the recommended amount) by 3.6 percent or 0.0363 (the percentage in the organic source), which yields 33. So, 33 pounds of chicken manure will do it. Next, figure out how much P and K is in the manure—multiply 33 by the percentage for P and do the same for K. It turns out that 33 pounds of chicken manure provide about 0.5 pound of P and 0.87 pound of K. To get more P and K, look up other organic nutrient sources, like rock phosphate and wood ashes, that are high in P and/or K and very low in N, and repeat the calculations. But don't get swamped with figures. Fertilizer recommendations are guidelines, and with organic materials, if you apply a little more or a little less, you'll still have healthy plants.

The Phosphorus Factor

Q. **How does phosphorus actually function in plants?**

A. Phosphorus plays an important role in photosynthesis—the process by which plants use light energy to synthesize carbohydrates (food) from carbon dioxide and water. This element also produces good flower and fruit growth. Its major influence is in helping plants mature.

Pulling Up
Phosphorus Levels

Q. **I recently moved to a new home. Soil tests show that the soil on my proposed garden site is low in phosphorus. What can I fertilize with that will make phosphorus readily available this year?**

A. To ensure an adequate supply of phosphorus for your plants this season, feed them every two weeks with a liquid fertilizer such as fish emulsion or manure tea. Poultry manure is especially high in phosphorus in a form readily taken up by plants. Dried blood is another source of phosphorus that becomes available soon after application. Incorporate rock phosphate into your soil this spring, too, even though your plants won't be able to use much of it this year. By next season, as long as your soil's pH is below 7.0, the rock powder will begin to release a slow, steady supply of phosphorus to your garden. Adding manure or compost to your soil along with the rock phosphate may increase availability of the phosphorus as much as 200 percent. Humic acids in organic matter convert insoluble phosphorus to a form that plants can use. Organic matter also "fixes" other elements, such as calcium and iron, which can tie up phosphorus in the soil.

A Piece of the Rock

Q. **What's the difference between rock phosphate and superphosphate?**

A. Superphosphate, a chemically processed fertilizer, has high levels of immediately available phosphorus and calcium. When the high concentrations of minerals are released into the soil, the pH of the area around the fertilizer is lowered to 1.0 or 2.0. This extremely acidic condition kills any microbes in the area and can also harm insects and earthworms. The high acidity also releases soil manganese and aluminum at levels that can burn root tips. Naturally occurring rock phosphate is a good source of phosphorus for your garden. The phosphorus is released slowly, and it doesn't have a drastic effect on pH. Follow the application rates recommended by your soil test.

Great Greensand

Q. People tell me that greensand is a good fertilizer and will improve my sandy soil. What can you tell me about it?

A. Greensand is excellent for building and conditioning both hard and sandy soils. This undersea deposit, also called glauconite, contains most of the elements found in the ocean. It has been used successfully for soil-building for more than 100 years and is a fine source of potash. The best greensand deposits contain as much as 6 to 7 percent potash, 50 percent silica, 18 to 23 percent iron oxide, 3 to 7½ percent magnesium, small amounts of lime and phosphoric acid, and traces of 30 or more other elements—most of which are important for plant nutrition. Part of greensand's benefit is its ability to absorb and hold large amounts of water in the surface layer of the soil where plant roots feed. It slowly releases the potassium necessary to stimulate photosynthesis, and it stirs up helpful soil organisms.

Greensand is so fine that it may be used in its natural form with no processing. However, it should be dried if the material is to pass through a fertilizer drill. Because it is versatile, greensand may be applied directly to plant roots (it never burns) or left on the surface as a combined mulch and compost. Combining it with a manure-phosphate rock mixture is often recommended. Apply no more than ¼ pound of greensand per square foot of soil at any time of year. Rodale Research Center gardeners have also used it to give special soil conditioning treatments to grapevines, fruit trees, and filbert bushes.

Gradual Granite Dust

Q. Is granite dust a good source of potash?

A. No. Granite dust, a by-product of the tombstone industry, contains about 5 percent potassium (potash) and smaller amounts of most micronutrients needed by plants. Since it is a rock product, its nutrients are locked up in complex minerals like feldspars and silicates and aren't readily available. Win Way, soils professor at the University of Vermont, points out that granite's resistance to breakdown by natural forces is the reason it's such a popular material for gravestones. To supply your plants with a reliable source of potassium, use manure, compost, and, for a quick fix, wood ashes.

Two Limestones

Q. What is the difference between dolomitic and regular limestone?

A. Regular (calcic) limestone contains calcium. Dolomitic limestone contains a rich supply of magnesium as well as calcium. They are equally effective in raising the soil pH. All plants need calcium and magnesium to perform vital functions, and dolomitic limestone could be used to provide the extra magnesium. Not all soils are deficient in magnesium, however, so a good soil test should be your guide when determining which limestone to apply. Hydrated lime and quicklime are also sold, but these forms of lime have undergone chemical processes that tend to adversely affect soil microorganisms instead of providing the favorable conditions ground limestone does.

Something Fishy

Q. I have access to a huge amount of fish tailings from a local hatchery. Would adding these tailings, mixed with sawdust, give fruit a fishy taste? What about vegetables?

A. The fish could provide many of the nutrients needed for the growth of your fruits and vegetables, agrees Dr. Homer Buck of the Illinois Natural History Survey. To get the best results, compost the fish with sawdust, leaves, or other organic debris. Under proper conditions, the fish will be quickly reduced to usable form. Fruit wouldn't have a fishy taste, since it doesn't touch the ground; only the mineral and organic content would be absorbed.

The Seaweed Bonus

Q. Since I live along the coast, seaweed is always easy to come by. What should I know about putting seaweed into my garden?

A. Seaweed is an asset to the compost heap, since it decomposes quickly and helps the pile heat up. As for its fertilizing value, fresh seaweed is nutritionally similar to barnyard manure, but it contains twice as much potassium. Because it is high in iron, zinc, and potassium and contains some iodine, seaweed is an excellent food for citrus fruits and roses. If you're using large amounts of seaweed, don't let it heap up while you wait for it to decay. Nutrients leach out easily during the decaying process, so dig the seaweed into the soil quickly. Many gardeners wonder if it's necessary to wash the salt off seaweed before using it in the garden. It really isn't necessary, since the amount of salt that might cling to the plants is minimal.

Dracula's Delight

Q. **How is dried blood beneficial in the garden? What does it contain?**

A. Bloodmeal and dried blood contain 15 and 12 percent nitrogen and 1.3 and 3 percent phosphorus, respectively. Bloodmeal also has 0.7 percent potash. These materials may be used directly in the garden, or they may be added to the compost pile. They should be used sparingly because of their high nitrogen content—a sprinkling is enough. Both are excellent in the compost pile, since the nitrogen in them stimulates bacterial action on woody, fibrous materials.

What a Grind

Q. **How do I make my own bonemeal?**

A. To grind your own bonemeal, you need a very heavy-duty grinder (a hammer mill or gristmill), butcher bones, and time. A new mill powerful enough to grind bones will probably be quite expensive. Regular grain and cornmeal grinders are not durable enough to break down bones. A shredder's blades are not strong enough either. Start by boiling bones to extract the fat that surrounds the marrow. Then dry the bones thoroughly in the oven at low heat. Finally, pulverize them in the grinder. There's a better way to use bones in the garden without making bonemeal, however. Burn them in a woodstove or hearth and add the ashes to your compost pile. Your garden needs only 2 pounds per 100 square feet each year.

Compost Is Best

Q. **What is the best substance for maintaining the organic content of the soil?**

A. Compost is the best all-around substance, but animal manure is the most popular. Compost is high in organic matter, and its organic matter is fairly stable. But compost must be made, which takes time and effort. Manure, on the other hand, is usually available in large quantities at minimal cost, and it contains more soluble nitrogen and potash than compost. So many gardeners apply manure for basic soil maintenance and use their precious compost where it's most needed. Green manure crops, especially legumes, are also very effective, but to grow them, you'll need space for two gardens—one plot in vegetables and the other in green manure for rotation every second year.

Peat Particulars

Q. **I notice that there are different kinds of peat. How do the differences affect my gardening?**

A. There are usually two types of peat for sale, peat moss (or sphagnum peat) and sedge peat (aquatic grasses). Peat moss is partially decomposed sphagnum or other mosses, which decay more slowly than aquatic grasses. Peat moss is usually coarser, lighter-colored (brown to reddish), and much more water-retentive than sedge peat. For potting mixes, milled sphagnum (finely ground) is best. Cold water will run off milled sphagnum, but hot water soaks right in. For tilling into the garden or mulching, use the cheaper, coarser stuff that comes in bales. A 6-cubic-foot bale will cover about 300 square feet 1 inch deep. Sedge peat, made up of decomposed aquatic grasses like reeds and sedges, is usually dark and thoroughly decayed. It looks like very fine, black soil and is a good ingredient in potting mixes. Sedge peat is often sold slightly moist in plastic bags under the names humus peat and Michigan peat.

Both of these peats are good soil conditioners. They lighten and aerate clay soils and help sandy soils hold water longer. Sphagnum peat is more absorbent and breaks down more slowly than sedge peat. Peat is quite acidic. That's good for plants like blueberries and azaleas. If you don't have compost for potting soil, use peat. In potting mixes, peat is best used with pasteurized topsoil and a little bonemeal, both of which help raise the pH.

The Trouble with Wood Chips

Q. **Last fall, I tilled in 3½ inches of wood chips and manure (bedding material from a barn) throughout my garden. I have been told that wood chips will use up the nitrogen in my soil. Do I need to add anything else to the soil before I plant this spring?**

A. Although you supplied some nitrogen when you added manure along with the wood chips, it won't be enough. You will have to add more nitrogen this spring, and probably for several years, until the wood chips have broken down. (They've broken down when they can be easily crumbled when rubbed between the palms of your hands.) If you don't add nitrogen, it will be taken from the soil and used to break down the wood rather than feeding your plants. Sources of nitrogen include bloodmeal, cottonseed meal, grass clippings, and manure. Watch your plants for leaf yellowing or stunted growth—indications of nitrogen deficiency. If you recognize these signs, side-dress your plants with compost or manure tea or with a weak bloodmeal solution.

Azobacter Blues

Q. I recently saw an inoculant called azobacter in one of my garden catalogs. What is it, and does it have beneficial effects in the garden?

A. Azobacter are soil-dwelling bacteria that fix nitrogen and produce growth-stimulating, hormonelike substances. Because of these two activities, they are helpful to plants. They are usually present in healthy soils that contain some organic matter. But buying these beneficial bacteria would be a waste of money. Soil microorganisms are highly competitive and will generally attack any intruders into their environment. Research studies have shown that when cultures of azobacter are added to the soil, their numbers decline rapidly. Where some azobacter existed before, the population usually drops to the original level. Soils that don't contain azobacter obviously don't have the right conditions to support them, and if added to such a soil, the bacteria will die. The best way to encourage azobacter and other beneficial soil organisms in your soil is to provide them with a steady diet of organic matter.

The Safety Factor

Aluminum Soil

Q. I've been using greensand as a source of potash for my garden. I understand now that greensand contains aluminum. Is there any danger of adding too much aluminum to my garden soil?

A. No. Although greensand does contain measurable amounts of aluminum—a mineral that can be toxic to plants—it is bound up in a form unavailable to plants. Greensand contains less aluminum than most garden soils, anyway.

No Joy in Gypsum

Q. Local nurseries advise me to use gypsum to break up clay soil. Can you advise me about gypsum from the organic standpoint? What are alternatives?

A. Gypsum, a hydrated calcium sulfate, does improve aeration and drainage, but at the price of putting extra sulfur in the soil. Gypsum causes an imbalance in most soils, which already contain sufficient sulfur. If your soil is heavy, use organic matter—peat moss, leaves, hay, straw, wood chips, chopped stalks, compost, or wood ashes—to break up the clay while improving soil structure. Earthworms, lured by the incorporation of organic materials, also help. Turning your clay soil into a friable planting soil will take work in both fall and spring, and it usually is a three-year process. If this is the first time you've worked with clay soil, consider adding the organic matter in selected places, such as planting holes or trenches. A good cultivation after wet spring weather, during that brief period when the soil is drying and crumbles easily, helps, too.

Chlorinated Soil

Q. Is it safe to use chlorinated water to irrigate my garden?

A. Yes. Dr. William Cooper of Florida International University, a specialist on the complex chemistry of chlorination, says there is minimal risk involved. Here's what happens: When you water your garden, some of the chlorine compounds escape as gases. Those that remain are washed into the soil, but according to Cooper, it is unlikely that they would be taken up by plants. Chlorine compounds break down when exposed to light, so the chlorine in water droplets on plants or near the soil surface degrades quickly on a sunny day. The soil can destroy chlorine that percolates through it much as an activated carbon filter does, preventing it from forming compounds with soil minerals.

Cadmium Concerns

Q. What's the story on cadmium these days? "Organic" sludge is available in my city, but I'm concerned about the effects it may have on the cadmium level of my soil.

A. Cadmium can be toxic to plants and animals, although it is innocuous at the very low levels normally present in the soil. High cadmium test levels usually come from the addition of cadmium-contaminated wastes, so the sludge should be tested for zinc and cadmium by the municipality. If the city is giving out untested sludge, don't take it! The safety factor is the ratio of zinc to cadmium. As long as the sludge contains at least 100 times more zinc than cadmium, the zinc content will be high enough to kill vegetable plants before cadmium becomes a danger to human health.

Bones Aren't *That* Heavy

Q. **I have heard that bonemeal contains lead. Does this mean it's unsafe to use in my garden?**

A. Lead in bonemeal is a problem only as a food supplement. Bonemeal is perfectly safe to use as a garden fertilizer. Rural soils naturally contain an average of 12 parts per million (ppm) of lead, while suburban soils may contain 50 ppm, according to Dr. Rufus Chaney, U.S. Department of Agriculture heavy metals specialist. Lead in gardens doesn't become dangerous until it reaches 500 ppm, when the blood lead levels could be increased in children who might get contaminated soil on their hands and transmit it to their mouths.

Arsenic and Old Cottonseed Meal

Q. **Our county agent told us that cotton is defoliated with arsenic, so cottonseed meal may contain up to 220 ppm of the poison. Must we stop using this organic fertilizer?**

A. Cottonseed meal is safe to use in your garden. In fact, it's a great source of nitrogen. It's especially beneficial for citrus and azaleas because it has a slight acidifying effect on soils. In very nitrogen-poor soils, apply up to 10 pounds of cottonseed meal to every 100 square feet the first year. Arsenic is used as a defoliant on cotton crops in California, Texas, and Oklahoma. But the poison doesn't get into the seeds. The seeds that are ground into meal contain levels of arsenic only in the 0.05-ppm range. Normal arsenic levels in soil are higher—in the range of 5 ppm. The high levels of arsenic that your county agent probably is referring to are those found in cotton "trash," the leaf and stem by-products of the ginning process, which uses arsenic as a drying agent. Cottonseed meal is produced in a completely different way, using no arsenic.

Softened Water
Hard on Plants

Q. Will watering my flowers and vegetables with softened water containing high concentrations of salt harm my garden?

A. Yes. It will put salt in your soil, and the salt can accumulate to levels that are toxic to your plants. Water softeners also remove calcium and magnesium from water, both of which are essential to plant health. If the minerals in your water are a severe problem, rather than softening your entire water supply, hook up a water softener to your hot water only. Your laundry and baths will benefit, but your plants won't suffer.

Coal's Not Cool

Q. I burn coal in my furnace. Is it OK to use the ashes in my garden?

A. No. Coal ash contains a number of toxic trace elements. Although the amounts vary widely, depending on the source of coal, heavy metals including lead, arsenic, mercury, and cadmium may be present. Coal ash also contains boron and alkaline salts, which are detrimental to plant growth. In addition, some samples of coal ash were recently found to contain small amounts of dioxin, a powerful carcinogen.

Barbecued Soil

Q. Are the ashes from the charcoal I use in my barbecue safe to add to my garden?

A. No. Briquets are composed mostly of wood but also contain coal with corn or wheat starch as a binder. The problem is in the coal. Some coals have toxic levels of sulfur and/or heavy metals which are taken up by plants (see "Coal's Not Cool," above). Sulfur combines with water to produce sulfuric acid, which lowers soil pH.

Danger in Plywood Dust

Q. Can the sawdust from plywood and particleboard be used in the garden?

A. No. It's best to avoid both kinds. The glues used in plywood and particleboard are formaldehyde-based. Softwood plywood contains a phenol-formaldehyde resin, hardwood plywood has a urea-formaldehyde resin, and particleboard a mixture, depending on the wood scraps used. Although the amount of glue is small (6 percent in particleboard and less in the plywoods), the formaldehyde-based resin is cause for concern. Phenol-formaldehyde takes many years to break down. The compounds will bind with organic matter and eventually be taken up by plants. The long-term effects of consuming these compounds are unknown. Urea-formaldehyde, on the other hand, breaks down quickly, releasing synthesized urea (a source of nitrogen) and formaldehyde gas. In an enclosed area, the gas is toxic to plants.

Herbicide-Dressed Garden

Q. **I would like to expand the area of my garden into a section of the lawn that has been sprayed several times with weedkiller. The last application was 12 months ago. What can I do to this contaminated area so that it can be used for growing food?**

A. Chances are, since there has been a 12-month lapse since the weedkiller was applied, that the chemical residue is no longer harmful. But just to be safe, you can start to improve the soil condition by rounding up organic fertilizer materials, which help detoxify soil. Some, such as commercial compost mixtures and dried manures, can be worked directly into your soil to increase its humus content. Others, such as hay, sawdust, and cocoa hulls, should be set aside for later use as mulches. Plan to start your own composting immediately. (To learn how, see "Composting 101" on page 39.) In less than a month's time, you can have a high-grade organic compost that will create a better-quality soil in your new garden area.

Chapter 3

Your Customized Compost Pile

Composting Quandaries

Compost 101

Cross Section
of a Compost
Pile

**Q. Last summer I made my
first compost pile. I used a
starter and put all of my garbage, shredded papers, cardboard boxes, and everything
else available into the pile.
Nothing happened. How about
some entry-level composting
information?**

A. Sure. Behind composting, as we know it today, lies the original Indore method, developed by the father of organic gardening,
Sir Albert Howard. The Indore method is still the most widely used,
and it is still practical and productive.

Howard found that by layering different organic materials,
their decomposition took place more quickly and more completely.
He first placed a 5- or 6-inch layer of green matter (such as grass
clippings), then a 2-inch layer of manure (bloodmeal, bonemeal,

sewage sludge, or other high-protein material may be substituted), and a layer of rich earth, ground limestone and phosphate rock, then repeated this layering process.

What you want to do is mirror Sir Albert's method in your backyard. There are many variables in compost-making, so let's go through them, and you should be able to see where you made mistakes.

- Timing: Compost is best started in fall, when ample plant material is available. In the summer, piles may dry out, while in the winter, extremely cold temperatures will slow down the composting process. During the winter, add extra manure to the heap to keep the temperatures high, and insulate it with a layer of plant material (such as straw).

- Ventilation: Ventilation is crucial to a good compost pile. The soil organisms that break down the plant and animal residues and convert them into compost must have oxygen to carry on their activities. If your pile does not allow oxygen to reach the inside, the process will not work. In fact, unpleasant odors may develop. One way to get oxygen into your pile is to prop wooden sticks or posts vertically like a teepee in a tall pile and build your compost heap around them; later you can remove the sticks, leaving air passages in the pile.

- Turning: If you turn your pile regularly, you'll be sure to have plenty of air in it for ventilation. Turning also mixes the ingredients to make sure all items are exposed to the highest heat in the center of the pile, so they compost faster.

- Watering: Your pile should be quite moist during the initial stages of composting. Later in the process, the pile may be somewhat drier but should never dry out. If you're not sure how much water to use, check to see that the inside of the pile doesn't get dry and powdery or become so wet that it mats together.

- Carbon:nitrogen ratio: Most plant matter contains high amounts of carbon. Soft green plant material, such as grass clippings and kitchen scraps, and animal matter, such as manure and bloodmeal, contain nitrogen. You need the right mix of carbon and nitrogen to get your pile to heat up. For a good working pile, you should have 20 to 25 parts of carbon (in the form of dried leaves, newspapers, straw, and so forth) for every 1 part of nitrogen (in the form of manure, bloodmeal, and so forth). The more you stray from this ratio, the more problems you are likely to have. Apparently your pile, with its shredded papers and cardboard boxes, was much higher than 25 parts carbon, and the pile never really started composting. If circumstances dictate that your carbon:nitrogen ratio must be off, make sure you have more nitrogen than needed, never less.

- Avoid meat: To keep rodents, cats, and dogs from wreaking havoc with your pile, don't include meat, bones, or fat. As an added precaution, cover the top layer of garbage with soil every day.

Cool Compost

Q. **My compost pile doesn't heat up. I've been using aged wood chips, horse manure, and cottonwood leaves. All of the materials are dry. Is it possible that there is not enough moisture? What do you recommend?**

A. If you have not added water to your compost pile, lack of moisture could very well be your problem. Water the pile thoroughly and evenly until it's as wet as a wrung-out sponge, but not so soggy that you can squeeze water from it. Covering the pile with black plastic will keep the moisture in and prevent nutrients from being leached out by rain.

If the compost pile still doesn't heat up, it lacks nitrogen, which the composting bacteria need. The manure you've been using may not be fresh, or you may not have added enough. To every 4 inches of leaves, add about 2 inches of fresh manure, mixing in enough wood chips to aerate the pile. Wood chips are not the easiest material to compost, but they will break down eventually and in the meantime will keep the other materials from clumping up, making turning easier.

Lawn clippings, vegetable wastes, and coffee grounds are other good sources of nitrogen, and they're usually free. If none of these is available, bonemeal or bloodmeal can be added to the pile.

Compost Concoctions

Q. **What is a recipe for compost to use in a potting mix for starting seedlings? Should I add manure or other nitrogen-rich organic fertilizers to the mixture?**

A. Any compost that undergoes a hot rot (above 140°F in the pile's center) will be free of disease organisms. A good recipe is four parts plant matter to one part fresh manure. Mix well and keep moist but not wet. Turn every week or so until the temperature comes down to 110°F. Screen and bag the compost immediately for later use. For your potting mix, make a blend of one part vermiculite and one part compost.

There is enough plant food in this mixture without adding manure or other fertilizers high in nitrogen. Used too soon, these can cause young plants to grow too rapidly and become spindly.

Shredder Shortcut

Q. I shred fruit and vegetable scraps, dry cow manure, and dry leaves, run it all through our trusty shredder, toss it with a small ash shovel, and pour the mixture into our cinder block bin. Is it necessary to layer soil into a compost pile?

A. While not absolutely necessary, layering of materials is the simplest way to ensure that you've mixed all the ingredients in your pile and to spread helpful microorganisms throughout, which encourages heat and decomposition. With your shredder, you've accomplished the mixing before you've made your pile. You still should throw a shovelful of garden soil into your newly shredded materials every so often to introduce soil bacteria and fungi throughout the pile for even decomposition.

A Good Pit
Makes Good Neighbors

Q. Gardening in my city yard is a challenge. I wonder, for example, how I can keep my compost heap alive and hot throughout the winter months without creating a backyard eyesore for my neighbors.

A. The best way to keep your compost heap active and out of view is by making it in a pit. During the winter, the pit sides keep compost warm and accelerate the decaying process. Even such resistant materials as ground corncobs and leaves will be ready for soil-building use by late spring with this method, especially if earthworms do the mixing.

The pit can be 3 feet deep, with the length and width about 4 feet. After placing the materials in the pit, cover them with soil, burlap bags, canvas, straw, or something similar to retain heat and moisture for faster decomposition.

Compost Minus Manure

Q. Living in the city, I don't have easy access to manure. Is it really necessary in making compost?

A. You don't need animal manures to make compost successfully. You can get by using nitrogen-rich sources like grass clippings or cottonseed meal. One easy method is to cut or shred fresh plant materials as finely as possible in order to expose a maximum amount of surface to the organisms of decay. As soon as the heat has subsided, the heap of finely ground plant materials may be given a nutritional boost by introducing some redworms and branding worms bred especially for the compost heap. These animals will supply the manure needed. You can also add such animal residues as bonemeal, dried blood, dried fish, and, if possible, dried manure to the heap.

Aerobicize Your Composter

Q. I built a barrel composter but find it doesn't work well. Why?

A. All compost needs air. A barrel composter, if filled to capacity, doesn't allow air to mix with the compost material when the composter is turned. Fill your composter only half to two-thirds full and see if that helps it to work better. To ensure good aeration, try turning the composter three to five times a day. Too much moisture, which can be a problem in barrel composters, will also slow decomposition.

Rotary Compost

Q. I gave my drum composter several turns a day, but two to three weeks later, the compost was still not finished. What went wrong?

A. Drum composters work best when the compost material is finely shredded. You can use one of the larger-size, heavy-duty shredders or, if you have only small amounts of materials, try one of the newer, smaller-scale models. And remember that bulky matter—long stems and clumps of organic debris—doesn't mix very well.

If bulk wasn't the problem, maybe lack of adequate nitrogen was. Fast compost requires a 25:1 carbon:nitrogen ratio. Many combinations of organic materials come close to the ideal proportions. For example, you can mix equal parts of garden debris, kitchen scraps, and leaves; half straw and half manure; or equal amounts of straw, grass clippings, and garden refuse. Layer the ingredients, wetting them down as you go, until the drum is almost full. The mixture should be as damp as a wrung-out sponge, not dripping wet. Turn the drum five times a day and add more water if the compost starts to dry out. In two to three weeks, it will be dark, crumbly, and ready to use.

Shred with Your Mower

Q. **What is an easy way to convert my lawnmower into a shredder for compost material?**

A. The easiest thing to do is not to convert your lawnmower at all. Just run the mower over your piles of weeds, leaves, straw, and manure, and your compost material is ready. It is helpful to do this job near a wall, which can prevent the cuttings from spreading out too much.

When shredding material with a rotary mower, it is best for two people to work together. One moves the mower back and forth over a given spot, while the other feeds material in front of it. You can tackle larger piles by tilting the mower back on two wheels, positioning the blades until they are directly over the pile, and then lowering the mower gradually.

Compost on Hold

Q. **Can compost be saved for several years and still retain its value?**

A. Yes, as long as you keep the pile covered. You can make a cover of weighted-down plastic sheeting, metal roofing, or wood that will keep rain and snow from leaching out water-soluble nutrients. However, no matter how it's stored, compost is still a valuable soil conditioner, improving the soil's tilth and its ability to hold water and oxygen.

Don't Rock Fast Compost

Q. **I want to make fast compost with leaves and pure horse manure (not bedding). What's the best ratio to get a good hot mix? Will rock phosphate and other additives help speed up the composting process?**

A. The best way to get the proper ratio for fast, hot compost with leaves and fresh horse manure is to alternate 3- to 4-inch layers of leaves with 1- to 2-inch layers of manure. The pile should be at least 3 feet square and 3 feet high to retain heat properly.

Mineral additives like rock phosphate, basalt rock, and bonemeal are more for compost enrichment than activation. They won't speed up the composting process, but they won't hinder it either. These substances increase compost's nutrient content, but they are not necessary. If your soil is low in phosphorus, for example, adding raw pulverized phosphate rock will give you compost with a slightly higher phosphorus level. Add these rock powders or bonemeal to compost only if a soil test indicates your soil needs boosting.

Keep the Lime Out

Q. Should I lime my compost pile? If so, do I still have to lime my garden?

A. We recommend that you don't add lime to your compost pile. Even if you put very acid materials like oak leaves or sawdust into your pile, the composting process will almost always turn out an end product with a pH of about 6.5—slightly below neutral.

Lime in the compost pile can also cause the formation of ammonia gas, resulting in a loss of valuable nitrogen. So lime your garden but not your compost.

Bacterial "Starters" for Compost Heaps

Q. I have recently started my first compost pile. I have read many ads for compost makers, tablets, powders, and liquids that claim to add beneficial bacteria to speed composting. A box of Rid-X is much cheaper and claims to add beneficial bacteria to a septic tank. Is there any reason I can't add Rid-X to my compost pile? Are they the same beneficial bacteria?

A. Of course you could add a box of Rid-X to your compost pile, but we doubt it would do anything. The beneficial bacteria needed for biological breakdown of human waste in a tank of water are completely different from those needed in a compost pile. It would be a lot like trying to raise fish on a good stand of alfalfa.

There is a great deal of controversy about the value of adding bacteria to compost heaps. Rodale researchers believe that, under normal circumstances, there is no reason to use a bacterial mixture in a properly built compost heap. However, the Bio-Dynamic Farming and Gardening Association strongly believes in the use of a biological starter, or preparation, on a compost pile. Although

Rodale researchers know of no university tests on the value of compost starters, the only point they see in their favor is that they may speed up the process in some cases. In the case of a poorly built heap, this could be of value, especially in the area of nutrient preservation. However, if you build your heap right and keep an occasional eye on it, you should not need any bacterial additions.

What Makes Good Compost?

Chips Ahoy!

Q. **I have access to wood chips and cow manure and would like to use them to make compost. In what proportions should I mix them?**

A. Composting wood chips is usually not practical because they contain a lot of carbon and relatively little nitrogen, explains Dr. Charles Michler, a researcher at the Forestry Sciences Laboratory in Wisconsin. You would have to mix 80 to 100 pounds of manure with every pound of wood chips to compost them within a month or so.

It's better to use wood chips as a mulch for fruit, perennial vegetables, and ornamental plantings. Since the chips break down so slowly (only about 1 percent a year), they won't rob a significant amount of nitrogen from the soil, Michler adds.

Cow manure, on the other hand, is an excellent ingredient for a compost pile. By layering it about half and half with materials such as straw, leaves, grass clippings, and kitchen scraps, you'll be able to produce fast, high-quality compost.

Composting Bermuda Grass

Q. **With the heat and dryness here in Yuma, Arizona, one of the few grasses that will survive is Bermuda grass. I've been saving all my lawn clippings but was recently told Bermuda grass is unacceptable as a compost material because its growing ability is not destroyed in the composting process. Is this true?**

A. Bermuda grass, an important pasture grass, can be a problem for home gardeners because it spreads both by creeping stolons (aboveground runners) and rhizomes (underground runners).

If your pile is properly composted, it should become hot enough to destroy both stolons and rhizomes, and there should be no problem using the compost. You might want to monitor the pile with a thermometer (such as a meat thermometer) to determine whether you're reaching a high enough temperature. Be sure not to mulch with Bermuda grass.

Diseased Plants: Compost or Destroy?

Q. I know that diseased plant parts should always be destroyed. But do they have to be burned, or can I compost them?

A. Most diseased plant material can be safely composted. Recent research suggests that nearly all plant pathogens are killed by temperatures of about 140° to 145°F—the range a well-constructed compost pile should reach in its initial stages. (You can use a meat thermometer to monitor your pile.) To make sure the outside of the pile heats up, we recommend covering it with black plastic for the first few days or turning it consistently and thoroughly. But don't worry too much if the temperature of your compost doesn't reach 140°F, because the competing microorganisms also do a pretty good job of killing pathogens.

Be aware, however, that composting won't kill fusarium or verticillium wilt. Any plants that have succumbed to these two diseases should be burned. If you're not sure of the disease, or if you compost by the "slow" method, burning diseased material will ensure destruction of all plant pathogens. You can then use the ashes in your garden.

Sawdust Savvy

Q. I'd like to use some sawdust in the garden. Most of it is from walnut and cedar trees. Will using it be a problem?

A. There should be no problem from the cedar sawdust. But you are right to be concerned about sawdust from walnut trees. Walnut wood contains a toxin called juglone that can kill or stunt your vegetables. A year's composting will break down the juglone, making the sawdust safe for the garden.

All sawdust should be composted before being added to the garden anyway. Because it is a high carbon/low nitrogen material, raw sawdust can cause a nitrogen deficiency in the soil as it breaks down. If you must put it directly on the garden, be sure to add a rich nitrogen source like bloodmeal, cottonseed meal, grass clippings, or manure.

Compost on Ice

Q. **What's the best thing to do with kitchen scraps in the winter?**

A. In regions that freeze during the winter, it's best to store the scraps until spring. Store them outside in a covered container. The scraps will freeze, and in the spring they can be composted. One *Organic Gardening* staff member uses a covered 30-gallon plastic trash can and finds it keeps all the scraps two adults and two children produce from December through mid-March.

If you have a basement or garage that stays above 50°F, you (with the help of some earthworms) can compost your kitchen scraps in containers throughout the year.

Which Style of Sludge?

Q. **I've been considering the use of sludge to fertilize my flower garden. What is the difference between digested sludge and dried-activated sludge?**

A. Digested sludge is given primary treatment by anaerobic digestion (occurring in the absence of free oxygen), but it's not heat-treated. The product is usually of relatively low quality as a fertilizer compared with products from an activated system.

In flower gardens, the digested sludge should be applied to bare land in the fall and lightly dug in, or composted. It is unwise to apply this sludge to vegetable gardens or to soils that will sustain an edible crop in the same season.

Dried-activated sludge is made from sewage that has the grit and coarse solids removed. After this process, the substance is inoculated with microorganisms and then aerated. The resulting organic matter is withdrawn from the tanks, filtered, dried in rotary kilns, ground, and screened. As you can imagine, properly heat-treated, dried-activated sludge usually draws a good price.

Caution: Whichever sludge you choose to use, make sure that the specific treatment system is not also involved in handling toxic materials (heavy metals) that are coming into it from industrial plants. Make sure sludge has been tested for the absence of cadmium, nickel, and lead. Also, raw, untreated, or improperly treated sewage sludge should never be applied as a fertilizer or soil conditioner.

The Safety Factor

Compost Cat Litter?

Q. **We would like to compost our cat's used cat-box filler for use in our vegetable garden. Is there a danger of introducing harmful organisms?**

A. Technically, the litter can be used in compost if you are sure that your materials compost thoroughly, the compost reaches a high temperature, and a good carbon/nitrogen balance of materials is used. However, we don't recommend composting the litter for vegetable gardens because cats, especially "outdoor" cats, occasionally carry diseases that can infect humans.

Toxoplasma gondii, a protozoan, usually causes few, if any, symptoms in man and remains unnoticed. But infection of pregnant women can lead to severe birth defects, and infection of a newborn may cause blindness and mental retardation. The cysts of *Toxocara cati,* a nematode, can infect the digestive tract of humans, leading to migraine headaches and visual impairment.

All things considered, we feel there should be enough safe compost materials so that you shouldn't have to use kitty's litter. And while we're on this topic, here's one additional caution: Pregnant women should never clean litter pans.

Toxic Tomatoes?

Q. **I understand there is a mild poison in potato and tomato vines and rhubarb leaves. Is it OK to compost them?**

A. It's safe to compost your potato, tomato, and rhubarb refuse. In the first place, the compounds are not toxic to plants. Furthermore, they break down quickly when composted. The toxin in tomato and potato vines is an alkaloid called solanine, which can cause vomiting, diarrhea, and abdominal pain. Rhubarb leaves have high concentrations of oxalic acid, which also can cause vomiting and stomach pain. Use only the fleshy main ribs for your pies.

Barrel Cleaning

Q. I have several 55-gallon steel barrels that I would like to recycle as composters and as a barrel root cellar. However, the barrels were used in the printing industry and contained chemicals (press wash and isopropyl alcohol). Is it possible to remove these residues so the barrels are safe to use?

A. No matter how these barrels might be cleaned, it is still not wise to use them for storage containers. Since strong chemicals were previously stored in them, you can never be certain that there are no harmful residues still embedded in the metal. Your best bet would be to get hold of some wooden barrels or build some simple wooden containers yourself.

Rust in the Barrel

Q. I've started some compost in my homemade barrel composter, but the barrel is rusty. Could I unknowingly transmit something harmful to my garden?

A. If anything, the rust from your barrel will probably give the iron content of your a compost a boost with the addition of iron oxide. However, a rusty barrel won't hold up over a long period of time. If you put a lot of effort into making your composter, replace the rusty drum with a good 55-gallon drum, preferably coated with a protective layer of lead-free paint.

Toxins in Mushroom Soil

Q. I use mushroom soil in my garden. The mushroom growers get their straw and manure from large horse farms that spray their stables, and I know that mushroom growers spray, too. Will pesticides end up in my soil?

A. Most mushroom compost contains pesticides. And while all of the insecticides commonly used break down into other compounds fairly quickly (most growers spread their mushroom soil in a field in a 2-foot-thick layer for a year or more before selling it), some of the residues may be harmful. Ask the mushroom growers whether they use a preventive spray program, which involves constant use of pesticides, or Integrated Pest Management (IPM), in which sprays are only applied if an insect problem occurs.

Toxicity, however, is not the only issue. Some of the pesticide compounds used, or their breakdown products, have been proven to be carcinogenic or mutagenic. In addition, an abundance of weed seeds usually finds its way into the compost while it sits in the field. And valuable nutrients such as nitrogen and potassium will have leached out, so mushroom soil will supply primarily phosphorus, some micronutrients, and organic matter.

Sludge Safety

Q. The municipal sewage treatment plant in our community makes composted sludge available to the public free of charge. I have put it on our flower beds, and it does wonders. Is it safe to use on the vegetable garden?

A. In most places, it's still not a good idea to use sewage sludge in your vegetable garden because of the possiblity of heavy metal contamination, most of it from industry. Not all sludges contain heavy metals, but how do you make sure that the sludge you use isn't contaminated? The federal government doesn't have regulations governing giveaway sludge problems. Some states and municipalities do, but the monitoring programs vary widely.

Metals in Milorganite?

Q. If I fertilize my lawn with Milorganite, can I use the clippings on my garden without a harmful buildup of heavy metals?

A. Yes. As long as you maintain the pH of your lawn at 6.5 or above, cadmium, which is found in the sludge product in small quantities (the level, tested daily, is about 45 parts per million), won't be taken up by the grass at all. When Milorganite production first began, cadmium levels were higher, but industries in Milwaukee now remove the metal from their waste before it goes into the treatment system. According to the Milwaukee Metropolitan Sewerage District (which produces Milorganite), even if you fertilized your vegetable garden directly with Milorganite at recommended rates, it would take 200 years for the cadmium level in the soil to reach the Environmental Protection Agency's unacceptable level.

Problems in the Pile

Antsy Compost

Q. **I've got ants in my compost pile. What can I do to get rid of them?**

A. Ants may be using your compost pile as a cafeteria—eating aphid honeydew, fungi, seeds, and other insects in the pile. They'll also eat moldy lollipops, buttered toast, and any goodies that might end up in your pile. So store your garbage until you have enough for a layer, then cover it with a 3- to 4-inch layer of material that won't interest the ants—such as weeds, grass clippings, or straw.

The compost can also provide shelter for nests and hills. The ants, however, will remain only while the pile is relatively cool. A hot pile will get rid of the ants as well as give you faster compost. If you turn the pile and it doesn't heat up, you have one of two problems. The most common is that your pile lacks sufficient nitrogen. Mix fresh manure or grass clippings into the heap and it should heat up. Turn the pile every three to five days and it will stay hot. If adding nitrogen doesn't work, the pile is probably too wet or dry. A good compost heap is moist, not soggy. To dry a waterlogged pile, turn it every day. When it dries enough, it will start heating up again. Cover the pile with plastic bags to shed the rain and increase the temperature. Ants won't be attracted to the finished compost.

Gnats in Compost

Q. **I live in a residential area and make compost with grass clippings, leaves, and kitchen scraps. My problem is that hundreds of flies and gnats hover over the pile, and I'm afraid the neighbors will complain. Any suggestions?**

A. While a few insects are to be expected, if large numbers are attracted to your compost, it probably isn't aerated well enough. Mix the grass thoroughly with the leaves so that it doesn't decompose anaerobically. (A foul odor is an indication of anaerobic, or oxygen-deficient, decomposition.) The pile should also be moist, but not dripping wet. To further reduce the number of flies and gnats in the area of your pile, you can cover it with a tarpaulin. You could also make or buy a compost bin, which your neighbors may find less objectionable.

Grubby Compost

Q. I mix grass clippings and leaves to compost slowly, and every year the pile is loaded with fat white grubs. How can I keep them out?

A. Slowly decaying organic matter is an attractive egg-laying site for various species of May and June beetles. The larvae of some species feed only on decaying plant material, but others can seriously damage plant roots. Prevent egg laying by covering the compost with plastic, though grubs may still migrate in from surrounding soil. Some gardeners have controlled grubs in compost by introducing insect-killing nematodes. Recent research indicates that these nematodes can control grubs in lawns and gardens as well.

Glass Compost

Q. I've read that glass is present in municipal compost. Doesn't the presence of these tiny razor blades pose a threat?

A. Glass, passed with refuse through a grinder, is either pulverized to the consistency of beach sand or shattered into highly polished fragments that have a surface much like that of a pebble. The polishing action is due to the abrasive nature of refuse. The principal objection to the presence of this glass in compost is that it detracts from the aesthetics of the product. While it might be ideal to eliminate all glass from compost in municipal composting, its presence will not constitute a hazard.

Chapter 4

Four for Fertility
Manures, Mulches,
Cover Crops, and Earthworms

The Right Stuff

Spring Manure

Q. I didn't get manure into my garden during the fall. Is it okay to manure the garden this spring, or will the fresh manure burn my early crops?

A. It's OK to put down a medium application of fresh manure (except poultry manure) if it's tilled into the soil at least two weeks before planting and rained on in the interim. If rain doesn't come, water the area deeply soon after tilling. But set a manure-free spot aside for carrots, which may branch excessively in freshly manured ground.

Keeping Up Appearances

Q. Is there any way to transform fresh manure into well-rotted manure without causing a neighborhood revolt due to smell and appearance?

A. We suggest piling the manure in an out-of-the-way corner of the yard and covering the pile with a tarpaulin or plastic sheet.

Unless there is plenty of straw already mixed with the manure, layer it with an equal amount of straw, hay, or leaves and allow it to compost for a year without turning. Surround the pile with attractive fencing for a neater appearance.

Aged, Not Composted

Q. I have access to manure from a horse barn. It's about a foot deep and has been there for some time. Is it composted manure? How should I use it?

A. Aging is not composting, so you don't have composted manure. Since it's been protected indoors, and the weather hasn't leached out the important nutrients, you can either till it into your garden four to six weeks before you plant, or layer it with other organic matter to make compost.

Making
Manure Tea

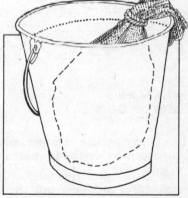

Liquid Fertilizers

Q. I would like to know the advantages of liquid fertilizer. Does it have any long-term benefits to the soil? How economical is it? Is it a practical alternative to organic fertilizer or composting manure?

A. The liquid fertilizers that are most beneficial include "tea," made from manure or compost, or seaweed or fish emulsion extract. Organic teas and sea extracts are excellent "pick-me-ups" during the summer when plants are growing fast because the liquids move through the soil quickly and are absorbed rapidly by roots. Liquid fertilizers also boost the productivity of intensive vegetable beds. There are some liquid chemical fertilizers that are so strong they will burn your skin on contact, so you can imagine what they will do to your soil. Don't use them.

Manure and compost teas are the least expensive liquid fertilizers. To make them, scoop manure or compost into a burlap bag and suspend it in a bucket of water. Steep one to two weeks, moving the bag around every couple of days. Use full strength or dilute to the color of weak tea.

Fish emulsion, made from soluble fish-canning wastes, is high in nitrogen. Fish emulsion is potent stuff—you should never use solutions stronger than 1 tablespoon to a gallon of water, and half of that for foliar feeding. As a foliar spray, fish emulsion has been found to increase tomato yields by 16 percent.

Current research into seaweed extracts shows that they benefit plants because, while lower in nitrogen than manure tea and fish emulsion, they contain a wide range of trace minerals (often more than 60). In work at Clemson University, foliar feeding of seaweed extract enabled tomatoes to survive temperatures slightly below freezing and provided considerable protection from insects. There are also products that combine both seaweed and fish emulsion for a balanced fertilizer. Apply any foliar spray once every three to four weeks.

These products are normally diluted for use, so the total cost is not too high. But liquid fertilizers don't improve soil structure, so they are not a replacement for incorporating organic matter into your soil. If you have a good soil management system that keeps your soil healthy, you could supplement it with an organic foliar-feeding program.

Horse Manure
Takes the Cake

Q. **I have access to horse, cow, sheep, and hog manure. Which one can provide the highest nutrient content in my garden?**

A. As a rule, horse manure is more valuable than the manure of other farm animals, but the nutrient content varies with the amount of grain that is included in the diet. Since grains are relatively high in all plant nutrients, the more grain, the better the manure.

Horse manure is richer in nitrogen than either cow or hog manure, and it ferments more easily. For this reason, it is usually referred to as a "hot" manure. Sheep manure also falls into the "hot" category and is generally quite dry and rich. Cow manure and hog manure are relatively wet and low in nitrogen, so these manures ferment slowly and are regarded as "cold" manures.

On the Wings of a Dove

Q. I have an old barn with a lot of pigeon manure on the floor. Is the manure a good fertilizer and safe to use?

A. Pigeon manure is a very good fertilizer, according to Marie Rotondo, secretary-treasurer of the International Federation of American Homing Pigeon Fanciers, who uses it regularly in her garden. It's more than twice as concentrated as chicken manure; apply 4 to 8 pounds fresh or 2 to 5 pounds dried per 100 square feet of garden area. Because it is so hot, it will burn young roots and leaves if spread directly on the garden.

Droppings from domesticated pigeons are safer to use in the garden than those from wild pigeons. Breeders strive to keep their birds healthy. Wild birds, usually found in cities, may be carriers of psittacosis, a severe form of pneumonia, and *Cryptococcus neoformans*, which can cause meningitis. To be safe, always compost pigeon droppings before you apply them to your soil.

Dr. Richard Fite, an avian pathologist at the University of New Hampshire, says that because dry manure is exceptionally dusty, you should wear a tight-fitting dust mask with a rubber apron and filter to keep from breathing airborne particles.

Dog Wastes

Q. Is it OK to use dog droppings in my garden?

A. No. Don't use dog feces in the garden. Theoretically, pathogens and parasites in the material would be killed if it were composted thoroughly at high temperatures. But there's too great a chance that some of the material won't be pasteurized or the high temperature won't be attained. Furthermore, the dog manure is dense and will not break down as readily as livestock manures.

The feces may contain tapeworms, roundworms, and hookworms, which are parasites of dogs. In their larval stages, they also infect humans and are generally contracted from infected soil. The organisms can survive in the soil for over a year or until the ground freezes.

Zoo Doo

Q. How safe is it to use manure from zoo animals for fertilizing a vegetable garden? The Portland Zoo sells this, and the Seattle Zoo is looking into the possibility.

A. There is no more danger of disease being transmitted from zoo animals to humans than there is from horses or cattle, so treat zoo manure as you would any other. The U.S. Department of Agriculture (USDA) regulates zoos, and according to Dr. Keith Sherman of USDA's Animal Care Staff, any zoo that takes sheep-, horse-, or cowlike animals from foreign countries after the normal quarantine period must meet strict post-quarantine regulations. These regulations require that the manure from these animals be disposed of at the zoo, either by burning, burying, or composting. Disposal is aimed at preventing the spread of hoof-and-mouth disease, which animals may carry but not suffer from themselves.

Animals that have been born in this country have no federal restrictions on their manure, and it may be treated the same as that from any other animal in that area, according to state and local laws. Thus it may be sold—as is done in Portland with elephant manure. Under the label of "ZooDoo Manure," the elephant manure is sold to help the zoo meet its maintenance costs. Although only elephant manure is sold at the Portland Zoo, all their animals have been born in this country with the exception of one giraffe, whose waste is handled separately. The remainder of the Portland manure is sold to area worm growers for composting in worm beds.

Mulch, Mulch More

What's for Mulch?

Q. **Although we mulched our garden with decayed plant materials, we were disappointed to find a good crop of weeds throughout the growing season. Is there a recommended amount of mulch or better mulching materials that would improve our track record?**

A. Determining the right amount of mulch and what type of mulch works best for a particular garden is often a trial-and-error procedure. However, there are basic guidelines you should follow for successful mulching. The first is simply providing enough mulch so that those weeds do not appear during the growing season. In your case, a thin layer of finely shredded plant materials would have been more effective than unshredded loose material. Eight or more inches of hay, straw, or a similar loose, "open" material would also work well. So will 1 or 2 inches of buckwheat or cocoa bean hulls or a 2- to 4-inch layer of pine needles. Leaves and cornstalks should be shredded or mixed with a light material like straw to prevent packing into a soggy mass. In a mixture, shredded leaves can be spread 8 to 12 inches deep for the winter. Other good mulches include sphagnum moss, a variety of weeds, crop residues, grasses, clovers, and different types of hay.

Peanut Shells Are Perfect

Q. Are peanut shells suitable as mulch around vegetables and flowers?

A. Peanut shells make a great mulch. Your soil will not only get the benefits of weed control, improved moisture retention, and ground cover, it will also be the beneficiary of added nitrogen. Peanut hulls contain 1.5 percent nitrogen. They also contain small amounts of phosphorus (1.2 percent) and potassium (0.78 percent).

If the hulls are ground or broken up, they will tend to pack down after rains to form a hard crust. Adding more nitrogen in the form of cottonseed meal—not bloodmeal or dried blood, which will burn plants—to the hull mulch will help decompose the compacted layer and break it up.

Yesterday's Papers

Q. Can household waste papers such as newspapers, paper bags, cardboard, and milk cartons be used as mulch? I recently purchased a shredder and wish to use all my waste papers as mulch, if possible.

A. Go ahead and mulch with newspaper, paper bags, and cardboard, provided none are covered with colored ink. Stay away from slick magazine paper and any dyed material such as comics, which may contain lead dyes. Milk cartons aren't recommended because they also contain dyes. On top of that, they are usually coated with paraffin, which is a petroleum product—certainly an undesirable addition to your mulch.

It's a good idea to add a layer of straw, hay, corncobs, or wood chips over the paper to keep it from blowing away and to aid in moisture retention.

A Hairy Subject

Q. I've been reading that the use of hair dyes can cause breast cancer in women. Is it safe to use clippings of dyed hair as mulch in the garden?

A. The questionable compound (2,4-DAA) in hair dyes breaks down rapidly when exposed to moisture and air. Considering the rather low concentrations of the substance and the rapid breakdown, there's probably no harm in using dyed hair as mulch. If you use it in the vegetable garden, we suggest you compost it first.

Is It Straw or Is It . . . ?

Q. What's the difference between straw and hay? Which is the better mulch?

A. Straw is the dry stems and leaves of a grain crop like oats or wheat, and hay is cut green from fields that are usually a mix of grasses, legumes (alfalfa, clover, and so on), and weeds. Because of weed seeds, mulching a garden with hay can sometimes introduce many more weed seeds as well as new weed species. So it is better to compost hay first. Straw isn't nearly as weedy, but it generally has some weed seeds and a few grain heads.

Hay is a little higher in nitrogen—it has 1 to 2 percent, while oat straw is 1 percent and wheat straw only 0.3 percent. Wheat straw could rob your soil of nitrogen if used as a mulch. Neither hay nor straw supplies much phosphorus, and they both contain 1 to 2 percent potash.

Basically, it's a choice between potential weed problems with hay and lower nitrogen with straw. The best choice is to mulch with straw, supplemented with compost or manure to make sure it doesn't deplete the soil.

Worth Its Salt

Q. I've heard salt hay is recommended as a mulch. Is it better than regular hay? Where can I obtain it?

A. Salt hay comes from a grass that grows abundantly in eastern coastal marshes. Its main advantage over regular hay is that it's relatively free of weed seeds. It also doesn't mat down like hay will. Although the grass grows only in saline conditions, it contains very little salt. You can buy it by the bale at a building supply store or garden center, or you can cut it yourself if you live near the shore.

New Jersey extension agent Richard Obal uses salt hay in his garden at home. He says, "I wait for the first flush of weeds in the spring and grub those out with a hoe." Then he applies a 2- to 4-inch-thick layer of salt hay in late June, when the soil has warmed up. Any thicker, he says, and the slugs become a problem because they like a dark environment. He figures that mulching with salt hay controls up to 90 percent of the weeds in his garden.

Pines and Needles

Q. I have an unlimited amount of pine needles and would like to use them to mulch my vegetables, berry bushes, and fruit and nut trees. I've heard they make soil very acidic—is this true?

A. Pine needles make a good mulch for all the plants you mentioned. The needles are slightly acidic because the trees take up relatively small amounts of the alkaline elments (calcium, magnesium, and potassium). They also release organic acids as they decompose, but since the process occurs fairly slowly, there is only a slight acidifying effect on the soil. This effect makes pine needles ideal for blueberry bushes and other acid-loving plants, while still suitable for those requiring a neutral pH.

Between a Rock and a Hard Place

Q. Is it true that you can mulch with stone? It sounds so unusual, I wonder how it compares with hay or straw methods. How is it done?

A. Stones have most of the advantages of other types of mulches, and they even do some things better. For instance, they are particularly good for conserving soil moisture. They allow the soil to heat up quickly in the spring and, because they absorb heat, help to protect tender plants during cool nights.

The bed to be stone-mulched must be cultivated deeply, just like any permanently mulched plot. Organic matter should be disked or tilled into the soil. If leaves are available, spread a thick layer over the soil and place the stones on top of the leaves.

The stones are set in rows 2 feet wide, leaving a foot between stone paths for planting. Spaces between the stones can be filled with compost or garden loam, and the rows can be mulched with compost, straw, or other mulches. While stones help keep weeds down, note that they add nothing to the soil's organic content.

Sawdust Smarts

Q. Since I do a lot of woodworking, I have a lot of sawdust. However, some of my friends cringe when I use it as a mulch in my garden. They claim it robs the soil of nitrogen, but it always seems to work fine for me. What is right in the long run?

A. The trick to using sawdust properly is to offset the potential nitrogen shortages by adding some compost, manure, bloodmeal, or soybean or cottonseed meal to the soil before mulching. An even better alternative is to compost the sawdust with nitrogen-rich materials and then apply the mixture as a mulch. If you apply sawdust directly to the soil after one of these treatments, don't till it in unless it's completely composted.

The trouble with sawdust is that it's relatively indigestible to soil microorganisms. They use so much nitrogen in their efforts to decompose the sawdust that little is left for the plants. The plants may then turn yellow—an obvious hunger sign. Since this isn't happening to you, maybe you've been adding nitrogen-rich materials to your sawdust all along.

Cover Crop Queries

Cover Crops

Q. **The man who plows my garden suggested that I plant rye this fall as a cover crop and plow it under in the spring. What is a cover crop, and what are the benefits?**

A. More gardeners are finding that cover-cropping—using a legume, grass, or grain crop to add fertility and organic matter to the soil while preventing erosion during the winter—keeps their gardens working year-round.

Rye, wheat, and ryegrass, all nonleguminous cover crops, are probably most popular with the small gardener. Sown in the fall, these crops are incorporated into the soil in the spring to provide organic matter.

Leguminous cover crops, like clovers and alfalfa, will not only supply organic matter but will also capture nitrogen from the air and fix it in your soil—a free source of nitrogen fertilizer. For the most benefit, however, leguminous crops should grow a full year, preferably in rotation with your regular vegetables and grains.

For the small gardener who wants to put his whole garden into production each summer, ryegrass is probably the best cover crop to sow in the fall. Let it grow to about a foot in the spring, then mow before plowing it in. The mowing is a big help in speeding decomposition.

Certain cover crops are especially suited to different areas and purposes, so check with your Cooperative Extension Service for varieties and planting schedules that work best for you.

Green Manure

Q. We have a large (90-by-100-foot) garden in desperate need of manure or some other source of nitrogen. The 12 pickup loads of manure we hauled last fall were not enough. Since we are far from any source of manure, what green-manure crop could we grow? Would such crops supply all the nitrogen our garden needs, or would we have to supplement with manure?

A. Gene Logsdon, author and green-manure expert, answers: "You do not say what kind of soil you have in your garden or what its pH is. If you have put 12 pickup loads of manure on a 90-by-100-foot plot, you should be growing a fair garden even if the soil was rather poor. If the weather has been quite dry, perhaps the manure has not rotted enough to give results. Have a soil test done; perhaps there is some other deficiency in your soil.

"I would suggest before you try growing any green-manure crop (if vegetables won't grow, the green manure probably won't either) that you test the pH and treat with lime if needed. Or, if your soil is too alkaline, treat with acidifying material. Then I'd apply 200 pounds of soybean meal over the garden to build in a source of nitrogen, plus bonemeal or rock phosphate for phosphorus and potash in whatever form you can get it. If the soil tends to be alkaline, use 200 pounds of cottonseed meal instead of the soybean meal.

"Then for green manure I'd grow soybeans, broadcast and disked or raked into the soil at about the same time you normally plant bush beans. When the soybeans are grown, but before the beans mature, plow them under. You may want to shred the plants with a rotary mower first. You should still have time to plant rye and plow that under the next spring and plant clover.

"Unless you can grow clover on your garden or part of it for two years, the first year mowing the clover and letting the clippings fall to rot on the ground, and the second year plowing the clover under, green-manure crops will not supply all the nitrogen you need. Some supplemental nitrogen is advisable until you build up the soil to a high state of fertility and it contains plenty of organic matter. Then a legume green manure allowed to grow a year and plowed under a second year will help sustain that level of fertility.

"If you cannot get manure but can buy fresh-cut alfalfa (good green alfalfa hay is a second choice), you've still got a solution. Using it as a mulch or working it into the ground as a soil amendment will increase both nitrogen and potash in the soil. Dry alfalfa meal is a pretty good organic fertilizer, too."

C'est Bon Buckwheat

Q. **Is buckwheat a legume? I've heard it is highly regarded as a green manure. What kind of nutrients will it make available in the soil, and when is the best time to plow it under?**

A. Buckwheat is not a legume—it's actually an herb. Organic growers often refer to buckwheat as the green manure crop par excellence. It has the ability to use phosphates in the soil unavailable to most other plants, according to University of Minnesota researchers, and it produces a lot of organic matter, kills off weeds, and grows quickly.

Buckwheat is well known for its ability to loosen hard clay soils and for growing well on marginal land. These assets are due to the large amount of vegetation that can be turned under, as it does not have an especially deep root structure. As a green manure, it will make three crops in one growing season. As a smother crop for weed control, it does best in the midsummer or fall. For a grain crop, it is best harvested after a frost has killed the plants and the mature seeds have had time to dry.

Which Rye?

Q. **I want to plant rye as a cover crop. Which is better, winter rye or annual rye? How late in the fall can I plant it?**

A. Traditionally, winter rye (*Secale cereale*) has been used as a cover crop. This is the kind of rye grown for grain. Annual or common rye (*Lolium multiflorum*) is a temporary lawn grass, but it also works well as a winter cover. Be sure not to plant *perennial* rye (*L. perenne*)—once planted, it is very difficult to get rid of.

If your soil is poor, winter rye will be a better cover crop, as it's a more efficient extractor of nutrients. An extremely hardy plant, it can withstand temperatures as low as 40°F. You'll get the best growth by planting four to six weeks before a frost, at a rate of 2 pounds per 1,000 square feet, although later sowings will also work. Mow or scythe down the rye and till it under as early in the spring as you can. Otherwise, the stems become coarse and hard to work with. You should wait a week or two before planting to allow time for the rye to decompose.

If this lag time is a problem for you, try annual rye. It will probably winter-kill anywhere that temperatures fall below 0°F. The dead grass is easily turned under, and you can plant right away. You'll end up with less organic matter, however, and some of the nutrients may have leached out. Since some of the rye seed will lie dormant over the winter, some sprouting will occur throughout your garden in the spring, which can be a nuisance. Sow at a rate of 4 to 8 pounds per 1,000 square feet four to six weeks before the first frost. If you can't get the rye sown then, later sowings will still give you a cover.

Uncovering Cover Crops

Q. **Last September, I sowed a cover crop of rye to enhance the fertility of my garden soil and protect it from erosion during the winter. What do I have to do now to prepare my soil for planting?**

A. If cover crop topgrowth is heavy, it's best to chop it before working it into the soil. Use a rotary mower and cut close to help kill the rye. Then use a tiller to work the material into the soil. Or you can just spade it under.

The time to work in a cover crop is usually determined by the time you plan to plant a main crop in that section. Since so much of the value of cover crops depends upon their large fibrous root systems, which add organic matter to the soil, it's best to postpone working them in for as long as planting schedules permit. The bigger they get, the more organic matter your soil gets.

Warm-Climate Covers

Q. **Which cover crops are best for warm-climate summers and winters?**

A. Because it germinates and grows fast in hot weather, buckwheat is hard to beat as a summer cover crop (green manure). Buckwheat crowds out weeds and can be turned under in six to eight weeks. Field peas also grow well in hot weather, boost soil nitrogen levels, and can be harvested in the green-shell stage before the plants are tilled in.

For winter cover, try berseem clover, crimson clover, or sweet clover, all of which fix large amounts of nitrogen. If you want an edible cover crop and if overwintering insects or diseases are not a problem, you can even plant kale, garden peas, turnips, or radishes. Sow thickly and harvest some for eating, but turn under most of the crop to enrich the soil.

Annual ryegrass and cereal grains can also be used in winter, but be sure to turn them under before they grow too tall and thick for your tiller to handle. Dig or till in all cover crops before they mature their seeds, and allow two or three weeks for them to decompose before planting vegetables.

Two's Company

Q. **My garden is in Delaware. Can I successfully grow vegetables and a cover crop of annual ryegrass at the same time?**

A. Yes, you can, by using a system developed by senior extension agent Tom Jurchak for northeastern Pennsylvania vegetable farmers. The key is to time the ryegrass so it won't compete with the vegetables but will make good growth before winter. Jurchak finds that late July is the best time to overseed most crops, but you can sow annual ryegrass until September 1. Cultivate the soil, then broadcast the seed at the rate of 1 pound per 1,000 square feet. You should have a thick stand of ryegrass by frost. Till it under in early spring.

This method works well for crops like beans, brassicas, peppers, potatoes, sweet corn, and tomatoes. It's better to mulch cucumbers, melons, and other low-growing crops to avoid weed competition and make harvesting easier.

Stop That Crop

Q. **Last year I planted alfalfa in my garden as a cover crop. I tilled it under in the fall and was surprised to see it come back stronger than ever in the spring. I let it grow last summer, but how can I stop it?**

A. You were right to try to till it in, because spading often does little more than move the earth around. Dr. James Elgin of the Beltsville Agricultural Research Center recommends that you cut off the crown of the plant with a shallow tilling (about 1½ inches deep) and follow with a deeper tilling to chop up the roots. Late summer is the best time to till in alfalfa, because the soil is firm and dry then. It's difficult to do a good tilling job in moist, soft soil. For winter cover, you might want to plant annual ryegrass. It will make a good start in cool weather and protect the soil over the winter. Till it under before it heads in the spring.

Keepers of the Soil

Cool Customers

Q. In the fall when I turn my garden, I dig up earthworms. They seem sluggish, and I'm afraid they will die in the cold. Should I wait until spring to till?

A. You can cultivate as long as the temperature will remain above freezing for several hours afterwards. The worms are sluggish because they are cold-blooded and their body temperature matches that of their surroundings. With a few hours' grace, they can burrow back into the soil, eventually migrating below the frost line, where they wait out the winter. Freezing temperatures, however, will kill them and their eggs.

Come Back Little Earthworm

Q. Four years ago I turned part of my backyard into a garden. The sod I dug was full of earthworms. Last year there were none. I add manure and mulch with organic matter. My crops do well and my soil looks rich. Why have the earthworms left?

A. What time of year did you dig for earthworms? The early spring and late fall are the best times to find your worm population in the top few inches of soil. When the soil temperature is over 60°F, they burrow down to cooler regions.

Earthworms require a moist, rich soil. Your mulched and manured garden seems to fit the bill. However, earthworms are also extremely sensitive to soil pH, and garden soils tend to be slightly acidic. Most species of earthworms do best in neutral to alkaline soil (pH 7.0 or slightly above). Common nightcrawlers and field worms won't survive below a pH of 5.4. The best range for most crops is pH 6.0 to 7.5. Check your soil pH and add lime if necessary.

Burned Worms

Q. Last fall, I learned of an old gardening practice called "burning over." All garden stubble is left to dry, covered with leaves or hay, and slowly burned. Is this a valid practice? What are the benefits?

A. "Burning over" or any type of field or garden burning is definitely not a recommended practice. It's harmful to earthworms, soil organisms, and the humus itself. Soil organic matter in the top few inches can be destroyed and moisture dried out of the soil. Besides, there's no reason to burn. Those plant "wastes," once decomposed through composting and worked in, are good organic matter for building your soil.

Potted Earthworms

Q. I've been told that earthworms can slow drainage in plant containers. Is that true?

A. Yes. To drain well, soil in containers must be coarser in texture, with larger pore spaces, than soil in the garden, and it should be uniform in structure from the top of the container to the bottom. Earthworms can gradually destroy this desirable structure by ingesting the soil and passing the undigested remains as fine-textured castings, which can compact with repeated waterings into a soggy layer that resists drainage. This condition is most likely to develop near the bottom of the container, where earthworms spend most of their time because the soil remains cooler and more moist there than nearer the surface. A few earthworms may have little effect on drainage in a large container, but the smaller and shallower the pot, the more likely they are to cause a problem.

Wormy Compost

Q. I'd like to make garbage-can compost this winter so I can recycle my kitchen scraps. I understand that you need earthworms to make this kind of compost. How do I do it? Do I need a special kind of worm?

A. The best earthworms for garbage-can compost are red worms (*Lumbricus rubellus*), also called red wigglers. They are sold by commercial worm-growers and are available through mail order sources. Use either heavy plastic or galvanized cans with tight-fitting lids. Two large cans should be enough to provide compost for a moderately sized garden. Punch several holes the size of a large nail in the bottom of each can. Then, set the cans up on concrete blocks in the basement or in another place where they won't be subjected to freezing temperatures. Put a plastic pan or other container under each can to catch the liquid that will seep out of the holes during composting. (You can use this "compost tea" to water your plants.) Put about 3 inches of soil in the bottom of each can, and add 500 to 1,000 red worms per can. Layer soil, shredded newspapers, shredded leaves, or coffee grounds over each layer of kitchen scraps to neutralize odors.

A Fine Cast

Q. **How do earthworm castings improve the soil?**

A. Earthworm castings, composed of digested soil particles, organic matter, and secretions, contain from five to ten times as much nitrogen, phosphorus, and potassium as the surrounding soil. They also have one-third higher beneficial bacteria, which speed the breakdown of organic matter and the release of nutrients. The fine texture of castings makes them an excellent medium for plant growth—some plant stores even sell bags of pure castings, which, like top-grade compost, improve potting soil. Because earthworms refine soil size in the casting process, an earthworm-rich garden creates better soil texture as well as adding plant nutrients. And earthworms do make a substantial contribution—they can produce up to 700 pounds of castings a day per acre.

Grow a Better Crop

Chapter 5

The Lively Nightshades
Tomatoes, Peppers, and Eggplant

Tomato Tactics

Tomatoes Once and Done

Q. I'd like to direct-seed tomatoes in our Phoenix, Arizona, garden. When is the best time to plant the seed, and should I use a row cover?

A. You can direct-seed tomatoes as early as the average last frost date, which is February 23 in your area, says Dr. Norman Oebker, a vegetable crops specialist at the University of Arizona. Enclosing the bed with a spunbonded polyester row cover, such as Reemay, will raise the air temperature and make the seedlings grow faster once they've sprouted. However, it won't affect the soil temperature, which should be at least 60°F for best germination. To warm the soil, cover the bed with black plastic before planting the seeds. Cut small slits in the plastic where the plants are to grow, and sow five or six seeds in the soil at each slit. When the seedlings are 6 inches tall, select the strongest one in each group and remove the others. To prevent overheating, cover the plastic with straw when soil temperatures reach 85°F.

Tomato Terms

Q. **Could you tell me what is meant by the terms determinate and indeterminate with regard to tomato plants? How can I tell the difference?**

A. These classifications refer to the growth habit of the plant. Determinate varieties include most *early* varieties. They have fairly short stems, and each stem ends in a flower cluster. Between the various flower clusters on determinate varieties there are fewer than three leaves. This growth habit leads to concentrated early set of fruit, which is usually low on the plant. Most determinate varieties tend to be bushy. They don't need staking, and they don't respond well to pruning. Determinate tomatoes tend to stop growing while the fruit sets and ripens. If you prune them, you are likely to reduce their fruit yield considerably.

Indeterminate varieties, on the other hand, have stems that grow as long as they live. They produce a flower cluster, then three leaves, then another cluster, then three more leaves, and so on. Indeterminate varieties produce later than determinate tomatoes. They respond well to staking, training, and pruning.

To Train or Not to Train

Q. **Should I prune my tomatoes?**

A. Determinate tomato varieties like 'Roma', 'Tiny Tim', and 'Floramerica' do not respond well to pruning and should not be staked. Indeterminate varieties should be staked and pruned or they become too difficult to manage. These so-called trained plants will have lower yields but will take up less space than untrained plants. By staking and pruning tomatoes, you will be able to get twice as many plants in the same area, so the final yield will be higher. The fruit size will be more uniform, with fewer small tomatoes. Pruning does not affect the rate at which the fruit ripens.

On the other hand, letting your plants sprawl also has advantages. Sprawling, viny plants that are unpruned are better protected from drying out and are less susceptible to cracking and sunscald than trained plants. Mulch well and allow the vines to ramble over the mulch.

More Tomatoes, Less Space

Q. I love tomatoes but have a small garden. What can I do to get maximum production from each plant?

A. Try varieties with an indeterminate growth habit, which yield more than determinate types, and stake the plants. Such well-known varieties as 'Beefmaster', 'Beefsteak', 'Better Boy', 'Burpee's Big Boy', 'Burpee's Big Girl', 'Early Girl Hybrid', and 'Manalucie' are indeterminate, as are the plum tomato 'San Marzano' and the cherry tomato 'Sweet 100'. Seed catalog descriptions tell whether a variety is determinate or indeterminate. Plant the tomatoes 2 feet apart in beds or at 18-inch intervals in rows set 3 feet apart. To prevent the staked plants from becoming top-heavy, they must be pruned. Pinch out all but a few stems that grow from leaf axils of the main stem. Two or more stems produce highest yields. After the soil has warmed up, mulch the plants, since staked tomatoes dry out quickly.

Setting Fruit under Lights

Q. We are trying to grow tomatoes indoors, but under our small light setup, they grow spindly and drop all their flowers. How can we get them to fruit in winter?

A. Increase the light intensity. Two 40-watt (4-foot) fluorescent tubes or a south-facing window may supply enough light to ripen a few salad tomatoes on a dwarf variety, such as 'Tiny Tim' or 'Pixie'. Four 40-watt tubes alone, or two 40-watt tubes hung in a south-facing window, will promote more fruiting. If you're interested in heavy production from a greenhouse tomato, such as 'Stakeless' or 'Starshot', you'll need eight 40-watt tubes.

To get the most from your light setup, keep the tops of the plants 6 inches or less below the tubes. If you have only a few plants, place them near the center of the fixture, where light intensity is highest. Various combinations of tubes will work, such as one cool white and one warm white or one cool white and one wide-spectrum plant light per two-tube fixture. The plants should receive light for 14 to 16 hours a day. Keep daytime temperatures between 70° and 80°F and allow a 10-degree drop at night. When plants bloom, pollinate the flowers by shaking the plants gently every day or two, or distribute pollen with a brush.

Saving Tomato
Seed

Saving Tomato Seed

Q. I'm saving tomato seed. What's the best way to separate the seed from the pulp?

A. The best way is to ferment the fruit, since this also destroys tomato canker bacteria, which can cause the plants to wilt and white spots to form on the fruit. Be sure your tomato is fully ripe, or even overripe. Cut open the fruit and scoop out the seeds and pulp. Put the mixture into a jar or glass with ¼ cup of water, and let it ferment at room temperature. Stir at least twice daily. The fermentation turns the pulp into a thin liquid and allows the viable seeds to sink to the bottom of the container. The fermentation will take four days at 60°F or three days at 70°F. At least three days are needed to destroy the canker bacteria. After the seeds have sunk to the bottom of the container, pour off the liquefied pulp and the seeds that are floating on the top. Spread the remaining seeds on newspaper or paper towels to dry. After drying, rub the seeds off the paper and store in an airtight container.

Winter Tomatoes

Q. I live in southern California and would like to grow tomatoes through the winter, since the temperature here rarely falls below 50°F. Are there any varieties that set fruit at low temperatures?

A. Even though you are in a frost-free climate, tomato plants don't set fruit well below 65°F and are injured at 55°F. However, you can harvest a crop of tomatoes during the winter by covering the row with a plastic tunnel.

Wayne Schrader, a farm advisor for San Diego County, California, suggests the following system, using 'Celebrity' tomatoes: Set out tomato plants in October or November in a row about 28 inches wide. Place 6-foot-tall stakes at 4-foot intervals down the center of the row. Tie a piece of heavy string to the row of stakes 26 inches above the ground. Then cut two pieces of 36-inch-wide clear plastic 6 feet longer than the length of the row. Lay one of the long edges of one piece along the outer edge of the row, leaving 3 feet of excess at each end, and either cover it with several inches of soil or weight it with stones or bricks. Do the same with the other piece along the opposite edge of the row. Attach the other long edges of the plastic to the string with clothespins, creating a "pup tent." Fold the excess plastic to cover the ends and secure with stones or bricks.

This row cover will increase the air temperature 6 to 20 degrees during the day and will warm the top 3 inches of soil 3 to 8 degrees at night, according to Schrader. When the interior temperature rises above 75°F, vent it by opening the ends or by removing the clothespins and pulling back the plastic. When the tomato plants flower, shake them so pollination will occur. By the time they outgrow the cover, the temperature will be warmer. Then you can remove the cover and train the plants to the stakes.

Hot Tomatoes

Q. **How can I grow a good tomato in Texas? I've grown delicious tomatoes in several states, but here they all end up thick-skinned and tasteless.**

A. According to John Dromgoole, an *Organic Gardening* contributor from Austin, Texas, you'll get better tomatoes if you time the planting so that they ripen before and after the hottest weather in July and August. For the first crop, start seeds or buy transplants early and grow them in milk cartons or other containers so that you'll have large plants to set out as soon as the weather is warm enough. Mulch the plants, irrigate often (thick skins indicate water stress), and work in plenty of water-holding organic matter—humus breaks down quickly during long, hot summers.

Before the summer heat ends fruit production, take cuttings of these plants to root. These vigorous replacements are ready to set out in time to produce a fall crop. If plants are in good condition, indeterminate varieties can be rejuvenated after the early crop by removing weak and broken stems and heading back the remaining shoots. A topdressing of fertilizer and regular watering should bring them back into production by autumn.

An Altitude Problem

Q. **How can I get my tomatoes to ripen earlier in our area, Idaho Falls, Idaho? We often have a frost right after Labor Day, just when the crop is beginning to turn red.**

A. Your difficulty in getting tomatoes to ripen in your area is understandable, with a 105-day growing season and an altitude of 4,800 feet. Choose the earliest varieties possible, such as 'Early Girl', 'Betterboy', and 'Better Girl'. Then add 20 days to the maturity date, because even though the average last frost occurs June 1, the soil temperature doesn't reach 50°F until midmonth, according to Bonneville County extension agent Charles Dunham.

Transplant seedlings started in early April into a south-sloping bed for maximum sun exposure, setting the stem below the soil surface to encourage more rooting. Dunham suggests covering the plants with hot caps and pinching the tops after fruit set. He's found that the Wall-o'-Water cloches help tomato plants grow faster.

Stop the Drop

Q. **What causes tomato blossoms to fall, and how can I stop them from doing so?**

A. Tomato blossom drop has a wide variety of causes. Low soil moisture with hot, dry winds will do it. A sudden shift from a hot spell to cool, wet weather is another cause. To prevent blossom drop, irrigate when the weather is hot and dry and plant tomatoes in soil that has good drainage. Certain varieties like 'Walter' and 'Floramerica' hold their blossoms better in hot weather.

The soil's mineral content also can play a role in blossom drop. Deficiencies of potassium, phosphorus, and nitrogen can all cause flowers to abort and drop off. But the most common mineral problem is *too much* nitrogen. It causes rapid, succulent growth and throws the plant's metabolism off balance, promoting blossom drop. Avoid applying high-nitrogen materials like bloodmeal or fresh manure during the early growth of the plant. If you use manure tea on your tomatoes, make sure it's weak.

Finally, both verticillium and fusarium wilt diseases can aggravate blossom drop. Many tomato varieties resist both diseases. These resistant varieties will be marked in most seed catalogs.

Sunscald

Q. **Why did many of my tomatoes have papery, blisterlike patches this past year?**

A. The patches are sunscald, which is caused by direct sunlight burning the fruit in hot, dry weather. The problem can also affect peppers. Plants that have lost their lower leaves or have been pruned and trellised are especially susceptible to this disorder. Sunscald first appears on green tomatoes as a yellow or white patch on the side facing the sun. The patch may remain yellow or white as the fruit matures, but usually the cells are badly damaged and the patch turns brown and papery. Often the damage opens the way for fungal infection.

Protect your plants from defoliating diseases by rotating your crops, planting disease-resistant varieties, and practicing good garden sanitation. Be sure your soil has enough nitrogen, but don't just pour on the fertilizer or it will stimulate leaf growth rather than fruit production. Plants without enough nitrogen will die back early, dropping their leaves before the fruit is mature. If the tomatoes become exposed to the sun, shade them with a cheesecloth awning or lathwork.

Green Shoulders

Q. **My tomatoes won't ripen on the stem end. What do you think the problem is?**

A. Most likely, the fruit is receiving too much sun, resulting in a physiological problem called "green shoulder." The first tomatoes of the season often have green shoulder because there's not enough foliage to shade them. Some staking methods tend to make the problem worse. You may want to try cages, which don't require pruning of protective foliage.

Catfaced Tomatoes

Q. **Here in Florida, I have beautiful tomato plants over 5 feet high, but the bottoms of the fruits are catfaced—puckered and veined with brown scar tissue. What causes this, and how can I prevent it?**

A. Catfacing results when environmental stresses during bloom cause young fruits to develop more than the usual number of cells. Exposure to temperatures below 55°F or above 85°F are the most frequent causes, but drought, high winds, and the herbicide 2,4-D can also produce catfacing. Heavy use of fertilizers high in ammonia, such as uncomposted poultry manure, may contribute to the problem.

The best way to prevent catfacing is to plant resistant varieties, such as 'Floramerica', 'Burpee's VF', and 'Big Set'. 'Floradel' and 'Floradade' are bred especially for Florida conditions.

Hounding Hornworms

Q. **My tomato patch is full of hornworms. The majority of the hornworms have white "tubes" on their backs, which I understand are the eggs of a parasitic wasp. How long does it take for the wasp to destroy the worm?**

A. The white "tubes" you see on the hornworms are the pupae of the braconid wasp, a beneficial parasite. Entomologist Bob Tetrault of Penn State University's Extension Service says that once the wasps reach the pupal stage, they've finished feeding on the hornworm and, though the worm may still be alive, its ability to destroy tomato and potato crops is basically a thing of the past. If the wasps have reached the pupal stage in your garden, let the cycle continue, allowing as many wasps as possible to reach adulthood and to continue breeding in the remaining hornworms. But if you have hornworms and see no white pupae forming, by all means, handpick the worms and destroy them immediately.

Stinkbug

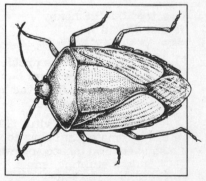

Attack of the Tomato Stinkbugs

Q. **Some of our tomatoes have small, irregular white lumps under their skins. Our neighbors have the same problem with some of their tomatoes. What's wrong?**

A. The white lumps on your tomatoes are caused by stinkbugs. Early in the season, the pest pierces the fruit to feed and leaves traces of saliva behind. The saliva in the wound breaks down the tomato tissue, causing the spots. You can still eat the fruit by cutting off the damaged part. Stinkbugs prefer damp places and generally attack the fruit closest to the ground. Control stinkbug damage by staking or trellising plants and pruning tomato suckers to avoid high humidity.

Trouble Spots

Q. **Last year, tomato spotted wilt hit our area. I planted 22 tomato plants, and 11 of them turned black and died. Can you offer any help?**

A. Since spotted wilt (*Lethum australiense*) is a viral disease transmitted almost entirely by tiny insects called thrips, you can control it by keeping the thrips off the plants, says Dr. Lowell Black, a vegetable disease specialist at Louisiana State University. He offers this suggestion. After you've prepared the bed in spring, cover it with black plastic. Then spray the plastic with aluminum spray paint, allow it to dry, and plant as usual. The reflective surface apparently confuses the insects as they fly over it, and most will not land on the plants. In Black's experiments, the treatment reduced the incidence of spotted wilt by 60 percent over the control.

Another effective technique, says Black, is to grow two plants per pot and set them out together. He has found that in a given area the same number of plants become infected, so doubled-up plantings yield better than conventional spacing. In areas where spotted wilt is severe, Black suggests combining the two methods.

Tomatoes Don't Smoke; Neither Should You

Q. **Last year, we had a problem with tomatoes started indoors. In midsummer they were healthy with green fruit. Gradually, they seemed to die from the base up. We've been told cigarette smoke may be a problem.**

A. Tobacco mosaic virus (TMV), which is highly contagious, is spread to tomato plants by people who've handled tobacco, including smokers and tobacco chewers. While it rarely kills the plants, TMV causes stunting, small fruit, reduced yields, and yellowing and curling of the leaves.

To prevent the spread of TMV, wash your hands thoroughly before you handle plants. Some TMV experts recommend dipping tomato transplants in milk before setting them out, since milk strongly inhibits the disease. Set out transplants where tomatoes have not been grown for at least two years. Remove and burn diseased plants and those surrounding them, since composting doesn't create temperatures high enough to kill the virus. Eliminate perennial weeds, and keep tomatoes away from their nightshade family relatives, including tobacco, cucumbers, and potatoes, which are possible disease carriers. Several TMV-resistant varieties now available include 'President', 'Celebrity', 'Big Pick', and 'Quick Pick'. Crop rotation will help prevent buildups of any of these diseases.

Seeing Spots

Q. My tomato leaves develop brown spots, turn yellow, and drop off from the bottom up. I believe this is early blight and wonder if the manure I got from a neighbor whose tomato plants also have this problem could be the cause.

A. Since you didn't notice any problems with the fruit, it's probably not early blight, which causes lesions in the stem end of the tomato and dark circular spots with targetlike concentric rings on the leaves. Your plants probably have septoria leaf spot (*Septoria lycopersica*), another fungal disease. Septoria thrives in warm, wet summers and usually appears just as the plants set fruit. Older leaves are attacked first, developing round spots 1/16 to 1/8 inch in diameter that are watersoaked at first, then turn gray with dark margins. The stalks are gradually defoliated from the ground up, and the fruit fails to mature or is spoiled by sunscald. The manure you used could have been contaminated with this fungus. Its spores are spread during watering or by contact with soil or tools.

To control septoria, buy disease-resistant varieties and practice good sanitation in the garden. Try to obtain manure from another source or compost it first, away from your garden. Septoria spores require a high moisture level for germination. If possible, water the plants with drip, rather than overhead, irrigation to avoid wetting the leaves. To enhance air movement, stake or cage the plants and prune back some of the stems. The fungus can live for at least three years on tomato refuse in the soil and indefinitely on weeds such as horse nettle and other nightshades. Burn crop residues and eliminate weeds. Finally, grow tomatoes in four-year rotations with unrelated crops.

Blighted Hopes

Q. My tomatoes have early blight. Are there any nonchemical ways to control this disease?

A. Yes. Use a three-year rotation with crops not in the tomato family (potatoes, peppers, and eggplant are all tomato relatives), and bury or compost all plant refuse immediately after harvest. Several resistant varieties are 'Early Cascade', 'Floramerica', 'Manalucie', and 'Red King'.

Tomato Wilt

Q. Before my tomatoes ripen, the leaves on the plants turn yellow and die from the bottom upward. The tomatoes are small and don't taste as good as healthy ones. What is the problem?

A. Your tomatoes are infected with a soilborne fungus called fusarium wilt (*Fusarium oxysporum* f. *lycopersici*). Although it is one of the most prevalent tomato diseases, it is easily controlled by using resistant varieties, often designated in seed catalogs and on seed packages by the letter F after the variety name.

Tomato Brown-Out

Q. My tomatoes develop small, light brown spots that appear to be skin-deep at first, then become larger and spoil the tomatoes when they ripen. What causes the spots, and is there a solution?

A. Round, sunken, water-soaked spots on ripening tomatoes are characteristic of tomato anthracnose, a fungal disease also called ripe rot. It attacks mainly the fruits, though you might find small dead spots with a yellow halo on the oldest leaves. The fruits can be infected when they're green but show no sign of spotting until they ripen, which usually coincides with hot, humid weather—perfect conditions for the fungus. Varieties susceptible to defoliation by leaf diseases are most vulnerable to anthracnose.

The fungus overwinters on decaying tomato vines and fruit in the soil, so clean up and burn or trash your tomato plants in the fall. Grow tomatoes on a two-year or longer rotation with other crops. When watering, soak the ground, not the plants. Since spores are spread by splashing water, overhead irrigation can greatly increase infection.

A Peck of Pepper Problems

Bitter Peppers

Q. Last year my bell peppers were small and bitter. Could dry conditions or low organic matter in the soil (it was a new garden) cause these problems?

A. Low organic matter combined with a dry season would mean that your peppers didn't get the two things they needed most for fruit production—a high moisture level and high humidity. Peppers are natives of the tropics, so they need warm temperatures (70° to 80°F during the day and 60° to 70° at night) and moist conditions. If stressed, the plants will never fully recover.

To avoid setbacks, young pepper plants should be set out after the soil is warm but before the plants flower. During dry periods, water them daily. Mulch and close spacing (16 inches apart is adequate) will also help maintain high moisture levels.

One other factor that can lead to plants' producing small, bitter peppers is a boron deficiency in the soil. As a safeguard, have your soil tested before you plant this year.

All Show, No Go

Q. My bell pepper plants grow large but don't produce peppers; instead, the blossoms fall off. Can you tell me what is wrong?

A. Temperatures below 60°F or above 80°F will cause blossom-drop, but your problem is most likely due to water stress. Large, blocky-fruited varieties like 'California Wonder' and 'Yolo Wonder' are especially sensitive to stressful conditions, according to pepper specialist Dr. Chris Wien of Cornell University. He recommends 'Lady Bell', 'Canape', 'Green Boy', 'Ace', and 'New Ace', which have somewhat smaller fruit but are more productive under stress. Make sure you mulch pepper plants and water regularly during dry spells.

Not-So-Hot Peppers

Q. I grow 'Hot Portugal' peppers. Some of the fruits are as hot as fire and some are as sweet as bell peppers, even though they were picked from the same bush at the same time. This is true whether they're picked green or red. What causes the variation?

A. Climate and, to a lesser degree, culture. Many hot-pepper cultivars produce less capsaicin—the substance that makes them hot—when grown under cool, moist conditions than they do under hotter, drier conditions. You may get more pungent peppers if you space the plants to get maximum sunlight and grow them fairly dry after fruit set.

A surer way is to experiment with cultivars until you find one that suits your climate. 'Long Red Cayenne' is consistently the hottest pepper grown at the Rodale Research Center, Kutztown, Pennsylvania. 'Sandia', a 7-inch pepper suitable for stuffing, is recommended by Dr. Roy Nakayama, now retired, a former chili breeder at New Mexico State University.

Get-Up-and-Go
Got Up and Went

Q. For the past two years my bell pepper plants have grown very slowly. The lower leaves turn pale green and fall off. I apply composted leaves to the bed twice a year. What do you suggest?

A. Acid soil, which stunts the growth of most vegetable plants, may be the problem, suggests Dr. Chris Wien, a pepper specialist at Cornell University. Have your soil's pH tested and if necessary, raise it to approximately 6.5 with dolomitic or calcitic limestone. (The correct amount to apply depends on the soil type and acidity and is usually included with the test results.)

Compost made from leaves may not contain enough nitrogen for peppers. To boost the nitrogen level of your next batch of compost, try adding some manure or grass clippings to the leaves, and cover the top of the compost pile with a tarp or boards to keep rain from leaching out nutrients. Until your compost is ready, you can sidedress the pepper plants with a sprinkling of bloodmeal after they've set several fruits.

Warped Peppers

Q. **Our garden is situated in California's moderate coastal climate. Some of my bell peppers are badly deformed. What causes this problem?**

A. Cold weather before or during flowering often causes peppers to be misshapen. Temperatures in the 40s and 50s or lower can damage developing ovaries or reduce pollination, resulting in undersized, flattened, or otherwise distorted fruit.

Choose pepper varieties better suited to your area. 'Golden Bell' and 'Staddon's Select' both set fruit under cool conditions better than other bell peppers. Make the most of available heat and light by planting on the south side of the house, away from the shade.

Drying Paprika

Q. **My red peppers turn brown or moldy when I hang them up to dry. How can I get them to dry red and mold-free?**

A. The peppers will naturally darken somewhat as they dry, but you should be able to get brighter paprika, free from mold, by drying the peppers in an oven or food dehydrator. Use only mature, sound peppers. Cut off the stems and halve the peppers. Remove the seeds and core for drying separately. Flatten the halves and place them in a single layer on trays in a food dehydrator at 140°F or on cookie sheets in a 150°F oven until they're crisp and brittle.

For the brightest color, grind the dried pepper halves alone. Adding the dried seeds will make a paler, more pungent paprika. Store in tightly sealed containers in a cool closet or the refrigerator.

Pepper Pests

Q. **In my New York State garden, I find brown, pinhead-size holes in many of my peppers just before they ripen. Affected fruits rot from the inside out. What's attacking them?**

A. Corn earworms are the most likely culprits, according to Dr. W. C. Kelly, a vegetable crops specialist at Cornell University. Though corn is their preferred food plant, earworms will also feed on peppers, eggplants, tomatoes (under the name of tomato fruitworm), limas, and other crops, especially in years when the pests are abundant.

In upstate New York, corn earworm moths appear in late July or early August and lay their eggs within one or two weeks. On peppers, the eggs are laid on the youngest leaves. After hatching in mid-August, the caterpillars feed briefly on the leaves, then tunnel into the fruits. Each caterpillar may damage several fruits before crawling to the ground to pupate. Tunneled fruits are quickly spoiled by bacteria and fungi, especially in wet weather.

You can avoid some damage by planting early varieties and harvesting the peppers green. If you have only a few plants, search for and rub off the eggs, which are yellowish and grooved with a flattened, spherical shape. *Bacillus thuringiensis* (Bt), a commercially available biocontrol, will kill the caterpillars, but it must be applied before they enter the fruits. Use according to directions on the package.

Since earworms vary in abundance from year to year, you can probably harvest a good crop of peppers in most years simply by watching for and culling infested fruits, says Kelly. Starting in mid-August, look for earworms in corn, which is usually attacked before peppers. As soon as earworms appear in the corn, begin to inspect your peppers for entrance holes. With only one earworm generation in the North, you can cull fruits with holes and leave sound fruits to ripen.

Eggplant Enigmas

Where's the Eggplant?

Q. **Last year the blossoms on my eggplants developed, wilted, and dropped off. What caused this, and how can I prevent it?**

A. The villain is probably the tarnished plant bug, a ¼-inch-long, greenish-yellow to brown insect that sucks on blossom stems and other plant parts, according to both Rob Johnston of Johnny's Selected Seeds and Dr. W. C. Kelly, vegetable crops specialist at Cornell University. Johnston offers two suggestions: Try adding more phosphorus to the soil, which will make the plants produce more flowers; and grow the eggplant under slitted row covers, which, despite the openings, will keep the tarnished plant bugs out.

Another possibility is lack of pollination due to extended periods below 65°F. Under these conditions, explains Kelly, either the pollen doesn't germinate or the pollen tube doesn't grow quickly enough. 'Dusky' is an early variety that should fare better than later-maturing varieties in cool temperatures. Using row covers will also raise the soil and air temperatures, ensuring good blossom set.

Phomopsis Phobia

Q. **Last summer, many of our eggplant fruits developed large, oval brown spots that sometimes rotted the whole side of an eggplant. What was the cause?**

A. Your eggplant had phomopsis blight, a fungal disease that attacks only eggplant and is most destructive in hot, wet summers. Before the fruits are attacked, the older leaves develop clearly defined, round gray or brown spots with pale centers. Badly infected leaves yellow and die. The fungus may also girdle the stem close to the soilline, killing seedlings and causing mature plants to fall over. Tools, insects, and splashed water spread the spores.

The fungus overwinters on seed, in diseased plant refuse, and in the soil, where it can persist for three years. In the fall, clean up all dead plants and burn, discard, or compost them in a hot pile. Grow eggplant in three-year rotations with other crops. Check seed catalogs for resistant varieties, which include 'Florida Beauty', 'Florida Market', and 'Florida High Bush'.

Chapter 6

Life with Legumes
Peas and Beans

Problems with Peas

Succession-Planted Peas

Q. **Every year my pea crop seems to mature all at once. Many of the peas get big and starchy before I can pick them. Can I make succession plantings to lengthen the pea season?**

A. Succession planting works well for peas only where summers are cool. Where summers are hot, later plantings will either catch up with earlier ones or the blossom-set will be poor and pods will dry up in the heat.

Instead, try planting several varieties with different maturity dates. 'Alaska', 'Maestro', and 'Sparkle' all begin bearing in about 55 days. Burpee's 'Blue Bantam' matures about 10 days later and will produce over a long period if the pods are kept picked. (All varieties should be picked every day for maximum production.) 'Wando' tolerates hot weather better than most varieties. It begins to bear 64 to 68 days after planting.

Fall for These Peas

Q. I garden in New Jersey. Last July I planted peas for a fall crop, but because of the heat, they didn't grow or produce well. Are there certain varieties to plant for late peas?

A. 'Wando' is a good choice because it is both heat- and cold-resistant. 'Perfection Dark Green' is another heat-tolerant variety. Plant breeder Dr. G. A. Marx of the New York State Agricultural Experiment Station in Geneva recommends edible-podded peas because you can begin eating the tiny pods as soon as they form, rather than waiting for the peas to develop inside. Another consideration in choosing a variety is disease resistance, especially to powdery mildew, which thrives under the cool, moist nights and hot days typical of late summer. 'Grenadier' is a good fall variety because it is resistant to powdery mildew.

The planting date for the best crop of fall peas is fairly critical. If planted too late, the flowers may be killed by frost. But if you plant too early, blossom set will be poor due to the heat. Estimate the ideal sowing time by noting days to maturity on the seed packet (the shorter a season the variety requires, the better) and then by counting backwards from your average first-frost date. Add a few extra days to account for the shorter days and cool fall temperatures. In your area, you should plant no later than the first week in August. Keep the peas well watered, and apply a heavy mulch so the soil will stay cool and moist.

Deep Worries

Q. My 'Sugar Snap' peas germinate poorly—only 60 percent of my seeds come up. Could I be planting too deeply?

A. Yes. At least 80 percent of your pea seeds should germinate, but planting too deeply could reduce the percentage significantly. Dr. Robert Becker, horticulturist at the New York State Agricultural Experiment Station in Geneva, recommends planting the seed no more than ½ to ¾ inch deep. He explains that edible-podded pea seed is smaller than English pea seed, so it has less food reserve and therefore tends to rot a little more easily if planted too deeply. Seed that is more than three years old is likely to germinate poorly.

Cowpea Curculio

Q. **Every summer most of my Southern peas have little worms in them. What are they, and how can I eliminate them?**

A. The worms are larvae of the cowpea curculio, a ¼-inch-long black beetle with numerous puncture marks on its humped back. Females lay eggs in the pods throughout the summer, and the larvae feed in the developing peas. The curculios also feed on related legumes, strawberries, and cotton. When disturbed, adult curculios drop to the ground and hide under litter, making them difficult to control with insecticides.

You probably won't be able to eliminate the pests from your garden, but you can reduce the number of wormy Southern peas (cowpeas) by planting resistant varieties such as 'Mississippi Shipper', 'Zipper Cream', and 'Freezergreen'. These varieties have thick, fibrous pod walls that resist puncture by the curculios. The heirloom variety 'Blue Goose' is also said to be resistant. To further control the pests, rotate crops and clean up debris in and around the garden after harvest to reduce overwintering areas for the adults.

Powdery Peas

Q. **Last summer my peas were covered with a white, powdery coating. What was it, and how can I keep it from coming back this year?**

A. Your peas had powdery mildew, a fungal disease that attacks many of the older home-garden varieties. Peas can become infected early in the season, but the disease usually strikes later, during the warmer and drier weather that favors its growth. The fungus is most common on mature vines whose productivity has declined. Pull up infected vines and compost them, or plow them under to control the disease. If younger plants are attacked, dust or spray with wettable sulfur. Some resistant pea varieties are 'Knight', 'Grenadier', 'Maestro', 'Olympia', and 'Mayfair'. Check seed catalogs for others.

Diseased Peas

Q. **For the third year in a row, the leaves on my peas turned yellow and died, starting at the bottom of the plant, and the pods were shorter than normal when they matured. Can you tell me what causes this?**

A. Several soilborne fungal diseases cause peas to become yellow and stunted. Plants infected with fusarium wilt (caused by *Fusarium oxysporum*) have downward-curling leaves, and if you split the stem lengthwise near the base, you'll see an orange to red discoloration. Various root rots attack peas, causing the lower stems and roots to turn brown or black. Seed catalogs list pea varieties with resistance to *F. oxysporum*. There are no varieties resistant to root rot (which can persist in soil for ten years or more); however, 'Wando' is said to be tolerant of *F. solani*, one of the most common rot organisms. Use five-year rotations and keep the soil well drained and aerated by adding plenty of organic matter to reduce infection.

If your peas showed no signs of disease, hot weather may have killed the plants before they could produce a full crop. Planting earlier will solve this problem.

Baffling Beans

What's the Right Dose?

Q. **Should I inoculate beans every time I plant?**

A. Yes. Rodale researchers recommend that you inoculate with each planting. Inoculant is made of rhizobial bacteria, which live on the roots of beans and peas and supply the plants with nitrogen. Inoculant is inexpensive, and it's insurance that your plants will be able to benefit from rhizobial nitrogen fixation. The commonly sold garden inoculant is good for green beans and related dry beans, scarlet runner beans, peas, and lima beans. There is also an inoculant for peanuts. Cowpea inoculant works just as well for adzuki and mung beans. Where cowpeas are commonly grown, you should be able to find the right inoculant at farm supply stores. Those stores often sell soybean inoculant also. Favas require their own inoculant.

Giving Treated
Seeds the Treatment

Q. **Can I use *Rhizobium* legume inoculant on treated seeds?**

A. Fungicides, such as captan, used to treat seeds are toxic to *Rhizobium* bacteria. If you must use treated seeds, sprinkle inoculant into the furrow before planting the seeds. Roots will be colonized by the bacteria when they grow beyond the treated seed coat.

Is the Captan OK?

Q. **This year I ordered some bean seed and noticed that it was treated with the fungicide captan. Is there a health question about using these seeds? Where can I get untreated seed?**

A. Yes, there may be a risk in handling seeds treated with captan. Although not highly toxic, captan is known to be carcinogenic. Related to thalidomide, it has also caused birth defects and genetic damage in laboratory animals. Since you already have treated seed, wear heavy gloves when planting (captan can cause a skin irritation). Wash your skin and the gloves immediately afterward. The fungicide on the sown seeds will break down in several weeks. For other reasons not to use captan on legumes, see "Giving Treated Seeds the Treatment," above.

Untreated seed is widely available. Many of the major seed companies sell it. Most companies that treat their seed will sell you untreated seed if you request it. The advantage of treated seed is that, unlike untreated seed, it can lie in cold, wet soil without rotting. But since all beans require a soil temperature of at least 60°F in order to germinate, there's no disadvantage in waiting until the soil is warm enough before planting untreated seed.

Fishy Beans

Q. **Why do my 'Blue Lake Bush' green beans curl up as they grow instead of forming straight pods?**

A. Your beans produce curled pods because they are not getting enough water. Under hot, dry conditions, curled pods (called fishhooks) and pods with seeds that don't mature to fill out the pod (called polliwogs) can develop. 'Blue Lake Bush' green beans are bred for cool, moist conditions, with daytime temperatures of 85°F and 50°F at night. They need at least an inch of water every week. Curled pods are not unique to 'Blue Lake Bush' green beans, however. All beans can develop fishhooks or polliwogs if stressed.

Snap Beans

Picking Primer

Q. Can I increase my bean yields by picking the pods a certain way? My wife claims that if you allow the stem ends to remain on the vines, you'll get a higher yield.

A. Dr. Mike Dickson, a snap bean breeder at New York State Agricultural Experiment Station, says it's not *how* but *how often* you pick beans that counts. Picking the pods while they're young keeps the plants productive. Pick when they are the width of a pencil and the seeds are barely visible. Letting beans grow past that stage puts the plants' energy into seed rather than flower production, and it's the flowers that give you more beans.

Blistering Beans

Q. When is the best time to water to keep my beans from blistering?

A. Blisters—brown, papery spots on the pods and leaves of your beans—are burns due to sunlight magnified by drops of water. The best way to avoid this is to water the soil, not the plants. A drip irrigation system will keep your beans burn-free. If you do use a hose or other overhead system, water early in the morning so the droplets on the plant will have evaporated by the time the sun is strong enough to cause a problem. If the sun comes up hot where you live, you can water in the early evening. But water early enough so the leaves dry before nightfall. If the leaves stay moist through the night, they'll provide the perfect environment for diseases to develop.

Pooped-Out Limas

Q. I've direct-seeded two varieties of 'Fordhook' pole limas the past two springs with poor results. One set only a few pods, and the other produced pods that didn't fill out. Any suggestions?

A. The problem is most likely due to excessive heat, according to lima breeder Dr. Vernon Fisher. While limas require warm temperatures to set pods, if it's above 80°F for more than 12 hours a day, the pollen die, and beans won't form. Baby limas and 'Fordhook' varieties like '242' and 'Concentrator' (both bush types) are less finicky, but Fisher suggests planting all other 'Fordhook' varieties no later than the end of May. Even though the plants won't set many beans during midsummer, they'll be sturdy enough to survive and should produce a satisfactory fall crop.

Soybean Subtleties

Q. What is the difference between edible soybeans and field soybeans?

A. Edible soybeans produce green, black, or yellow seeds that are usually larger and more tender than the small, hard, yellow seeds produced by field soybeans. The most popular of the edible types are the green-seeded vegetable soybeans, which were developed for use in the greenshell stage, though they can also be eaten as dry beans. Because of their more tender texture, vegetable soybeans are easier to cook than field types. They're also milder, sweeter, and more digestible, says Dr. Yun-tzu Kiang, a soybean breeder at the University of New Hampshire. Field soybeans have a strong, disagreeable flavor and contain a higher percentage of indigestible, gas-producing starches than vegetable soybeans. The nutritional value of field and vegetable soybeans is about the same.

Growing Garbanzos

Q. After frost last September here in Utah, our garbanzo beans were still green and had flowers and pods. Should the beans be picked green and then dried, or should they dry on the vine?

A. Garbanzo beans are usually allowed to dry on the vine, but the growing season in your area may be too short or too cool and moist to mature a crop in the field. In a hot, dry climate, most garbanzo beans mature in 115 to 120 days, says U.S. Department of Agriculture (USDA) plant geneticist Dr. Frederick J. Muehlbauer, who works with this crop in eastern Washington. In a cooler, damper climate, the same varieties may take 140 to 150 days because the plants remain vegetative longer. They develop beans, but the crop won't dry. If you want dry garbanzos, you may have to pick the pods as they fill out or pull the plants late in the season (they're very tolerant of frost) and dry them on wire racks or in a dehydrator. The beans have reached full size if you can feel them when you squeeze the puffy pods. The variety 'U.C.-5' is said to be adapted to shorter, cooler growing seasons.

However, it isn't necessary to wait for the beans to mature—they're very good eaten in the greenshell stage, when they can be cooked like peas. Though not as sweet as peas, they are sweeter and much less starchy than mature garbanzo beans, and they have the distinctive garbanzo flavor, says Muehlbauer. His favorite way to eat garbanzos is to pull a plant, then shell and eat the young beans right in the field.

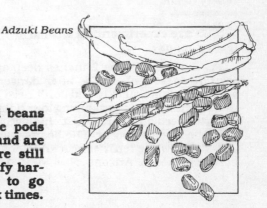

Adzuki Beans

Harvesting Adzukis

Q. **I'm growing adzuki beans this year. A few of the pods have dried on the vine and are shattering, but most are still green. How can I simplify harvesting—I don't want to go down the rows five or six times.**

A. Most varieties of adzuki bean tend to ripen over a longer period than other dry beans. They also shatter more easily. If you want to harvest just once, wait until most of the pods have turned brown. You'll just have to sacrifice a few immature and shattered pods. Pull the entire plants and hang them in a warm, dry place.

Sprouting Mung Beans

Q. **I would like to grow mung beans for sprouting. Can you tell me how to grow them and where I can purchase seeds?**

A. Mung beans grow best in hot, dry weather. Maturity dates will vary with the climate. In Oklahoma, where mung beans are grown commercially and the weather is ideal, they mature in 70 days. In cooler or wetter weather, they can take as long as 95 to 100 days to mature. Mung beans can be grown as far north as Maine—though you can't expect a crop every year. Johnny's Selected Seeds of Albion, Maine, lists 130 days to maturity for northern gardeners.

Warm, sandy soils are best, but it's possible to bring in a crop in any well-drained soil. Plant the mung beans 6 to 8 inches apart after the soil warms up. Mung beans are untouched by Mexican bean beetles, which attack many other garden beans. Harvest the mature beans when the plants have died back. The pods will be slightly curved and the beans will appear olive green. They will mature at different rates. To avoid a low yield, watch the pods and pick the beans as they ripen. Once the pods get too dry, they burst open and scatter the beans on the ground.

Tepary Beans

Q. **We are experimenting with arid-land crops. How do I grow tepary beans?**

A. Plant the beans 2 inches deep and 2 to 3 inches apart in rows 18 to 24 inches wide after danger of frost has passed. The seeds germinate quickly and don't need irrigation. These beans do well in arid climates, producing four times as much as other beans. Teparies need little care—just shallow cultivation to control weeds until the blooms appear. The beans will mature in 60 to 70 days. The small, white teparies resemble navy beans and are native to northern Mexico, Arizona, New Mexico, and Texas.

A Bean Beetle Predator

Q. **Last year my beans were destroyed by Mexican bean beetles. What's the best way to control them?**

A. A small imported predatory wasp, called *Pediobus foveolatus*, is your best bet against Mexican bean beetles. Studies in Maryland and Florida found these wasps to be extremely effective against the beetles in commercial bean fields. And Dr. Robert Schroder of the USDA's Beneficial Insect Introduction Laboratory claims the wasps also work in home gardens.

When adult beetles start eating holes in your bean leaves, they're preparing to lay eggs. Then is the time to place your orders for wasps. The unhatched wasps will arrive as "mummies" (parasitized larvae of the beetles). If the mummies arrive before your bean beetle larvae are ¼ inch long, they may be held for several days outside in a cool, sheltered place (keep the lid on the container).

The nonstinging wasps lay their eggs in the beetles' larvae. The young wasps kill the larvae by eating their way out. The wasps complete a life cycle every two weeks, so there may be as many as six cycles before they're killed by frost. The wasp is not a native and can't live through the winter in most areas, so you need to release them each season. Control without predators may be achieved with extremely conscientious handpicking and with rotenone or pyrethrum sprays.

Chewing a Blue Hairstreak

Q. A ½-inch, slightly fuzzy, yellow-green caterpillar has been chewing round holes in my green beans. What is the culprit, and how can I combat it?

A. The caterpillar is the larva of the cotton square borer, also called the gray hairstreak butterfly. It is found throughout North America. The adult is blue-gray with black and orange spots and two "tails" on each hindwing. The wingspan is about 1 inch. There are two or more generations each year.

Besides beans and cotton, the caterpillars feed on apple, citrus, and several wild plants. They're seldom numerous enough to cause serious crop losses. Handpick or spray with *Bacillus thuringiensis* (Bt), a widely available biocide, according to package directions.

Weevils Hot, Weevils Cold

Q. How can I prevent bean weevils from getting into beans I grow for drying?

A. Bean weevils lay eggs on maturing bean pods in fall. Spraying with rotenone in early September will help reduce the number of egg-laying adults but will not give total control, says Dr. Art Muka, an entomologist at Cornell University. Usually only about 1 to 2 percent of the beans are infested with eggs when they come out of the field, and few adults or larvae come in with the harvest, says Muka. But if the beans are stored at room temperature, the eggs will hatch, and the weevils will grow and reproduce as long as there are beans to feed on.

Either heating or chilling the beans directly after harvest will prevent most weevil damage. To kill the pests with heat, place shelled beans in a layer 1 inch deep on a cookie sheet, heat in the oven at 120°F for 20 minutes, and then store the beans in airtight containers in a cool place. Alternatively, store the shelled beans in airtight containers in the freezer. Two weeks at −10°F will kill the weevils.

Slugging the Slugs on Beans

Q. Last year my green beans were full of round holes, although the leaves didn't seem to be affected. I couldn't find the culprits. Any ideas?

A. Slugs probably chewed holes in your beans. You won't catch them in the act because they're nocturnal, but you might notice slime trails near the holes. You can handpick them within three hours of dawn and after dusk, when they're most active. Because they suffer from a "Dracula complex" (avoiding light), they seek out cool, moist, dark conditions, according to Dr. David Rollo, a biologist at McMaster University in Ontario. Don't mulch your beans until the average temperature is above 60° to 70°F (the ideal range for slugs), and break up soil clods, which they like to hide under. Surround the plants with a band of diatomaceous earth—the sharp crystals will pierce their soft bodies and dehydrate them.

Bean Mold

Q. The stems of my bush beans acquire a moist fungus that kills the plants at the peak of production. What is it, and how can I control it?

A. The fungus is most likely white mold (*Sclerotinia sclerotiorum*, also known as cottony rot). Plants usually look water-soaked at first and later become covered with a white fungus. At the end of summer, you'll often find black sclerotinia (the overwintering stage) about the size of a small pea on the plants or soil surface. Potatoes, peppers, lettuce, carrots, crucifers, and cucurbits are also susceptible.

Since the disease overwinters in the soil, Dr. Robert Carroll, a plant pathologist at the University of Delaware, suggests planting beans in an area where susceptible crops have not been grown for at least five years. Don't overfertilize with nitrogen, he adds, since the disease tends to attack lush growth. Space the rows 24 to 30 inches apart to provide good air circulation.

Failing with Favas

Q. Here in Florida, my fava bean plants get 8 to 12 inches high, then suddenly turn black and die. New shoots come up but they die, too. What's the problem?

A. Probably a virus, says Dr. Richard Hampton, a virologist at Oregon State University. But, since many viruses produce similar symptoms, it's impossible to say which one your plants have. Fava beans are attacked by about 20 different viruses—more than any other bean, and unfortunately, no resistant strains have yet been developed. However, Hampton adds, you may be able to get a crop by growing favas in fall or late winter in your area. Most viruses are spread by aphids, which are less active during cool weather.

Chapter 7

The Cool Cucurbits
Cucumbers,
Squash, and Melons

Close Calls for Cukes

Crazy Cukes

Q. **Last year my cucumber plants were healthy, but the fruit was curled up, yellow, and inedible. What went wrong?**

A. Water stress often causes poor fruit formation, says Robert Mulrooney, extension pathologist at the University of Delaware. Insufficient pollination is another possibility. If bees aren't visiting the flowers, you could hand-pollinate using a small artist's brush to transfer pollen from male flowers to the stigmas of female flowers. Or plant bee-attracting plants, such as borage, thyme, or buckwheat, nearby.

Seeing Double
(Cucumbers, That Is)

Q. **This summer I harvested a cucumber that looked like two cucumbers stuck together. Is this common? What happened?**

A. "Siamese twin" cucumbers aren't unusual. The fruit of a cucumber is actually a developed ovary (the slightly swollen part beneath the female flower). When you see a double fruit, it means

100

the plant produced a flower with two ovaries fused together. Sometimes there is a double flower as well.

A Case of Cuke Bitters

Q. **How can I keep my cucumbers from tasting bitter?**

A. Cucurbitacins (compounds found in cucumber leaves, stems, and roots) cause the bitterness. When the plant is stressed by hot, dry weather, cucurbitacins spread into the fruit. Since the bitterness enters through the stem, cutting off some of that end will eliminate most of the off-flavor if you harvest your cukes before they have been stressed for long. If the whole fruit has turned bitter, peeling it can help, because the bitterness is usually concentrated just under the skin.

Some cucumber varieties, such as 'Marketmore 80', have no cucurbitacins and will not turn bitter. Two other varieties with a bitter-free gene are 'County Fair' and 'Spartan Salad'. 'Sweet Slice' and 'Burpless' both produce less bitter cukes, although they don't have the bitter-free gene.

Worn-Out Cukes

Q. **I planted a gynoecious (all female-flowered) cucumber along with two regular varieties. After one good picking, the gynoecious variety produced only small, curved cukes. Was poor pollination the cause?**

A. The two regular (monoecious) varieties you planted should have ensured good pollination. Most likely, quality declined because the heavy initial fruit load exhausted the plants, says Dr. R. W. Robinson, cucumber breeder at Cornell University.

Because every flower can produce a fruit, gynoecious cucumbers need extra care for sustained yields. Dig plenty of manure or compost into the hills and space plants generously. Keep the soil moist all season. After fruit set, begin feeding with manure tea or fish emulsion to stimulate new vegetative growth. Pick the fruits young—once the seed coat hardens, the plants are much less likely to go on producing.

Sorting Out Squash, Pumpkin, and Gourd Problems

Mystery Squash

Q. **Last summer one of my 'Early Prolific Straightneck' yellow squash produced fruits with light green flesh and skin. Could this be a mutation?**

A. It's unlikely that your green squash was produced through a mutation, according to Dr. Dean Knavel, cucurbit breeder and vegetable crops specialist at the University of Kentucky. Most probably, a seed from a green variety, such as 'Senator', was accidentally packaged with the 'Early Prolific Straightneck' seed.

Baby Zukes

Q. **My first hybrid zucchini of the season grew about 3 inches long and then rotted. Later in the season, I got a bountiful harvest of normal-size fruit. Why?**

A. Your early zucchini were produced from unpollinated female flowers. The blossoms of most zucchini hybrids are all female when plants first flower, explains Dr. Henry Munger, noted squash breeder at Cornell University. He recommends picking the tender young zucchini as soon as possible after the flowers open. Male flowers, which (unlike the females) have no swelling beneath them, should begin to appear within several weeks and will pollinate the females, so you can let later-developing zucchini grow as large as you like.

No Zukes

Q. **Last year our zucchini squash produced lovely orange blossoms but no fruit. Where did we go wrong?**

A. Squash does not set fruit when the blossoms aren't pollinated. Normally, bees carry the pollen from male to female squash flowers. But if it is too early in the season, or if your area's bee population has been decimated by pesticides, the female blossoms will wither without being pollinated. After two days, a deformed miniature squash forms. If this happens, pick the fruit immediately and compost it. Otherwise, it will drain energy from the plant.

X-Rated Seeds

Q. We would like to use sunflower and pumpkin seeds toasted and salted, but can't find any varieties that produce hull-less seeds. Have you heard of any?

A. Yes, but only in pumpkins. Harris' 'Lady Godiva' variety produces small pumpkins with "naked" seeds. They have no hulls and thus do not require shelling. Sorry, no hull-less sunflower seeds yet.

Bitter Pumpkins

Q. Our 'Small Sugar' pumpkins were so bitter that we had to compost them. We planted them in March here in California and harvested after they turned orange in July. What happened?

A. Slow growth caused by drought or insufficient nitrogen can concentrate strong flavors and lower production of sugars that normally mask bitterness, says Dr. Dean Knavel of the University of Kentucky. Water pumpkins regularly and work in manure or compost to provide slow-release nitrogen and moisture-holding organic matter.

Pumpkins need a long season of warm, sunny weather to develop high sugar content. Plant your next crop in May to mature in September, and don't harvest until the rind resists puncturing with your thumbnail, suggests Dennis Pittenger, extension urban horticulture specialist at the University of California.

Pumpkins and Corn

Q. I planted 'Triple Treat' pumpkins in the rows of corn in my Indiana garden. They blossomed, but not one pumpkin grew. What went wrong?

A. The most likely reason your vines didn't produce pumpkins is lack of pollination, suggests Dr. Dean Knavel of the University of Kentucky. Honeybees are generally active only between 70° and 90°F. Daytime temperatures in your area were probably in the 90s by the time the pumpkins began to flower, and they would have been even higher between the rows of corn. Since shading can also affect fruit set, interplanting pumpkins with corn should be more successful if the pumpkin seed is planted as early as possible (or even started indoors) and the corn sown several weeks later.

Drying Luffa Gourds

Q. My wife and I grew a great crop of luffa gourds this year, but we can't find any information on how to dry them.

A. If you want to dry luffas for sponges, place boards or something similar under the developing gourds to keep them dry. Harvest each gourd when the stem turns yellow and the skin starts to lose its green color. Green skin gives a tender sponge, but very yellow luffas are too wiry.

Cut the gourds from the vines. Slice off the larger end and shake out the seeds. Dry until the skin hardens and browns—about two weeks. Then soak the sponges overnight or longer, until you can peel the outer skin off easily in large pieces. Stand the sponges in the sun or in a well-ventilated place to dry again for several days. Then they'll be ready to use.

If you'd rather process them immediately, you can obtain a softer sponge by boiling the harvested gourds in water for several minutes. Remove the outer skin, wash out the center, remove tissues and seeds, and dry gradually in a shady place.

Gourd Birdhouse

Homegrown Birdhouses

Q. Last year I harvested only two large birdhouse gourds, and both had rotted where they touched the ground. This spring, I planted a whole packet of seed and none germinated. What am I doing wrong?

A. To keep gourds from rotting, American Gourd Society member Mary Ann Rood suggests either placing boards or straw under the developing fruit, or trellising the vines. Gourd vines usually produce more than two fruits. Perhaps you overfertilized last year, producing lush vines at the expense of flowers. However, if there were many flowers, a lack of pollination by bees could be the problem. Using a paintbrush, you can transfer pollen from the male flowers to the female flowers (the ones with a swelling where the stem meets the blossom). Your gourd seeds may have failed to germinate if you planted them in soil that was too cold. The ideal soil temperature range is between 70° and 95°F. Also, if the seed was stored improperly, it may have lost its viability.

Gourds Eternal

Q. Is there any way to preserve the color and design on gourds and still dry them out? Mine just turn brown.

A. Color and design always fade as gourds dry, but you can easily make dried gourds more decorative, according to the American Gourd Society. Enjoy the fresh gourds until the colors begin to fade, then put them aside in a dry place. Wipe off any mold that forms and throw out gourds that shrivel. When the gourds feel light and the seeds rattle, soak them in warm water. Scrape off the softened skins with a knife, then rub the gourds with steel wool and set them aside. When they're dry, sand lightly. You can wax, shellac, paint, or carve the dried gourds, or decorate them with woodburning equipment.

Crossover Cucurbits

Q. If I plant squash, pumpkins, and watermelons next to each other, will they cross-pollinate? Can I plant different varieties of pumpkin on the same hill?

A. Basically, squash or pumpkins and watermelon won't cross. Squash and pumpkins, both of the genus *Cucurbita*, will. This cross won't show up in your vegetables the first year, but it will ruin the following year's crop if you plant seeds saved from this year's plants. To keep varieties coming true from seed, separate the squash and pumpkin varieties.

The Great White Worm

Q. A fat white worm, about ½ inch long, gets into the stems and destroys my squash and melon vines. I read that the organic way to kill the worm is to "search and destroy" with a small knife, but I end up ruining the stem as well. What is this worm and how can I get rid of it?

A. Your worm is the larval form of the squash vine borer, a large, orange-and-black flying insect in the moth family. It lays eggs on the stems of squash vines. The larvae hatch and burrow into the stems, where they feed. A gummy, sawdustlike substance oozing from holes in stems and leaves near the base of the plant is a sure sign that squash vine borers are at work. Leaves of infested plants will droop severely on sunny days.

Slitting the stems and killing the worms (there may be three or four worms in one tunnel and two or three tunnels per plant) is in fact an effective control. Kill the worms with your knife blade or a piece of wire, then bandage the slit with tape. Other controls that don't require you to slit squash stems are injecting *Bacillus thuringiensis* (Bt), a caterpillar-killing biocide, or predatory nematodes into the base of affected stems.

Another preventive measure is to pinch off the growing point while the plant is young and before the borers attack. That forces the plant to branch out, becoming multistemmed. Then cover the stems with soil as they grow. This encourages the vine to root at the joints from which the leaves grow. Or try a delayed planting, which may miss the egg-laying moth. Earlier plantings (under cloches or spunbonded row covers) can work, too, because the adult borer doesn't begin laying eggs until July, by which time the plants are larger and much more tolerant of attack. When a plant dies, find all the larvae inside and kill them so none overwinter.

Winter squash varieties like 'Hubbard' and most summer squash varieties are severely damaged by attack. 'Baby Blue' and 'Butternut' are somewhat resistant.

Squash Bug

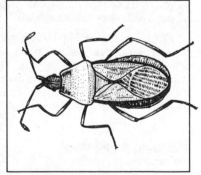

Squash Bug Strategies

Q. Every year I try to grow winter squash, but the plants are always attacked by squash bugs and die before I get any fruit. What can I do?

A. Insecticidal soap works well against squash bugs. The brownish-black, flat-backed adults fly into gardens in late spring or early summer. They suck the juices out of cucurbit leaves, causing them to wilt and turn blackish-green. After mating, the females lay yellowish-gold eggs on the undersides of squash leaves in geometric patterns. Within a few hours, the eggs darken to a bronze-brown. Green nymphs with crimson legs hatch in 5 to 14 days. They have voracious appetites and generally feed in groups.

Keep a hand-sprayer filled with insecticidal soap handy. Check the plants daily and spray the adults at their first appearance in spring. Continue watching for and spraying adults and nymphs through the season. The eggs won't be affected by the soap, so "squash" them between two hard surfaces. If you move quickly, you can also handpick or crush the adults and young. Avoid deep, cool mulches like straw and hay, which provide a refuge for the insects. After the harvest, burn or compost vines to help rid the garden of shelters for breeding and overwintering.

Banishing Mildew

Q. Every year I lose squash, pumpkin, and cucumber plants to powdery mildew. How can I curb the disease?

A. First, plant resistant or tolerant varieties. Resistant cucumbers are widely available. The zucchini varieties 'Zucchini Select' and 'Ambassador' are mildew-tolerant. There are no resistant winter squash or pumpkins, but squash like hubbard and buttercup are somewhat more mildew-tolerant than pumpkins, according to Dr. Brent Loy, a cucurbit breeder at the University of New Hampshire. In a small planting, you can slow or stop the spread of powdery mildew by pruning infected leaves as soon as the disease appears, says Loy. Don't crowd the plants, and make sure they're well fed and watered to reduce stress and stimulate early fruiting.

Researchers in Japan found that baking-soda sprays, applied weekly at the rate of a scant teaspoon of baking soda per quart of water, controlled powdery mildew on cucumbers and other crops. In the experiments, the baking soda both prevented infection by mildew spores and stopped development of the disease when it was present in an early stage.

Bringing Up Melons

Hot Soil, More Melons

Q. Cantaloupes don't yield well in my Harrisburg, Pennsylvania, garden. Do you think a black plastic mulch would help?

A. Yes. Melons need warm soil to grow well. Researchers at Virginia Tech found that melons direct-seeded through black plastic yielded earlier and twice as heavily as those planted in bare soil. The plants in the plastic mulch plots also grew faster and began running much sooner. Fruit size and flavor were identical. Black plastic absorbs heat from the sun, holds it in at night, keeps down weeds, and retains soil moisture. Clear plastic does a better job of soil heating, but weed seeds sprout. In the tests, using transplants rather than direct-seeding provided earlier fruits but didn't increase overall yield.

Bland Cantaloupes

Q. **I garden in Florida. My cantaloupes grow vigorously and produce good-looking fruits, but they taste bland, not sweet. Why?**

A. High rainfall during ripening can cause bland fruit, but sweetness is mainly dependent on variety, says Jim Stephens, extension vegetable specialist at the University of Florida. Perhaps the best choice for home gardeners is 'Planter's Jumbo', which combines sweetness and good disease resistance, says Stephens. Of the other varieties recommended by the Florida Extension Service, 'Ambrosia' and 'Smith's Perfect' are very sweet, but they're also susceptible to mildew and other diseases. Less sweet but more disease-resistant and productive are 'Hale's Best Jumbo', 'Edisto 47', and 'Super Market'.

But When Are They Ripe?

Q. **I've read that true cantaloupes like 'Charantais' don't slip from the vine when ripe. How do you know when they're ready to pick?**

A. Harvest 'Charantais' cantaloupes when the skin color at the stem end and in the ribs has changed from pearly gray-green to gold and the fruits have a strong melon fragrance, says Rose Marie Nichols of Nichols Garden Nursery, Albany, Oregon. In addition, the area around the stem will separate slightly and begin to look coarse as the fruit ripens.

Bacterial Wilt Woes

Q. **I have tried to grow cantaloupes without success. Each year beautiful vines grow, then almost overnight wilt and die. Why?**

A. Your melon vines had bacterial wilt. The disease affects all members of the cucumber family and is most common east of the Rockies, but it may also occur from Arizona to Idaho and Washington. Since striped and 12-spotted cucumber beetles spread the disease, control of wilt depends on keeping them off your plants. The bacteria overwinter in the beetles' intestines and are transferred to the plants through their feces. Bacteria enter the plant through wounds like those caused by chewing beetles.

The best protection is to keep the plants covered from setting-out to harvest with spunbonded row covers such as Reemay or a tent of fine-mesh cheesecloth. Commercial growers usually plant 10 to 20 percent more cucurbits than they need, because the disease usually affects only a few plants. If you have the space and choose this strategy, simply pull up and compost dying plants. There's no need to burn them.

Melon-Patch Plague

Q. Every year a disease shrivels my cantaloupes and Crenshaw melons when they're softball size and then kills the vines. My pumpkins develop pits in the skin and rot, but the vines survive. What's the problem?

A. Dark pits ¼ to 2 inches across on fruits and rapidly spreading yellow or brown spots that kill foliage or leave ragged holes are symptoms of anthracnose, a fungal disease that thrives during wet summers in the East. Watermelons, cucumbers, muskmelons, and gourds are much more susceptible to the disease than pumpkins and squash. Anthracnose overwinters on dead plants, so burn all infected crop residues. Destroy wild cucumbers near the garden. Spores of the fungus are spread by insects, gardeners, and splashing water. Grow cucurbits on trellises to keep the vines and fruit dry. Control insect pests and don't work among the plants in wet weather. Also, purchase and plant resistant varieties.

Cracking Crenshaws

Q. I like to grow Crenshaw melons, but eight out of ten crack before they are ripe. Why? How can I keep them from cracking?

A. Crenshaws are most likely to crack when heavy rain or irrigation follows a dry spell, so the best control is to maintain even soil moisture levels through the growing season. According to Ted Torrey, director of vegetable research for W. Atlee Burpee Co., susceptibility to cracking is a genetic trait of the Crenshaw melon, and no resistant variety has been developed. Torrey recommends using black plastic to conserve moisture, control weeds, and ensure the warm soil temperatures required to grow 'Crenshaw' melons. However, you can use any mulch if you wait to apply it until early summer, when the soil has warmed.

Hollow-Hearted Melons

Q. How can I control hollow heart in my watermelons?

A. Hollow heart, characterized by a cavity at the center of the fruit, is a genetic trait, says Dr. J. D. Norton, a fruit breeder at Auburn University. You can eliminate the problem by planting varieties that don't get the disorder, such as 'Crimson Sweet', a large, early, disease-resistant variety that is widely available, or the small icebox-type watermelons 'Mickylee' and 'Minilee'. If you save seeds from your own crop, you may gradually be able to eliminate the trait by planting only seeds from fruits that don't have hollow heart.

Blossom-End Rot

Q. For the past several years my watermelons have had blossom-end rot. What can be done?

A. Blossom-end rot first appears as a water-soaked area at the end of the fruit. The area will appear dark and will spread until the fruit begins to ripen. As the patch grows, the fruit tissue shrinks and becomes dry and leathery. Bacteria and fungi may grow on the decay, causing rot or mold.

Water stress or calcium deficiency can cause blossom-end rot. Test the soil for calcium deficiency. Calcium is not available to the plants at a low pH. Watermelons prefer a soil pH of 5.5 to 6.0, but will tolerate a range from pH 5.0 to 8.0. To correct for low calcium, add lime. Dolomitic limestone is a good source, and it also supplies magnesium, an essential nutrient for watermelons. If you want to plant a watermelon crop this year, use a fine grade of limestone. The finer the limestone, the faster it breaks down in the soil and the more it raises the pH and provides calcium. For example, 100-

mesh-size particles are extremely fine, so the calcium should be available within two weeks. Most of the calcium in 40-mesh particles will become available in about a year. The grade of limestone is usually marked on the bag.

If your calcium level is OK, water stress is the problem. Watermelons need a steady supply of water, ideally an inch a week. Periods of drought or heavy rain can cause blossom-end rot. Plenty of organic matter in the soil and mulching will help maintain even soil moisture.

Chapter 8

Some Like It Not
Asparagus, Rhubarb, Cabbage, and Other Cool-Weather Crops

Cool-Weather Crop Queries

Cool Crops, Hot Weather

Q. What can be done to prevent beets, chard, Chinese cabbage, and radishes from bolting in the late spring?

A. These vegetables are basically cool-weather crops with a tendency to bolt, or go to seed, as the weather warms and the days lengthen. To get the most from these crops, always choose varieties that produce well at the time of year you want to plant them. (For instance, if you plant Chinese cabbage in spring, don't choose a variety that has been bred for fall planting.) Look for varieties that are bolt-resistant. A good technique for spring planting is to provide shade as the weather gets warmer, mulch heavily, and use floating row covers or lath, or sow on the north side of a building.

Halloween Planting
Scares Up Spring Harvest

Q. Our garden is in Iowa. What vegetables can we plant in October that will be ready to harvest next spring?

A. Northern gardeners can harvest an early spring crop of spinach, lettuce, kale, garlic, parsley, and chervil if they make their last plantings just before the cold weather hits. Protect young plants with a coldframe or thick mulch throughout the winter, and remove this protection when soil temperatures reach 40°F. Water the plants well. Southern gardeners can sow those crops throughout the winter, too. In addition, they can plant brassicas, fava beans, and peas for an extra-early spring harvest.

About Asparagus

The Crowning Touch

Q. **Can you tell me how to grow asparagus crowns from seed sown outdoors?**

A. Sow the seed 1½ inches deep and 2 inches apart in loose, well-drained soil in late April or early May. At soil temperatures of 70° to 75°F, emergence will begin in 10 to 20 days. When the plants are up, mulch to control weeds and keep the soil moist through the summer. After frost kills the tops, mound 3 or 4 inches of soil over the crowns to prevent freezing and waterlogging. Mulch after the ground freezes. Transplant the crown in spring about the time you set out tomato plants.

Asparagus Overhaul

Q. **We are wondering how to handle our six-year-old asparagus patch, which is producing less each year. We have many pencil-size shoots and a few good thick spears. When should asparagus be cut down, in summer or fall? Should the berries be allowed to develop?**

A. If you take good care of your asparagus bed, it will keep producing. Some asparagus beds are reported to be in good production more than 100 years after the original bed was established.

First, never cut the growth down in the summer or fall. Asparagus shoots grow on the energy stored in the roots by this growth during the summer, fall, and even winter. Even though the tops may look dead in fall, they are storing energy for better production next spring. In the early spring or the very end of winter, break off the dead topgrowth and add it to your compost pile. Berries should be allowed to mature on the plants. If you have too many new plants starting from the dropped berries, thin them out each year, but allow some new plants to become established and replace older plants.

A deficiency of phosphorus or potassium could be responsible for asparagus decline if you aren't feeding your patch. To combat this, you should apply a winter mulch of about 3 inches of aged manure and some compost. In the spring, after harvesting, each plant should receive a good feeding with an organic fertilizer, because the summer growth will determine how good next year's spears will be. A good organic mixture for asparagus is three parts greensand, one part dried blood or two parts cottonseed meal, and one part bonemeal. Apply this mixture at the rate of about 2 pounds per 50 square feet of bed space. This combination of a winter manure mulch and a localized late-spring feeding will give your plants both the fast-acting nutrients they need for topgrowth in summer and slow-release nutrients during the rest of the year.

Last, you should give the bed a good cultivation before harvest in spring. Apply 4 to 6 inches of a mulch that's neutral in pH, like hay or straw, during the summer to preserve moisture, keep down weeds, and prevent too many new plants from getting established. Asparagus prefers a pH of 6.5 to 7.5 (neutral is 7.0). Shallow plantings can also cause poor growth. Set crowns at least 6 inches deep.

Florida Spears

Q. I've recently moved to central Florida from Michigan. Can I expect homegrown asparagus like we had back home?

A. Yes, you can grow asparagus, but expect lower yields than you got from your Michigan garden. To produce long, thick spears, the plant needs to store carbohydrates. In the North, the plant produces and stores carbohydrates during the summer for the following spring. During the winter, cold temperatures cause the plant to go dormant. But in the South, asparagus stores fewer carbohydrates because the plant uses them more rapidly in the hotter weather. That means less energy is available for the following spring's surge of growth. Although the winters are cold enough to bring on dormancy, Florida also experiences sudden warm spells when the plants will break dormancy. Small shoots appear, which are then killed as the temperature drops to freezing again. This continual shoot production wastes carbohydrates that might have gone into lush spring spear growth.

Bugged by
Asparagus Beetles

Q. **Last spring, whenever I went out to pick my asparagus, the tips were covered with asparagus beetles. What can I do to keep them from destroying the spears this year?**

A. If your planting is recent, take heart: Beetle damage is usually less serious in older beds. Both the common and the spotted asparagus beetles overwinter as adults in the stems of asparagus plants, under tree bark, and in garden debris. The most important way to control them is to scrupulously remove all the mulch and dead plant material from the garden in the fall.

Common asparagus beetles are found east of the Mississippi and north of North Carolina. Eggs are laid in April or May, soon after the adults emerge. Young asparagus shoots are sometimes blackened with tiny eggs standing on end. Within a week, the grayish, sluglike larvae hatch and begin feeding on the asparagus tips. They eat for two weeks, pupate, and emerge as adults a week or two later. There are two to five generations per season.

Handpicking is not effective for these beetles, since the adults fall to the ground when disturbed, and the young have usually done their damage by the time you notice them. You should pull out all volunteer plants and cut the shoots close to the ground every day to remove the eggs before the larvae can establish themselves. If you cleaned up the beds the previous autumn, gauze netting supported on a framework or spunbonded row covers will also give good control; however, you must put it up before egg laying begins. Rotenone controls the beetles, but we recommend it only as a last resort because it also kills ladybug larvae and chalcid wasps, important predators of the asparagus beetle.

The spotted asparagus beetle's range and life history are similar, but the greenish eggs hatch a little later and the orange larvae bore into and feed strictly on the berries. Only the adults, which are tan with 12 prominent spots, damage the spears. The insect can be controlled by removing and destroying the berries that form on the fernlike fronds of the female asparagus plants. The berries are green, later turning red.

Bedridden Asparagus

Q. My first asparagus bed died out after ten years. The new one is four years old, but the spears are pencil-thin and the plants grow only 18 inches tall. The crowns are brownish. Could this be the problem?

A. Fusarium crown rot is the most common reason for poor results in asparagus that is given proper care. "Almost all asparagus gets it eventually," says Dr. Stephen Garrison, an asparagus specialist at Rutgers University. Plants that are otherwise healthy can stay ahead of the disease for several years, then decline slowly. This is probably what happened to your first, and now your second, planting. Brown or yellow tissue on the crown (it should be white) indicates crown rot. Buy only certified disease-free crowns. The main home-garden varieties, 'Mary Washington' and 'Martha Washington', are very susceptible to fusarium, but two new hybrids, 'Jersey Giant' and 'Greenwich', are resistant.

Asparagus Wilt

Q. Our asparagus spears came up this year looking strong and healthy—at first. Then they started to get limp and wilted. It was just a matter of days until this wilt progressively hit each stalk after it reached about 3 inches tall. This has been happening for three years now. What's going on?

A. Stunting and yellowing or wilting are symptoms of asparagus wilt or root rot caused by fungi like *Fusarium* and *Verticillium*. These fungi invade the roots and stems of plants, interfering with the upward movement of water. In effect, the plant is dying of clogged arteries.

These fungi build up in infested soil where asparagus is established or where an old asparagus bed has been plowed under in recent years. After the asparagus dies, the fungi produce masses of spores that may live on humus in the soil for several years. As a result, seedlings that are grown nearby may be killed in great numbers.

The only way to "cure" the diseased section of your garden is to remove and destroy your asparagus planting. For your next asparagus bed, start with certified disease-free plants and put them as far from the old bed as possible. Choose a site with soil that's rich, deep, and well drained.

Rhubarb Right and Wrong

Your First Rhubarb

Q. A friend with a huge rhubarb patch has offered me some plants. How do I transplant them?

A. Dig rhubarb crowns as early as possible in the spring, before they break dormancy, or in the fall before the ground freezes. Divide the crowns, including as much root as possible. Each piece should have at least two large buds. Four to six pieces can usually be split from each crown. Don't allow the divisions to dry out before planting them 2 to 3 inches deep in a well-drained location.

Rhubarbering

Q. Should I cut the leaves off rhubarb in the fall?

A. Don't be too anxious to cut them. Rhubarb plants manufacture carbohydrates all summer, taking in sunlight and carbon dioxide through their leaves. These nutrients are stored in the root system, providing energy for next year's stalks. When the leaves turn completely brown in fall, you may cut them if they look ugly to you. However, because rhubarb leaves don't harbor diseases, it's not necessary to remove them after they've been killed by frost.

Bolting Rhubarb

Q. What causes rhubarb to bolt?

A. Bolting, or flowering, is a normal part of the rhubarb plant's life cycle, although it may not happen every summer. It is often triggered by stressful conditions, such as hot, dry weather. If a flower stalk appears, pinch or prune it off so the plant's energy will be concentrated on vegetative growth.

Worn-Out Rhubarb

Q. **My red rhubarb stalks are small, porous, and tough, and they appear to have sting spots on them. What can be wrong?**

A. Your plants may simply be worn out and need dividing, especially if they've been growing in the same location for five years or more. In early spring, dig them up and split the crowns into well-rooted pieces having two or more eyes or buds on each. Cut out any diseased or dead roots. If you replant in a new location, choose a very well drained site where tomatoes, peppers, and strawberries have not been grown for several years. (All these plants can harbor verticillium wilt, which rhubarb might contract if it follows them.) Dig in a few inches of compost, and apply rock fertilizers or bonemeal if necessary. Plant the crowns 2 or 3 inches deep and 3 feet apart, and keep the bed weeded and watered. Begin pulling stalks in the second year.

If the sting spots on the stalks are small, black blotches with holes, they may be egg-laying punctures of the rhubarb curculio— a slow-moving, ½- to ¾-inch-long, snouted black beetle that looks as though it's been dusted with yellow powder. Look for similar spots on the roots and crown. The curculio uses rhubarb only for egg laying. It feeds on a weed, curly dock, to which the larvae also migrate after hatching. Control the insects by handpicking and by eliminating curly dock near the garden.

Brassica Basics

Direct-Seeded Brassicas

Q. **Most gardening books suggest starting seeds for plants like broccoli and cauliflower indoors six weeks before the last frost. When should they be planted if I want to sow the seeds outdoors?**

A. Broccoli and cauliflower seeds take about 2½ weeks to sprout when the soil temperature an inch deep averages about 50°F, ten days when it is 59°F, and six days when it is 68°F. If you plant them outdoors 2 weeks before the last frost date (about the same time you would set out transplants), the seeds will sprout in about a week. You can plant the seeds outdoors earlier, but they will take longer to germinate. Though outdoor-sown seedlings will grow faster than transplants, they won't catch up with them, so your harvest will mature 2 to 3 weeks later.

Clubroot Clobbers Brassicas

Q. Last year my broccoli, brussels sprouts, cabbage, and cauliflower had clubroot. Can you tell me more about the disease and how to control it?

A. Clubroot is caused by a soilborne fungus that attacks the roots of crucifers, including radishes, turnips, mustard, and the brassicas. Severely infected plants develop large, clublike swellings on the roots, and the stunted, yellowed topgrowth wilts on sunny days. The fungus produces spores inside the clubs, and these are released into the soil when the roots decay. The spores can remain viable for ten years or more.

Because of its persistence and ability to infect plants under a wide range of conditions, clubroot is very difficult to control. There are no resistant brassicas yet available. Raising the soil pH with lime to 7.0 or above can reduce or prevent infection where spore counts are low. (To help keep spore counts low, pull and burn clubbed roots.) Since the lime must be mixed uniformly throughout the root zone to suppress the fungus, this technique works best with sandy or loam soils. Clay and muck soils are well buffered against chemical change, so it takes more lime and often more than one year to raise their pH significantly. Depending on soil type, you may need to add lime every year to maintain a high pH. Your county agent will be able to recommend application rates based on soil test results.

Headless Broccoli

Q. My early broccoli didn't produce heads this spring. Why?

A. Head formation in broccoli (and cauliflower) depends on three factors—cool weather, plenty of water, and adequate calcium. Hot weather, drought, and/or a soil calcium deficiency can all produce nonheading broccoli plants. Broccoli prefers cool temperatures, particularly at night. A sudden hot spell can result in no heads at all or cause the plant to bolt to seed within a few days. Early in the season, broccoli needs at least an inch of rain per week. Broccoli planted for fall harvest needs slightly less water, but the supply must be just as steady. To correct a calcium deficiency, spread crushed limestone over your future broccoli patch in the fall, then till it in.

Buttoned-Up Broccoli

Q. **Last year I started seeds of 'Green Comet' broccoli at the end of March and set vigorous transplants into my garden in May. They grew into lush 3-foot specimens, but not one of them produced anything more impressive than a button head. What went wrong?**

A. If broccoli plants are exposed to cold weather when very young, they may make small "buttons" (or miniature flower heads) instead of heading up. "Buttoning" can be induced by chronic temperatures of 50° to 55°F or by a few days at 40°F. Seedlings in a cool greenhouse or coldframe are especially susceptible. The ideal range for broccoli transplants is 70°F during the day and 60° to 65°F at night. Once a plant has buttoned, it won't produce a primary head, but it will form an abundance of smaller lateral heads if given good care throughout the summer.

Bugs in Broccoli

Q. **My harvested broccoli was full of aphids and worms last fall. How can I keep these pests out of the edible parts of broccoli?**

A. Broccoli, like other cole crops, attracts aphids and a variety of worms. The aphids cling to the undersides of leaves and flower heads, stunting plants and killing seedlings. A fine, forceful spray of water from the hose, companion plantings of mint, and finely ground limestone sprinkled over the heads and foliage of broccoli all discourage aphids. For worms, protective netting or spunbonded row covers can keep moths away from plants during their egg-laying cycle, and tilling the soil several times in fall and spring should expose and kill any remaining eggs. *Bacillus thuringiensis* (Bt) also stops cabbageworms ("A Cure for Cabbageworms" on page 123). But no matter how you try, some insects *will* find their way into the kitchen after harvest. Plunging broccoli into warm water with a little white vinegar should float the bugs to the top. Never soak more than 15 minutes. We suggest warm water because hot water will destroy nutrients, and cold water, from experience, doesn't clean as well.

Blowup in Brussels

Q. Shortly after I topped my brussels sprouts last fall, several of the topmost sprouts on each plant opened and elongated to form new leaders. What caused this?

A. Topping too early can cause the upper sprouts to "blow up," as commercial growers call the response. To produce a stalk of fairly uniform sprouts for once-over harvest, J. A. Cutcliffe of Agriculture Canada advises eastern Canadian growers to top their plants when the sprouts in the seventh to ninth whorl of leaves from the bottom are about the size of a small pea. At that time, the sprouts at the bottom of the stalk are ½ to ¼ inch in diameter. California growers also top when the lower sprouts are about ¼ inch in diameter. In both cases, the crop is harvested about a month later, yielding sprouts ½ to 1 inch in diameter, the preferred size for freezing.

Cabbages Hate Maples

Q. Each fall I cover my garden with 10 to 20 inches of leaves, mostly maple. I've had very disappointing yields from all of the cabbage family. Can leaves stunt cabbage?

A. Yes. Maple leaves contain phenols, which reduce the growth and yields of brassicas and other vegetables by inhibiting root elongation, says Dr. David Hill of the Connecticut Agricultural Experiment Station. Early crops are most vulnerable because the phenols are quickly released when the leaves begin to degrade in spring. Fall crops are usually not affected because most of the phenols have leached by midseason, says Hill. Large quantities of raw leaves can also inhibit growth by tying up nitrogen as they decompose and by keeping the soil too wet, especially if the season is cool and rainy.

You can solve all three problems by composting the leaves for at least nine months before putting them on the garden. In that time the phenols will leach, nitrogen levels will stabilize, and the leaves will degrade into drainage-enhancing humus. Shred the leaves if possible and turn the pile occasionally to keep it hot. A cold, compacted pile may take a year or more to decompose sufficiently.

Saving Cabbage Seed

Q. How do I go about saving seed from cabbage?

A. Cabbages are biennial, flowering the second season, and must be overwintered to set seed. No protection is needed where winter temperatures stay above freezing (32°F). In severe climates, store the plants in pots in a root cellar or in a pit in the garden. When you replant in early spring, cut an inch-deep cross in the top of the head to let the seed stalk come through.

Since some cabbages are self-sterile, plant at least two. If other brassicas (wild mustard, broccoli, cauliflower) are blossoming nearby, you'll need to keep insects off your cabbage flowers. Shield the flower heads with gauze or other fine mesh, and cross-pollinate the plants by hand, using an artist's camel's hair brush. After the flowers have faded, remove the mesh. In 30 to 40 days, the seed-pods will yellow and turn brown, then split and scatter the seed. Since the pods ripen at varying rates, it's best to remove them as they darken. After they've dried, separate seed from the hulls by rubbing the pods over a screen. To prevent seed-transmitted diseases like black rot and blackleg, put the seed in a loosely tied cloth and soak in 112°F water for 30 minutes. Dry the seed thoroughly right away and store in a cool, dry place.

Cabbage Maggot Control

Q. In my Illinois garden, the roots of my cabbage and broccoli are severely attacked by cabbage maggots. Is there some way to rid the soil of them?

A. You can protect brassicas from the egg-laying parent flies by tenting them with fine gauze (at least 20 threads to the inch) tacked to a wooden frame around the bed and supported by wires across the beds at 5-foot intervals. Rodale Research Center tests showed that Reemay, a spunbonded polyester material, is a very effective barrier. Plant crops where brassicas (or their wild relatives like wild mustard) were not grown the previous season, since the insects overwinter in the soil.

About mid-May in your area, the ¼-inch-long adults emerge and fly close to the ground, then lay small white eggs in the soil near the brassica stems. Four-inch tarpaper disks can reduce egg laying in the immediate root zone. Eggs hatch in three to seven days, and the larvae seek out the roots, feeding on them for three to four weeks. Of the three generations per season, the first is the most destructive, since the maggots thrive in cool, moist soil.

A promising new control is Seek, a beneficial nematode that destroys cabbage maggots and other soilborne larvae and remains active in the soil from six months to two years. The nematode comes mixed with cedar shavings. It can be applied as a mulch or by adding water and spraying the strained mixture on the infested soil. The nematodes enter the maggots, killing them within a day or two.

A Cure for Cabbageworms

Q. Is there a cure for cabbageworms?

A. For cabbageworms, the most effective treatment is to spray plants with *Bacillus thuringiensis* (Bt). This biocontrol is commercially available in garden stores and from many mail-order sources under a variety of names, including Dipel, Biotrol, and Thuricide. The spray is completely harmless to all life forms except caterpillars and will not upset the natural insect balance in your garden.

Trichogramma in Your Garden

Q. I've read about the trichogramma wasp controlling cabbage loopers on a large scale in Texas. Are they effective in the home garden? Do they survive colder climates?

A. The tiny trichogramma wasp, which destroys a variety of worms by laying its own eggs in theirs, can be effective in home gardens. The gardens should be large (or in a more rural setting) to attract enough cabbage loopers and cabbageworms for the wasp to establish itself. If you're raising a dozen or so cabbage plants in a suburban backyard, the wasp may not have enough insects to feed on all season. Also, you must know the life cycles of the insects you want destroyed and release the wasps during the pests' egg-laying period. Your county extension agent can help you determine the time for optimum wasp releases in your area. As far as survival in cooler climates goes, the trichogramma wasp survives wherever the cabbage looper does. If you have a small cabbage crop, it may be more effective to handpick the worms. *Bacillus thuringiensis* (Bt) is an effective control.

Burned-Out Cabbage

Q. **What is causing the edges of my cabbage leaves to turn brown? When I cut the cabbage in half, the inner leaves are brown-edged, and I have to compost them.**

A. It sounds like your cabbage is a victim of a cabbage disorder called tipburn. The discolored leaves are caused by using too much nitrogen or general-purpose fertilizers, which produce large plants with big outer leaves. That creates a condition where insufficient calcium is transported to the leaf tips in the head, resulting in tipburn. Tipburn usually develops only when a period of heavy rain is followed by warm and relatively dry days. Such conditions stimulate the movement of calcium to the outer leaves but not to the rapidly growing leaves within the head. Use slow-release organic fertilizers like compost and aged manure to keep from overdosing your plants with nitrogen, and mulch your patch to keep soil moisture even.

Color My Cauliflower Purple

Q. **My white cauliflower picks up the color from my purple cauliflower. Should I plant them farther away from each other?**

A. The neighboring purple variety isn't the problem. Sunlight on the cauliflower head (called the "curd") causes it to turn from white to purple, yellow, or green, depending on the variety. Blanching will prevent it from coloring. To produce the best-looking white curd, start blanching as soon as the developing head begins to push back the inner leaves. Make sure the head is dry, then blanch by gathering up the longest leaves around the head and holding them in place with a strip of cloth, soft twine, or clothespins. You can also rip off a large bottom leaf and place it over the head. Many newer cauliflower varieties are self-blanching. They have longer leaves that protect the curd.

Keeping Cauliflower Cool

Q. **In my growing season, days are hot (80° to 85°F), and nights are cool (40° to 60°F). My cauliflower grows only 4 to 5 inches high, then develops tiny florets that turn brown. How can I get them to produce larger heads?**

A. Good-quality cauliflower is difficult to produce where night temperatures are so cool. At 50°F or below, the plants become susceptible to a physiological reaction known as "buttoning." Transplant seedlings no more than 30 days after germination, as older plants seem to be more prone to buttoning, says extension horticulturist Orville McCarver of Montana State University. He also recommends a black plastic mulch, which raises the soil temperature about 7 degrees. Clear plastic or polyester row covers raise air temperatures 10 to 15 degrees during the day and 3 to 4 degrees at night in spring. Plant in full sun and use both plastic mulch and row covers to get the plants off to a fast start. Check plants daily and don't allow the temperature inside to exceed 75°F. Even if button heads form, says McCarver, leave the plants alone, because they may produce normal-size heads later.

Wait for Kale

Q. **When should I plant kale, and how much should I plant?**

A. Kale is very frost-hardy, and seedlings can be set out unprotected as early as four weeks before the last frost date. But for the best eating, you should plan for the crop to mature in the cool season. A light frost greatly improves the flavor of the leaves, and kale retains its good eating qualities through intense cold. People often report brushing the snow from plants to harvest leaves in midwinter.

You should plant seedlings *no later* than eight weeks before your first autumn frost date. But if you've got the space, you can plant them earlier and let the plants get much larger before the harvest begins. Start seeds in flats in late spring and transplant them four weeks later. An earlier planting gives you a much longer harvest. Cook the large leaves. Small leaves are tender enough to include in salads. Kale should be eaten immediately after picking, like sweet corn, because the sugars convert rapidly and the leaves become bitter. Plant 6 to 12 plants per person.

Spotting Kale

Q. My kale gets alternaria leaf spot. Can you tell me what spreads the disease and how to prevent it?

A. Alternaria is caused by a fungus that attacks almost all the crucifers, including the brassicas, oriental cabbages, radishes, turnips, and horseradish. Leaf spots start as round yellow pinpricks and enlarge in concentric circles to 2 or 3 inches in diameter. These circles gradually become sooty with fungal spores. The disease can also cause cankers on cabbage stems and browning of broccoli and cauliflower heads.

Seeds from infected plants carry the fungus, which kills seedlings or causes them to develop wire stem, a lesion near the soilline. Discard infected survivors—they never grow to full size and don't yield well. Seeds can be cleansed of the fungus by immersing them in water held at a constant 120°F for not more than 30 minutes. In the garden, alternaria is spread by wind, splashing water, and gardeners working among their plants. Space plants generously and avoid overhead watering to keep the leaves as dry as possible, since the spores need moist conditions to germinate. Because older leaves are usually infected first, you may be able to limit the disease by picking them as soon as spots appear. If the disease has been severe, dust with sulfur. Grow kale and other susceptible plants in a two-year rotation with noncruciferous crops.

Leads on Lettuce and Chard

Too Late for Lettuce

Q. I can't get head lettuce to form heads. What could be the problem?

A. You may be planting it too late. If hot weather sets in before head lettuce matures, it won't develop firm heads before bolting to seed. One week can make the difference. In field trials conducted at Cornell University, lettuce plants set out on May 12 produced a larger number of firm heads than plants of the same cultivars set out on May 17.

Plant during the first week of May if the ground isn't too wet, Cornell extension agent Roger Kline recommends. Space vigorous, hardened transplants 12 inches apart in rich, porous soil and protect them from frost. Make sure the soil stays moist until the heads mature. You can improve your chances of success by planting relatively heat-tolerant cultivars like 'Ithaca', 'Minetto', and 'Montello'.

Head Start on Lettuce

Q. **For the past two years I have tried to grow head lettuce, but it rots just as it is starting to head. What causes this?**

A. Dr. Jim Utzinger, extension horticulturist at Ohio State University, says it's likely that your plants succumbed to bacterial soft rot. Since this disease is enhanced by constant moisture and warm weather, the solution is to set out transplants six to eight weeks before the average last frost date. Head lettuce is fairly frost-tolerant and will survive night temperatures as low as 29°F. Grow the plants under row covers or hot caps to protect them from frosts.

A Miner Disaster

Q. **Leafminers attack my beets and Swiss chard. I've tried everything to stop them, but nothing is working. Please help!**

A. The best way to protect your plants from miners is to screen the pests out. Spunbonded row covers like Reemay, anchored around your bed with soil, work well to stop miner attacks. Since leafminers usually pupate in the soil, you should plan to grow beets and chard in a different area for the screening to be successful.

If leafminers have already gotten to your crops, burn or compost any miner-infested leaves. (You can recognize these by the pale tunnels winding across the upper surface.) Also keep weed hosts cut down, especially lamb's-quarters, one of the miner's favorite snacks. Because the miners are leaf chewers, you could try dusting the leaves with sabadilla dust, an insecticide made from the seeds of a tropical plant in the lily family.

Chapter 9

Storage Staples
Potatoes, Onions, and Other Root Vegetables

Potato Problems

**Use Seed,
Not Feed, Potatoes**

Q. What is the difference between seed potatoes and potatoes from the grocery? Can't I just use grocery-bought potatoes for planting?

A. When you buy certified seed potatoes, you're buying a known variety of potato, guaranteed to carry minimum risk of disease. Plain seed potatoes, by comparison, are not classified or certified, so you know the variety, but not if it's disease-free. Potatoes from the grocery store are the poorest risk for planting. You don't know the variety, whether the potatoes are diseased, or if a sprout inhibitor, which prevents normal sprouting in the bag (and in your garden), has been applied. A viral disease in a potato is not harmful to you when you eat it, but if you plant a virus-infected potato, the disease will appear when the plant is growing. It will be transmitted to other plants by insects, usually aphids, and can ruin the crop. So rely on good seed potatoes—not the grocery store—when planting.

When to Spade Spuds

Q. **How do I know when my potatoes are ready to be harvested?**

A. For storage, potatoes are ready to harvest when the tops of the plants have died back completely. In the northern part of the country, harvest time usually starts in September, when the days are getting cool and frost is not far off. Wait for a warm, dry day to start digging them up. In damp weather, bruised tubers have a greater susceptibility to rot. Cloudy days are ideal, since too much light will green newly dug potatoes and alter their flavor after a few hours. If you're using potatoes for storage, their skins should be tough enough so that they cannot be rubbed off with your finger. Use a potato fork or pointed shovel. Be gentle as you dig. Each bruise decreases storage life. "New" potatoes—the earliest crop of the season—may be dug anytime after the blossoms form. Although these potatoes are no more than an inch in diameter and don't store well, they are delicious and go well with many midsummer garden vegetables.

Fall Potatoes

Q. **Seed potatoes are hard to find in fall, and I can get very few of them to sprout. How can I turn part of my spring crop into seed potatoes for fall planting and harvest?**

A. Failure of spring-crop potatoes to sprout in fall is a common problem, says Malcolm Beck, commercial composter and organic farmer in San Antonio, Texas. The tubers' natural dormancy is reinforced by the high soil temperatures that prevail at fall planting time. You can help the tubers break dormancy by placing them in the refrigerator 30 days before the fall planting date, says Beck. After two weeks, remove the potatoes from the refrigerator and expose them to light in a cool place to induce sprouting, then plant. You may not get full rows, but you'll get a crop. Use golf-ball-size potatoes for planting; smaller ones don't yield as well, and larger potatoes cut into pieces are more susceptible to dehydration and rot.

Explorers in Mulch

Q. I'd like to try the new 'Explorer' potato that is grown from seed. Usually I plant my tuber pieces on top of the ground and then cover them with mulch. Can 'Explorer' be grown this way, too?

A. No one we know has tried it yet, but we don't see why mulching 'Explorer' potatoes shouldn't work. Either plant the root ball of your potato seedling right in the soil as you would a tomato seedling or simply set the root ball on top of the soil and, to prevent drying out, surround it with compost. Then add layers of mulch as the plants push out their leaves. The mulch should be deep enough to prevent light from reaching the newly formed potatoes. Mulch will keep weeds down and preserve the moist and cool soil temperatures potatoes like. The developing tubers won't have to fight heavy soil, and they should be right where you need them for an easy harvest.

Heartless Potatoes

Q. The white potatoes I raised last season were very large, but most of them were hollow. Can you tell me why?

A. Hollow heart—a star-shaped cavity at the center of the tuber—results when conditions such as high rainfall (especially after drought), excessive fertilization, and wide spacing overstimulate growth. Varieties that produce large tubers, such as 'Katahdin' and 'Kennebec', are most susceptible. Early varieties like 'Norland' and midseason varieties like 'Superior' and 'Chieftain' produce smaller tubers and are much less prone to the disorder. The best control is to space plants 7 to 10 inches apart, depending on the variety. Close spacing increases competition, encouraging slower, more uniform growth and smaller tuber size. Don't overdose the plants with nitrogen, but maintain high potassium levels and keep the soil evenly moist.

Slushy Spuds

Q. My 'Nooksack' potatoes were a healthy crop, but they became a slushy mess when I boiled them. Why?

A. 'Nooksack', a russet, was developed primarily for french fries. Slushiness is due to the potato's high proportion of dry matter, explains Joseph Pavek, U.S. Department of Agriculture (USDA) potato breeder at the University of Idaho. 'Nooksack' potatoes will taste all right when boiled if you cook them in the minimum amount of water, watch them carefully, and remove them from heat and then drain them as soon as they are cooked. "I've found that potatoes with high dry matter tend to cook faster than the ones with low dry matter," says Pavek. Try harvesting 'Nooksack' earlier to limit the amount of dry matter.

Spotty Potatoes

Q. Although my homegrown potatoes seem healthy, they have a little circle of dark specks around the edge when cut in half. Are they safe? What can I do to prevent this?

A. The dark ring is probably caused by the quick death of the potato plant itself. Rings can occur if the immature plant dies rapidly from disease, air pollutants, or cutting off the foliage. Killing the plant cuts off the nutrients that the developing tubers received from the vines. In the North and East, an early frost will quickly kill the plants. Another possibility is too little water—once the potatoes are fully grown, we tend to forget that they still need plenty of water. As for safety, though their appearance may not be perfect, the potatoes are fine to eat.

Green Potatoes

Q. We decided to follow mulch maven Ruth Stout's advice last year to use unworked ground for potatoes. We placed our seed potatoes on the weeds and covered them with a thick layer of dry grass from a recently thatched football field. The potatoes grew beautifully, but under the red skins some of the potatoes were bright green. What do you think caused this?

A. Sunlight is the culprit. Potatoes exposed to light begin to photosynthesize, and like the leaves of the plant, they'll turn green. The green on both the leaves and tubers of potatoes is solanine, a substance that can be toxic. You can eat these potatoes if you peel away the green parts before preparing them. This year, increase the amount of mulch you use to prevent light from filtering through to the tubers.

Wiry Worms

Q. In our Washington State garden, our potato crop is regularly decimated by wireworms. What can we do to control this pest?

A. Wireworms are the larvae of the click beetle. These tough grubs live in the soil for a number of years and feed on a variety of plant roots. They are generally at their worst in sod ground and land recently plowed out from sod crops. Their numbers decline under row crop and small grain cultivation and can sometimes be substantially reduced by frequent tilling. Wireworms frequently appear to be more damaging to root crops such as carrots and potatoes when these crops are left in the ground after the harvest is mature. Prompt harvest, thorough cultivation, and rotations relying on green-manure crops of annual plants like winter rye rather than sod crops can effectively if gradually lessen losses caused by this beetle grub.

Colorado Potato Beetle

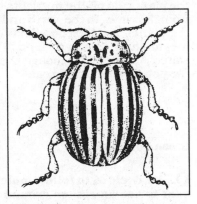

Beetlemania

Q. Where does the striped potato beetle come from? We planted two patches of potatoes this year, about 200 yards apart. Neither place was used for potatoes in the past, as far as we know. One patch had no beetles, the other was covered with them. Why?

A. Though it may seem that the potato beetles just descend in great numbers out of the sky, they actually build up populations gradually for the first couple of years, then stage a population explosion. You may have had a few potato beetles the year before last and not noticed them. You don't have to raise potatoes to have potato beetles—they also eat ground-cherry, horse nettle, and other weedy members of the nightshade family, as well as potatoes, tomatoes, peppers, and eggplant.

Fortunately, on a smaller patch, potato beetles are not hard to control by hand if you *scrupulously* kill all egg clusters of the first generation, or at least kill all the red grubs that hatch in May or

June from those first clusters of orange-yellow eggs. If this first invasion force is not exterminated, each grub will pupate in three weeks and become an adult. And these adults will lay the eggs that give you a beetle baby boom. In the South, the situation is worse, since a third generation is possible. For the squeamish or those with larger plots, rotenone provides effective control.

Unknown to you, a few of this year's beetles probably did move over to the other patch in the fall, ate a little, and hibernated. They'll be out in force next year. Should you continue to have beetle problems in one garden and not in another 200 feet away, then you may have a potential breakthrough in bug control. First, check such things as: Are you growing the same variety in both plots? Is there more groundcover to harbor predators around one patch? Are there different weed species around one garden and not the other? Did you use the same fertilizers? And most important, are the soil types the same? If you have differing soil types, you may find that a deficiency in one soil is weakening the plants and encouraging the beetles, while the other soil has no such detrimental effect on the plants. Last, check to see how many flea beetles were active in the two gardens. Some gardeners have found that where flea beetle populations feed on potatoes, the potato beetles don't feed. If the leaves of your potatoes are all peppery with little holes, that's flea beetle injury.

Picking at Potato Scab

Q. I have a problem with potato scab that seems to get worse every year. How can it be controlled?

A. Common potato scab (*Actinomyces scabies*) is a disease that occurs everywhere potatoes are grown. The disease has no aboveground symptoms, but affected tubers have sunken or raised corky areas. You can eat the potatoes if you cut away the diseased parts. The disease organism thrives when the soil's pH is between 6.0 and 7.5. It is not active below pH 5.2. But like most vegetables, potatoes do best at pH 6.0 to 7.5, so lowering your soil's pH isn't the solution.

The best steps you can take to control potato scab are to plant scab-free seed potatoes and rotate your crop. In the rotation, avoid other root crops like turnips, beets, and carrots, which are also susceptible to scab. Also, research has shown that potatoes grown in dry soil are more susceptible to the disease. Dr. Richard Cole of the Department of Horticulture at Penn State University says that you can foil the disease by maintaining adequate soil moisture at the time of tuber set (one or two months after planting). Don't use fresh manure if you think the livestock may have eaten scabby potatoes. No variety is truly resistant to scab, but tolerant varieties include 'Cayuga', 'Cherokee', 'Chieftain', 'Early Gem', 'Menominee', 'Norland', 'Onaway', 'Ontario', 'Russet Burbank', 'Sebago', 'Seneca', and 'Superior'.

Late Potato Blight

Q. **Our potato plants start out vigorous, then develop brown spots on the leaves, shrivel, and die. Do you have any suggestions for this year's crop?**

A. Your potatoes are being infected by the late-blight fungus (*Phytophthora infestans*). This blight can kill plants within a week or two under ideal conditions (100 percent humidity and temperatures between 61° and 72°F). First, plant only resistant varieties like 'Kennebec', 'Cherokee', 'Essex', and 'Pungo'. To reduce the humidity, don't use overhead watering on your plants. Clean up thoroughly after harvesting, and burn or cull infected potatoes to help control the disease, since the fungus overwinters in infected tubers and is spread when they sprout. Don't dig the crop until two weeks after the tops die to prevent harvested potatoes from developing blight and rotting in storage.

Asking about Onions and Garlic

Storing "Splits"

Q. **When I try to dry onions that have twin bulbs in one outer casing, they seem to retain moisture between the bulbs and go bad. The only way that I've found to save them is to take off the outer casing, separate, and clean each bulb, then freeze them. Is there a sure way to dry twin-bulb onions?**

A. The best thing you can do is correct your growing habits so you don't have to fool around with split onions. Splits are formed when the soil is allowed to dry out during bulb formation. This year, when the tops get about 10 inches tall, put a thick mulch around them, and periodically check to see that the area doesn't go completely dry. That way, you shouldn't have any problems.

Flowering Onions

Q. **Why do my onions, planted in our Santa Rosa, California, garden, want to make flower heads instead of nice, plump bulbs?**

A. Your onions have been fooled. Fall-planted onions can grow too much before winter, especially in your mild climate. When spring comes, they act as if a season has passed and go to seed. The same false maturity will show up in spring-planted onions if a late cold spell persuades them that winter is coming. Plant your onions later in the fall and spring or space your plantings over several months so part of your crop escapes bolting. If you grow your onions from sets, perhaps they are too large or were stored in too warm or too cold a place by the seedsman. If so, many will go to seed no matter when you plant them. In general, sets less than ½ inch in diameter resist bolting, so you should resist the temptation to buy the biggest sets.

Onions Won't Keep There

Q. **Can I leave mature onions in the ground through the winter if I mulch them like carrots?**

A. No. Carrots need cold (32° to 40°F) and very moist conditions (90 to 95 percent relative humidity), but onions keep only when it's cold and dry (60 to 70 percent humidity). The earth is too damp for onion storage—they'll rot. It's especially important that the necks of onions be kept thoroughly dry to keep out decay-causing organisms. If onions freeze, they'll deteriorate rapidly soon after thawing. Onions will keep well in a dry root cellar, a basement, or a cool attic. If you harvest in summer, you may have to move the onions around the house to provide good storage conditions through several months.

Off with Their Heads!

Q. **Some of my onion sets produced big onions, but others sent up a fat flower stalk and produced very small bulbs. Will I get larger onions if I cut off the stalks?**

A. Yes. The plant uses the food stored in the bulb to produce flower stalks and seeds. Onions that flower are also likely to have woody centers and keep poorly. Cool weather stimulates flower-stalk production, so avoid planting in the fall or early spring. Snip off flower stalks as they appear. Cutting the stalks promptly will give you larger bulbs, but you should still use them before onions that didn't produce stalks.

Pick a Peck of Pickling Onions

Q. **Can you tell me how to grow the little white onions used for pickling?**

A. You can grow pickling onions the same way you would grow onions for sets—by seeding directly into the garden at close spacing to keep the bulbs small. Buy seed of an early white onion and sow thickly in a bed or 4-inch-wide band so the seedlings stand ¼ to ½ inch apart. Go easy on the fertilizer to avoid lush growth. Choose a weed-free area if possible—weeding crowded onion seedlings is tedious work. Plant 4 weeks before the last spring frost if you want pearl onions by the time the peas come in. The rest of the crop will mature at pickling size about 12 weeks after sowing.

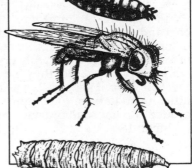

Onion Maggot: Pupa (top), Adult (center), Maggot (bottom)

Curtains for Onion Maggots

Q. **Last spring my onion plants turned yellow, and when I pulled a few up, they had small white maggots in them. How can I prevent this?**

A. Rotate plantings and cover emerging crops with fine mesh netting or a spunbonded polyester row cover such as Reemay. Seal the material securely by mounding soil around the edges. This prevents most emerging adult onion maggots from laying eggs at the base of the plants. Since the insects thrive on decaying organic matter, don't mulch, but do keep down weeds and harvest the crop completely. Onion maggot populations tend to be higher during very rainy periods, so row covers may be unnecessary in a dry year.

Onions Neck and Neck

Q. Last year I had a beautiful crop of 100 red and white onions, but half of them rotted at the neck in storage. How can I store my onions successfully?

A. Neck rot is the most common cause of onions spoiling in storage. The botrytis fungus that causes neck rot can infect an onion through any wound but most often enters through the wound left when the top is cut off. The fungus grows down into the onion, causing the inner scales to soften and turn brown, as though they had been cooked. The onions may look normal on the outside until decay is well advanced. The foul odor characteristic of spoiled onions is produced by bacterial soft rot that often follows the fungus.

Spores of the neck-rot fungus won't germinate under dry conditions, so the best way to protect your onions is to cure and store them properly. Avoid bruising the onions during harvest, and cure them in a single layer on slats or screens in a dry, well-ventilated place. Make sure the necks are completely dry before clipping or bunching and tying the dried tops. Store the onions in a cold, dry place where air can circulate around them. Temperatures close to freezing coupled with low humidity (60 to 70 percent) help to inhibit the fungus. If you've consistently had problems with neck rot, grow thin-necked rather than thick-necked onion varieties for storage. Thick-necked onions are more vulnerable to infection because they dry more slowly (and sometimes less completely) than thin-necked types. And hold off on nitrogen-rich fertilizers, which can produce soft, lush topgrowth.

Chilled-Out Garlic

Q. My summer-planted garlic won't come up. What's wrong?

A. Garlic won't sprout unless it's given a cold period of several weeks at no warmer than 50°F. It doesn't matter when the cloves are treated. For a strong stand of summer-planted garlic, store the cloves in the refrigerator for a few weeks before planting. Fall-planted garlic sprouts readily in the spring because it has been well chilled by winter temperatures.

Green Elephants

Q. **When I dig my elephant garlic bulbs, the skins are split and the cloves inside are green. Why does this happen?**

A. You may be feeding the garlic too much nitrogen and not enough phosphorus and potassium. To get strong skins and large cloves, work in bonemeal for phosphorus and greensand or kelp meal for potassium before planting. Exposure to sunlight due to shallow planting turns garlic cloves green. Green cloves are usually too bitter to eat but can be used for planting. Set cloves 4 inches deep, harvest as soon as the tops wither, and dry the garlic in a shady place before storing.

Invisible Garlic

Q. **Last fall I planted garlic, but it never came up. Do you think it rotted? How can I prevent this?**

A. It probably did rot. For the best results, select grocery- or nursery-bought cloves that are fresh, firm, and show no sign of any kind of rot, says garlic specialist Dr. R. E. Voss of the University of California at Davis. The bigger the cloves, the larger the bulbs will be. Fluctuating winter temperatures can heave the plants right out of the ground, so set cloves 2 to 3 inches deep. They usually sprout within two weeks. Plant about a month before you expect heavy frosts, at which time you should cover the garlic with a winter mulch. The bulbs will be ready to harvest in early July.

Moldy Bulbs

Q. **I plant garlic in the fall, but in mid-May the tops dry up and the bulbs begin to mold. Can you help me solve this problem?**

A. Because garlic requires good drainage, your soil may be too wet, according to Betty Walker, manager of Nichols Garden Nursery in Oregon. She suggests that you make a raised bed in another location, incorporating lots of compost to improve drainage. And don't leave the garlic in the ground too long: Harvest the bulbs as soon as the tops die.

Water-Soaked Cloves

Q. **The skin between the cloves of my garlic bulbs rots. What is the problem?**

A. The most common reason for rot between the garlic cloves is too much water just before harvest. Garlic needs ample water while the bulbs are developing, but when the tops start to die, stop watering. If it rains, pull the bulbs. If the rotting occurs after harvest, high humidity, such as in a refrigerator, could be the problem. Garlic keeps best in a cool (40° to 60°F), dry place.

Carrot Quandaries

Speeding Carrot Sprouting

Q. **The weeds always get ahead of my carrots. Is there some way to get the seed to sprout faster?**

A. Try soaking the seed overnight. When sowing carrot seed, cover it with vermiculite, sawdust, or peat. Many soils tend to crust over, preventing the delicate seedlings from emerging. Radishes planted at the same time will sprout ahead of the carrots and break the crust. If you plant in furrows, the quick-sprouting radish seedlings will mark the carrot row. Hoe between the rows until the radishes emerge, then apply mulch. Just be sure to pull them up before they start to crowd the carrots. The bed-planting technique requires more diligent weeding at first than row-planting, but within about six weeks, most weeds will be shaded out by the carrots' ferny foliage.

How to Harvest Carrots

Q. **I want to grow carrots this year. How do I harvest and store them?**

A. Don't harvest carrots until the ground has had a good frost or two. Cut the tops anywhere from ½ to 2 inches from the top, and don't wash the carrots. Store in dry sawdust or straw, or in moist sand, peat, or moss. The carrots should be stored at a temperature of 32° to 40°F and a relative humidity of 90 to 95 percent. They should last six months or more when stored this way.

Embittered Carrots

Q. **I have grown carrots for a good many years, but they are always bitter. I would be grateful for a solution to this problem.**

A. Carrots with an uneven supply of moisture or nutrients will become bitter. Under these stressful conditions, the plants produce a bitter substance called isocoumarin. Besides providing water at the first signs of drought, prepare your seedbed by digging in rotted manure. That will supply both nutrients and moisture-holding organic matter. Check regularly for signs of insects and disease, which can also stress the carrots and cause bitterness, and control them promptly.

Avoiding Split Ends

Q. **Almost all my carrots split open last year. What was the problem?**

A. Deep drying of the soil followed by heavy rain or watering causes carrots to split. To prevent drying, mix completely rotted manure or compost into the soil at planting time, mulch the plants, and water regularly and generously during drought.

Undercover Carrots

Q. **This season my carrots and parsnips were destroyed by maggots tunneling into them. What can I do to keep this from happening again next year?**

A. The best way to protect your root crops is to cover them with a spunbonded row cover such as Reemay, cheesecloth, or wire mesh screen. The damage is caused by the larvae of the shiny green, yellow-headed carrot rust fly. Adults emerge from the soil in May and lay eggs, which hatch in 3 to 17 days, around the base of the plants. The maggots work their way into the soil, attacking tender root tips and leaving rust-colored burrows. Second and third generations emerge in August and September. The flies also attack celery, parsley, dill, and fennel. Grow carrots and parsnips in an area where host plants were not grown the previous season. Some gardeners also report success with spraying a solution of ground wormwood on the soil around the plants before eggs are laid.

A Blight on Carrots

Q. **The foliage on our last three crops of carrots died back just as the roots were sizing up. After a while, the tops grew back. Can you explain this?**

A. Leaf blight is the problem. It can be caused by two different fungi (*Alternaria dauci* and *Cercospora carotae*) or a bacterium (*Xanthomonas carotae*). All three diseases overwinter in carrot residues and in soil. Clean up infected tops and roots and compost them in a hot pile or bury them outside the garden. If possible, grow carrots in three- or four-year rotations with other crops. Plant in rows instead of beds to improve air circulation around the plants. Water early in the day so the foliage is dry by nightfall, and don't work among the plants while they're wet. Though there is no blight-resistant cultivar, 'Orlando Gold' is tolerant of the blight fungi, according to USDA carrot breeder Dr. Clinton E. Peterson.

Catty Carrots

Q. **Cats have used my carrot bed as a litter box, and I'm afraid they might carry *Toxoplasma gondii*. Are the carrots safe to eat?**

A. Carrots and other root vegetables from infected soil are safe to eat if you scrub and peel them first, says Dr. J. P. Dubey, the USDA animal parasitologist who discovered the disease cycle of *T. gondii* in cats. Boiling or steaming for a few minutes removes all risk by killing the one-celled protozoan parasites. *T. gondii* is carried by as many as 40 percent of all cats in the United States. The protozoan is excreted in their feces, through which it can infect humans and other warm-blooded animals. If contracted by pregnant women, the parasite can cause brain disease and impaired vision or blindness in the unborn child. Young children and adults with damaged immune systems are also at risk, but healthy adults are resistant. The parasite can remain infective in cat feces outdoors for 12 to 18 months, says Dubey.

Gardeners are more likely to pick up the parasite on their hands directly from the soil than from eating vegetables, says Dubey. Wear gloves when gardening and wash carefully afterward, especially under fingernails. Try to keep cats out of the vegetable and flower beds by using fences, repellents, or mulches (such as cardboard or plastic) that they can't dig through. If they get through your defenses, removing the feces along with the soil immediately surrounding them will remove most of the parasites.

Sweet Potato Sagas

Skimpy Sweet Potatoes

Q. **My sweet potato plants produce mostly vines and very few potatoes. Why?**

A. Too much nitrogen in the soil promotes vine rather than root growth. Prepare the soil for sweet potatoes with moderate amounts of compost and some wood ashes or other potassium-rich material, but don't add high-nitrogen sources like manure, cottonseed meal, and bloodmeal.

Sweet Potato Primer

Q. **What nutrients do sweet potatoes need, and what pH is best for them?**

A. Although they aren't known as a poor-soil crop, sweet potatoes do not like too much nitrogen. The soil should have adequate amounts of phosphorus and potash, but heavy potash fertilizing makes the roots short and chunky. Sweet potatoes prefer a slightly acid soil, growing best when the pH is between 5.2 and 6.7. Sweet potatoes do best in a light, sandy soil and require a long, hot growing season. They need 140 to 150 warm days and nights from the time transplants are set out. Too much water during the last few weeks before harvest will cause the roots to crack.

Shot-Holed Sweet Potatoes

Q. **Some of my 'Allgold' and 'Centennial' sweet potatoes have dark brown skin, and some have small holes about the size of a common nailhead. What's the problem? Also, how long does it take these varieties to mature?**

A. Brown or tan skin can be caused by high organic content in the soil, according to Dr. Ron Robbins, director of the Sweet Potato Research Station in Chase, Louisiana. Small holes are often the work of grubs. However, both problems are cosmetic, and neither should affect the eating or storage quality. Because sweet potatoes are swollen underground stems rather than fruits, they do not mature or ripen but can be harvested as soon as they are large enough. Most popular varieties, including 'Allgold' and 'Centennial', reach harvestable size in about 120 days. 'Travis', a relatively new variety, is ready to eat in only 90 days.

The Evils of Weevils

Q. How can I keep weevils out of my sweet potatoes?

A. The best control is to plant a resistant variety like 'Regal', advises J. M. Schalk, a research entomologist at the USDA Sweet Potato Laboratory in Charleston, South Carolina. Though the roots of 'Regal' are about 80 percent resistant, you'll still find weevils in the vines, says Schalk. Sweet potato weevils are ¼-inch-long, antlike beetles with long snouts, blue-black heads and backs, and reddish legs. Adults lay eggs in sweet potato stems and tubers, and the larvae spoil the potatoes by tunneling through them in the ground and in storage. There may be up to eight generations a year. Inspect your plants regularly and begin spraying weekly with pyrethrum as soon as weevils appear, making sure to cover all leaf surfaces. When you dig the sweet potatoes, store only those that show no sign of weevil damage. Clean up and destroy dead vines and potato pieces. Control weeds, especially wild morning glory, in and around the garden to deprive the weevils of wild hosts.

Soft Touch
with Sweet Potatoes

Q. Though I try to avoid bruising my sweet potatoes when I dig and store them, most of them develop hard, dry, black sunken spots that may go deep into the root. How can I get them to keep better?

A. The black spots are a sign of fusarium surface rots. Careful digging, curing, and storage are the best defenses against these rots. These diseases are soilborne and usually infect sweet potatoes through wounds at harvest time. They can enter through an injury as small as that left by a broken hair root. After infection, the diseases grow slowly in storage. No commercial variety is resistant. Dig your crop when the roots have reached an acceptable size in September or October. Don't wait to dig until cold weather sets in— that only makes the potatoes more likely to rot. Handle them carefully to avoid injury. For a week after digging, cure the potatoes under conditions as close to 85°F and 100 percent humidity as you can manage. One way is to seal a basket of sweet potatoes in a plastic trash bag and keep it in a warm room or shed. Curing helps the potatoes seal off wounds and resist decay. After curing, store the potatoes at 55°F. Cooler temperatures may cause chilling injury, while warmer temperatures encourage soil diseases. Try to keep the humidity high. If you store the potatoes in a dry basement, keep them in an unsealed plastic bag.

Radishes, Rutabagas, and Other Robust Roots

Bearded Radishes

Q. Why do my radishes sometimes develop many fine roots that look like beards?

A. Soil compaction and crowding are the most likely causes, according to Dr. Hasib Humaydan, a vegetable breeder and the vice president of research at Harris Moran Seed Company. Plant radish seeds 1 inch apart in soil loosened to spade depth. Work in compost, but keep out large chunks of undecayed organic matter that could check taproot growth. If the radishes are undersize and the edges of the older leaves are dead, your soil could be low in potassium. Have a soil test performed and add wood ashes, greensand, manure, or compost if necessary.

Mild-Mannered Radishes

Q. My radishes are too hot to eat, no matter what variety I plant, when I plant them, or how I prepare the soil. Can you tell me how to grow a mild radish?

A. The "heat" or pungency in radishes is controlled primarily by genetics, so you should continue your search for a variety you like. Contrary to popular belief, soil preparation and planting time don't have much effect on how hot your radishes are. Young radishes are actually hotter than those left in the ground longer. But while mature radishes are milder, their texture becomes woody and pithy. A new variety called 'Fancy Red' is reportedly milder than many others. 'Faribo White Snoball', a white-fleshed variety, is also said to be extremely mild. If these are still too hot, prepare radishes for eating by slicing them, setting them in a bowl of cold water, and putting them in the refrigerator for 30 minutes. In addition to making the radishes crisper, the water will draw out the compound responsible for the pungency, resulting in an even milder radish.

Rootless Root Crops

Q. I got plenty of greens but no roots on my radishes and turnips. What am I doing wrong?

A. You're probably crowding the plants or giving them too much nitrogen. Space the seeds or thin the plants so radishes grow 1 to 1½ inches apart and turnips 3 to 6 inches apart, depending on the cultivar. Use high-nitrogen fertilizers sparingly, or skip them if the previous crop was heavily fertilized.

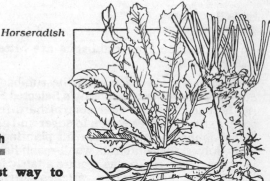

Horseradish

Homemade Horseradish

Q. What is the best way to grow, harvest, and prepare horseradish?

A. Horseradish, a perennial herb of the mustard family, must be started from a root cutting. Plant the cutting early in the growing season (as early as February) in deep, moist loam with a high organic content that will allow roots to grow long and straight. Poor soil can cause gnarled roots, which are harder to prepare. For best results, horseradish needs the cool weather of autumn, so don't plan to start the harvest until after September. Some gardeners gather a few roots at a time, leaving the other hardy roots stored in the soil. Others harvest all the roots they'll need, storing them in sawdust or damp sand in the root cellar or refrigerator. Horseradish tastes best freshly grated in a blender and mixed with vinegar to the consistency of a sauce. It can also be mixed with oil, lemon juice, and chopped hard-boiled eggs as a sauc, or served with grated beets. Try adding other spices, including dill and mustard.

Tried-and-True Turnips

Q. Do you have a "tried-and-true" method for storing turnips in the ground during the winter to keep them fresh for the table?

A. We don't recommend in-ground storage for turnips because the succulent roots are prone to rot and frost damage. The protruding shoulders of turnips are also an easy meal for hungry mice. Turnips are best stored in a cool basement or root cellar. Roger Kline of Cornell University has found a container of moist vermiculite ideal for storing his turnips. Moist sawdust or dry leaves also work well.

Rude Rutabagas

Q. My 'Purple Top' rutabagas are bitter and strong-tasting. Can you help?

A. You may be harvesting the rutabagas too early, says Rob Johnston, president of Johnny's Selected Seeds in Albion, Maine. It's best to dig them after several hard frosts, because the cold temperature changes starch to sugar and gives the roots a sweeter flavor. Johnston suggests delaying planting until the end of June or early July so the rutabagas won't reach harvestable size until fall. For best flavor, rutabagas require a fairly fertile soil, he says. You might also want to try some varieties with improved flavor, such as 'Laurentian' or 'Pike'.

No-Wax Finish for Rutabagas

Q. When I harvested my rutabagas, I cut the leaves off close to the body, washed the dirt off, and let them dry for half a day. I dipped them in hot wax, but within a week they began to spoil. What did I do wrong?

A. Perhaps the cut surfaces did not have a chance to form their natural seal before you waxed them, says Vince Rubatzky, extension vegetable specialist at the University of California at Davis.

Wait a day or so before waxing, until newly exposed areas no longer look wet but are milky and scalelike. Your wax may also have been too hot, suggests James Hicks, post-harvest physiologist at Cornell University. The wax should be no hotter than 270°F. If your storage area stays at 32°F and has high relative humidity (98 to 100 percent), you may not have to wax the rutabagas at all, says Hicks. In fact, USDA research shows that they keep best when left unwaxed in the proper atmosphere. If you have an area with cold, humid conditions, just slice off the leafy tops, being careful not to cut into the root, and store. Don't trim the lateral roots or wash the rutabagas until you're ready to eat them.

Ice-Bound Parsnips

Q. The ground froze solid before we finished eating all our parsnips. Is there a way for us to harvest them?

A. If the frost has penetrated only a few inches, try freeing your parsnips by using a heat-trapping black plastic mulch to thaw the soil. If that fails, forget them until spring. Trying to break the roots out of frozen ground is futile and is almost certain to ruin them. But when the ground thaws, dig them all promptly and store them in the refrigerator. Overwintered parsnips are one of the first plants to sprout in spring, and the sprouting will ruin their eating quality.

Chapter 10

The Staff of Life
Corn, Grains, and Other Crops

Corny Concerns

Skimpy Corn

Q. My corn grows well, but 90 percent of the ears are short and poorly filled. How can I correct this problem?

A. Short, poorly filled ears are caused by spacing plants too closely, poor pollination, insufficient water, and low fertility. For best pollination, plant corn in blocks of four or five short rows rather than in long double rows. Work in plenty of manure or compost and space plants 15 to 18 inches apart in all directions. Control weeds while the corn is young and make sure the root zone stays moist. To be sure you're planting the best variety for your area, ask your county extension agent for a list of locally recommended corn varieties.

The Indians Got It Right

Q. I want to use fish as a fertilizer for corn. How do I do it?

A. Plant one fish in each corn hill or lay the fish in a trench between rows and cover with soil. Put fish at least 6 inches under the surface, well away from young plants' roots but close enough for mature plants' roots to penetrate. Fish are a good source of nitrogen and phosphorus. Their wastes on the ground can attract animals, so keep the fish in a bucket while digging the holes. If you have problems with animals, put screening over the seedbed and weight it with stones.

The Supersweet Corn That Wasn't

Q. **Last year, I planted 71-day supersweet 'Crusader' corn alongside 110-day 'Rainbow' ornamental corn. Both varieties tasseled at the same time, and the 'Crusader' corn didn't taste sweet at all. Any suggestions?**

A. Most supersweet corn, including 'Crusader', loses much of its sweetness if allowed to cross-pollinate with other corn varieties. Isolating the planting usually isn't practical (varieties tasseling at the same time need 400 yards between them), but planting the 'Crusader' corn a month later than 'Rainbow' is one solution. You could also substitute a different type of supersweet corn, one with a sugar-extender gene, such as 'Miracle', 'Incredible', and 'Silverado' (a white variety). These don't require isolation to develop maximum sweetness.

Pooped Popcorn

Q. **I'm going to plant popcorn again this year, and I'd like to know how to dry it properly for popping. Last year, half popped and half didn't.**

A. Moisture content is important to popcorn. Even if you let the ears dry on the stalk, they might need extra drying. Remember, too, that popcorn takes longer than sweet corn to mature. Seed catalogs usually feature varieties that take a minimum of 90 and up to 120 days. Growers are usually cautioned to dry popcorn without artificial heat, but one reader claimed success by drying the kernels (removed from the cob after a period of natural drying) in an oven, at the lowest setting, for two hours. Store popcorn in glass jars.

Prepopped Corn

Q. When we harvested our popcorn last fall, we found that some of the kernels had split and the starch had pushed out and hardened. What caused this?

A. Too much water during kernel enlargement is the most likely cause of splitting, but the disorder seldom reduces yields significantly, according to Dr. Bruce Ashman, a popcorn breeder at Purdue University. The older, thick-hulled cultivars resist splitting, but they make tougher popcorn than modern selections.

Maggots Maul Corn

Q. Maggots destroy my corn before it even comes up. What can I do about them?

A. Keep planting. Seed-corn maggots, the larvae of a small grayish-brown fly, tunnel into the seeds of corn, peas, and other large-seeded vegetables. If infested seeds sprout, the seedlings are weak and soon die. Usually, injury is worst early in the season in cold, wet soil high in manure or other organic matter. The flies, which emerge in spring, are attracted to organic matter for egg laying. After feeding for one or two weeks, the maggots pupate in the soil and emerge as adults about two weeks later. There can be several generations a year. To make the soil less attractive to the adults, turn under manure, compost, or cover crops in fall so they can decay by spring. Delay planting until the soil has warmed up, and plant seeds in shallow furrows to speed emergence. Monitor germination closely. If there is heavy maggot damage, replant immediately so the seeds germinate before the next generation of adults emerges.

My Corn Has Fleas

Q. Last summer, tiny black beetles damaged my corn, especially the ears at the silk end. What can be done to control them?

A. If the beetles jumped away at your approach and some of the corn leaves were riddled with shotholes, the pests were flea beetles. Since their numbers can vary greatly from year to year, the population may not reach damaging levels in the coming season. Research has shown that mulching crops with chopped clover and companion planting with other vegetables, herbs, or cover crops such as clover or annual ryegrass can reduce flea beetle numbers. Flea beetles stop feeding and hide in wet weather, so you may be able to discourage them from feeding by giving your corn frequent light waterings with a hose or overhead sprinkler. Dusting the plants lightly with wood ashes or lime or spraying them with a garlic/hot pepper solution may also help repel the pests. If these methods fail, dust or spray with rotenone to kill them.

Derailing a Double Pest

Q. How do I control corn earworms, which I understand are the same pests as tomato fruitworms?

A. They are one and the same. On corn, the worms feed on tassels first, disrupting pollination. But most of the damage is to the ear. Late-season corn is particularly susceptible. Keep them out of your ears by applying a few drops of mineral oil into the silk just inside the tip of each ear, after the silk has wilted. The oil, which is completely tasteless and will not affect the flavor of the corn, suffocates the worms. You can also handpick the worms after the silk begins to turn brown and pollination is complete. Corn varieties like 'Country Gentleman' and 'Silver Cross Bantam' have long, tight husks that prevent earworms from penetrating. *Bacillus thuringiensis* (Bt), the bacterial disease that kills many caterpillars, works well as long as you apply the powder or spray while the insects are feeding. You can also plant a row of earworm-repellent cosmos flowers near your corn and tomatoes. If the infestation gets more severe, use a garlic spray before spraying or dusting with rotenone.

Ban Backyard Smut

Q. What can I do to prevent smut in my sweet corn?

A. Remove and destroy all affected corn plants before the gray boils burst and release thousands of fungus spores throughout your garden. You can recognize ripened spore masses because they have an oily appearance. Corn smut is a common fungus that causes kernels, tassels, husks, and ears to grow monstrous galls or boils. The disease spores spread to other cornstalks by the wind when the membranes break (spores germinate best at between 80° and 92°F). Wherever a spore lands, a new boil forms. A dry spring followed by a wet spell when corn reaches a height of 1 to 3 feet creates the perfect conditions for the fungus.

Although smut spores can remain viable in corn debris, soil, or even manure for five years, they are destroyed by the high internal temperatures of a compost pile that reaches 150°F. You can also burn infected crop residues. Do not till contaminated residues into the soil. Make sure that you thoroughly clean up and properly dispose of all crop debris in the fall, too. If your corn was hit by the disease last year, smut spores are probably dormant in your garden. Never grow corn in the same place year after year. A three-year rotation plan will cut down the chances of reinfection.

Growing Tips for Grains

Swatting Small Grains

Q. My father planted a small plot of wheat and triticale last spring that gave us a very nice harvest. The problems came, however, when we tried threshing it with everything from baseball bats to tennis shoes. Nothing seemed to produce much for the time and labor involved. Isn't there a more effective way to thresh and clean small quantities of grain?

A. We usually recommend threshing (breaking grain away from the husks) small amounts of grain by some kind of a beating action, which you've tried. There's no doubt about it—while this action is the least complicated, it seems clumsy and time-consuming. But small-scale threshers aren't made in this country anymore except for precise experimental work. That kind of engineering puts them way out of the gardener's price range. Old models can be found at farm auctions, in the back corners of some old barns, and sometimes in farm swap listings.

Amaranth Mixup

Q. I'm confused about amaranth. I received some seed that I planned to experiment with as a supplemental sheep feed. An agricultural extension agent here in Mendocino County, California, convinced me not to, because of what he called "toxicity and nonacceptance." What is the story on amaranth?

A. The botanical genus *Amaranthus* has several different species. Most of us know the native pigweed (*A. retroflexus*). It is quite different in plant type from grain (*A. hypochondriacus*) or vegetable amaranths (*A. caudatus* and *A. cruentus*). Pigweed tastes very bitter and is well known for deleterious effects on animals, particularly swine, if eaten in large amounts. Cultivated amaranths—both grain and vegetable—are safe for people and animals.

Amaranth Bash

Q. I'm growing grain amaranth in my garden this year. How can I tell when the seeds are mature, so I'll know when to harvest? Also, how can I separate the seeds from the seed head?

A. Seed heads should be harvested at the early stages of maturity. Pull off a small portion of a head and rub it lightly between your fingers. If the seeds come off easily, it could be time to harvest. To make sure, try the "dough stage" test. Chew on a seed. If it's doughy, it's not quite ready to be harvested. Mature seed should be firm. But don't wait too long—if the plants become too dry in the field, too much seed will fall to the ground. When harvesting, collect the seed heads with as few stems and leaves as possible. Hang the heads in clusters or put them in a burlap bag. Store in a dry place. A simple method of threshing is to put the heads in a cloth bag and beat it against a concrete floor. Seed can be separated from the chaff by sifting through a common 16-mesh household screen.

Questioning Quinoa

Q. Can you tell me more about a cereal grain commonly grown in the South American Andes that scientists are experimenting with as a high-altitude crop?

A. The plant you are referring to is no doubt quinoa (pronounced kee-no-ah), a crop that has been cultivated by the Peruvians for thousands of years in high altitudes where amaranth (traditionally the staple grain) doesn't grow well. Though more closely related to lamb's-quarters, quinoa is grown and used in much the same manner as amaranth. The seed heads are smaller than amaranth's, but the seeds themselves are larger—about the size of a grain of millet. They can be ground into a flour or cooked like rice. (Quinoa is being test-marketed in Denver under the name "Incan Rice.") It has a nutty flavor and a texture like wild rice, according to agronomist Duane Johnson of Colorado State University, who is working with the plant. If you live in the mountains, give quinoa a try, but if you're a flatlander, don't bother. The plant grows poorly below 6,000 feet.

Grow Your Own Broom

Q. I want to make my own brooms. Is broomcorn difficult to grow?

A. No, growing broomcorn is as easy as growing sweet corn. After the soil has warmed up, plant the seed in hills 12 inches apart or sow 4 or 5 inches apart in rows. Cut the heads about three months later when they begin to fill out but the seeds and sweeps are still green. Fully mature broomcorn will have red heads, which make an attractive broom, but the fibers are not as strong as green ones. Cut the stalks about 3 feet from the top. Hang the heads or lay them flat to cure. Cured outdoors, the heads will bleach. Broomcorn mildews easily, so if you let it dry outside, take it in at night and during rainy weather. To make a broom, you'll need about 30 stalks.

Peanut Problems
and Sunflower Solutions

Peanut Roast

Q. How can we roast our homegrown peanuts?

A. After you dig the peanuts, let them dry in the shell on the vine for three to seven days in a sheltered but airy spot, says Melanie Miller, home economist for the National Peanut Council. The moisture content will drop from about 30 percent when freshly dug to 12 or 15 percent after three or four days. It's best to store peanuts in the freezer until you want to roast and eat them, says Miller. To roast, spread one layer of dry peanuts on a cookie sheet and place in a 350°F oven. Roast unshelled peanuts for 20 to 25 minutes and shelled peanuts for 15 to 20 minutes. Once roasted, peanuts become stale in about six weeks. Don't eat moldy or damaged peanuts. They may contain aflatoxin, a carcinogen.

Not a Nut in Sight

Q. When I dug peanuts in my New York State garden, I found that the shells were watery and soft. Many had no nuts inside, while others had small nuts that shriveled when dry. What went wrong?

A. Your peanuts were immature. You may have planted them too late for your area, chosen a long-season variety, or dug them too soon. Try growing Spanish peanuts this year. They usually give good results in northern climates, since some varieties mature in as few as 100 days. Plant the seed as soon as possible after the last frost date in your area. Then, when the plants are a foot high, hill the soil up around them. That will enable the fruiting pegs to start forming peanuts earlier in the season. Don't dig them until after the leaves have been killed by frost. Mature peanuts have a well-defined shell that is dry and hard. The nuts inside should fill the shell, and their papery hulls (the red "skin" on dry peanuts) should be brownish.

Sunflower Seeds

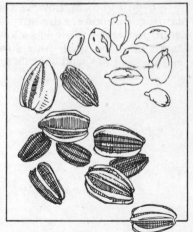

Shelling Sunflowers

Q. I have a large crop of sun-flowers this year. I'd like to shell them mechanically but can't locate any shellers. Can you help?

A. As far as we know, there aren't any sunflower shellers for small-scale use available, but a grain mill will work. You can use any mill, as long as the stones open wide enough to accommodate the largest seeds. Because seed size varies, smaller seeds tend to slip through the mill, so it's necessary to grade them first and process different sizes separately. Three sizing boxes should do it. Make a wooden frame and staple ¼-inch hardware cloth to the bottom. The second and third boxes should have two layers, moved slightly to narrow the mesh openings. After shelling, winnow seeds outdoors or in front of a fan.

Weevil Woes

Q. When I was shelling my sunflower seeds, I found that they were infested with small white larvae. How can I control them? I shell my seeds mechanically, so even a few would ruin the whole crop.

A. Your sunflower seeds are probably infested with seed-weevil larvae. You should be able to obtain close to complete control through a combination of fall plowing and early planting. Since the larvae overwinter in the soil after dropping from dry sunflower heads, plowing or tilling 6 to 8 inches deep will kill up to 40 percent of them. Adult weevils emerge in early summer and will fly in from more than a mile away to lay eggs on your developing sunflower heads during July and August. They won't lay eggs on seeds that have begun to form, however, so the other key to control is early planting. Sunflowers are surprisingly frost-tolerant and will grow when the temperature is as low as 50°F. If you sow them by late March or early April, your sunflowers should already be setting seed by the time seed weevils are ready to lay eggs.

Chapter 11

Special Vegetables
Celery to Salsify

Celery Queries

Lime Your Celery

Q. What caused the center stalks of my celery plants to turn brown and rot all the way to the ground last summer?

A. Blackheart. This disorder is caused by a calcium deficiency in the young, rapidly growing leaves at the center of the plant. It is most likely to occur if the soil pH is 6.0 or lower. Add lime to raise the pH to between 6.5 and 6.8, so plenty of calcium will be available. Stressful growing conditions like hot weather, alternately wet and dry soil, and high salt (especially potassium) levels can cause the disease by preventing celery from taking up calcium even when it is available. Try planting your next crop so it will mature late in the season when the hottest days are past. Dig in plenty of finished compost, mulch the plants, and water regularly to maintain the high moisture levels celery demands, especially during the last month before harvest. If your soil tests high in potassium, avoid fertilizers like wood ashes and manure.

Sickly Celery

Q. What's wrong with my celery plants? The leaves become mottled, then develop brown spots, turn yellow, and shrivel. Three varieties in different places have all had the same problem.

A. Your celery probably has late blight (*Septoria apiicola*). Cool, moist conditions promote this disease. The blight is caused by two types of fungus, which can appear alone or together. The large-spot fungus starts as small, yellowish specks that turn pale brown as the leaf dies. The spots may reach ½-inch in diameter before producing small, black dots that are fruiting bodies. When these become wet, they release spores that cling to tools and clothing and are spread to other plants or are splashed onto plants from rain or irrigation. The small-spot fungus is similar but spreads faster, and the fruiting bodies appear before the yellow spots.

The best way to control the blight is to use seed that has been aged two years. By then, any spores that were on the fresh seed will have died. Seed companies don't routinely age celery seed, so store your seed for a season under cool, dry conditions or soak it in hot water (122°F) for 25 minutes before planting. Seeds remain viable for five years. When you water your plants, make sure you don't get any water on the leaves. Wet foliage is more susceptible to the growth of celery late blight. If you find the fungus in your garden, burn infected vegetation and rotate your crop. The disease can overwinter in garden refuse and soil.

All about Okra

Cracking the Okra Germination Code

Q. I have heard that you can speed up okra germination by using freezing and hot-water treatments. How do I do it?

A. Put okra seed in the freezer overnight, then soak it in hot tap water for ½ to 1 hour. The point, says Elizabeth Whittle of Hastings Nursery, is to crack the hard seed coat. It's this outer covering that inhibits germination. Just soaking the seed at room temperature for 24 hours will also improve germination. And you can rub the seed lightly between two pieces of sandpaper, or nick the seed coats with a sharp knife before planting.

Picking Okra Pods

Q. This is the first year I've grown okra. Could you tell me how it should be harvested?

A. Okra pods are ready to pick a few days after their flowers fall. Harvest them promptly while they're young, and pick them daily to ensure the best quality and keep the plants producing until frost. The pods should be soft and the seed no more than half-grown if you're going to serve the pods whole. Once the pods have reached their prime—on or off the plants—they quickly become woody. Use them at once or freeze, can, or dry them promptly. To dry okra, slice the pods or leave small pods whole and string them. Hang the strings in a well-ventilated place, out of the sun, until the okra is dry.

Okra

Too Cold for Okra

Q. I planted 'Lee' okra in March. It began blooming when it reached about 30 to 35 inches tall, but the pods fell off when they were only ½ inch long. What was wrong?

A. You probably planted too early. Though okra grows in cool weather, it doesn't produce enough pollen to set seed at soil temperatures below 70°F and air temperatures below 75°F. The unpollinated pods just drop off. Since early planting does not increase production, time your next crop so the first bloom coincides with summer temperatures.

Okra Mummies

Q. **We waited for warm weather to plant our 'Clemson Spineless' okra. It grew to treelike proportions but produced a lot of mummies—small, undeveloped pods that fell from the plants. Why did this happen, and what can I do about it?**

A. First, since okra pods are almost 90 percent water, make sure your plants are watered regularly and deeply. Second, you mentioned that your okra grows to near tree size. If you are putting on too much manure, there will be too much nitrogen available, and the growth will go into the plant, not the pods. You also may not be harvesting the pods promptly. If you allow some to overripen on the plant, new production will stop. Last, if your area had a lot of rain over a long period during the growing season, the problem could be inhibited pollination, in which case pods would not develop properly.

Bottoms Up for Okra

Q. **When my okra gets about knee-high and begins producing, the leaves start dying from the bottom up and the stalk turns brown inside. Can you help?**

A. Your okra plants are probably suffering from the soilborne disease fusarium wilt. Wilting, curling, and the slow death of the plant are symptoms of fusarium. The fungal disease invades the host's vascular system, showing up as dark streaks if the stem is split lengthwise. No resistant okra variety is available. Plant pathologist Dr. Donald Sumner of the University of Georgia recommends controlling fusarium wilt with a two-part program. First, add as much compost to the soil as you can. Compost contains beneficial fungi and nematodes that will kill fusarium organisms. Second, try crop rotations. This year, plant okra in an area where corn, mustard, or collards grew last year. These crops aren't hosts to fusarium wilt fungus, so the population in the soil should be relatively low. But since the fungus can live in soil for ten years or more and is easily spread by cultivation, controlling it by crop rotation may not be possible in a home vegetable garden. Okra is an attractive plant—try growing it along the back of a flowerbed that is not infested with fusarium.

Fun with Fennel
and Other Gourmet Treats

Fennel

Flummoxed by Fennels

**Q. How many kinds of fennel
are there? How are they used?**

A. There are three edible fennels—common fennel, Sicilian
fennel (*Carosella*), and Florence fennel (*Finocchio*). Sweet fennel,
the common garden fennel grown as an herb, is prized for its seeds
and leaves. Its uses are varied, but it primarily serves as a flavoring
in soups, tea, breads, cookies, candies, and even liqueurs. Its feath-
ery foliage also makes a lovely garnish. Sicilian fennel, cultivated
in Italy and usually eaten raw, produces tender young stalks similar to those of celery or asparagus. Florence fennel, with its thick
stalks and bulbous, celerylike base, can be chopped for salads,
braised, stir-fried, or steamed. All fennel has a sweet, slightly anise
flavor.

Fall-Ripened Fennel

**Q. My Florence fennel went to seed in late August without
forming bulbs. What went wrong?**

A. Hot weather causes fennel to bolt without bulbing. Since
Florence fennel needs a 90- to 100-day season, it may not be possible to plant early enough to harvest a spring crop before the heat
sets in. Time your next crop to mature in fall. Start seeds in a flat in

June and set out the plants in July. Fertilize heavily with compost or manure, mulch the plants to cool the soil, and water regularly to stimulate fast growth.

Blanched Endive

Q. **Every time I try to blanch endive, the outer leaves rot by the time the center is blanched. What am I doing wrong?**

A. You can reduce the chance of rot by keeping the leaves dry. Pull off any injured or decaying leaves, and cover the plants to exclude light and rain. Roomy containers like boxes, buckets, or trash cans work better than small ones because the air underneath is less humid. Cover a few plants at a time, and don't wait too long before picking—endive spoils quickly once it's blanched. Blanching takes one to two weeks in summer.

You should also try growing some endive to mature in late fall in a coldframe or cloche. You'll find it a little less bitter than the summer crop, and it may suit your taste without blanching. Broad-leaved cultivars do well under cool fall conditions, and their tightly packed inner leaves blanch naturally by the time the head matures. If they're still too bitter, blanch them by covering the cloche or coldframe with any material that keeps out light.

Witloof Woes

Q. **What is the secret of growing tight chicons? I forced witloof chicory roots in my cellar this past winter, but their leaves were loose.**

A. To form compact heads, chicory roots must be planted 6 to 8 inches deep in sand, fine soil, or sawdust. Keep the box or container covered to exclude light. The heads will reach a height of 6 inches in three or four weeks. Harvest the chicons by cutting them from the root. 'Zoom F-1' is the only cultivar that doesn't need to be planted deeply or covered.

Where to Grow Jicama

Q. My neighbor invited me to try an unusual vegetable called jicama. It was fairly large and crisp, and it seemed to be a somewhat sweet, watery tuber. He said it is grown in Mexico. What is jicama, and what is its nutritional value? Can it be grown in Michigan?

A. The jicama (pronounced hee-kah-mah) is a tropical plant that is grown primarily in Mexico, the Philippines, Hawaii, and Formosa. Since it requires a frost-free, nine-month growing season to produce large tubers, that leaves Michigan out of the market—unless, of course, you have a greenhouse. If you're willing to settle for smaller-size tubers, jicama can be grown as far north as Massachusetts if you start the seeds inside and harvest them before the first frost. This vegetable is virtually unknown to cooks and gardeners in the East, and it's still relatively new to California markets. A brownish root shaped like an irregular turnip, jicama has a very tough, thick skin that peels off easily, leaving the sweet, white flesh beneath. Roots range in weight from 1 to 6 pounds and in diameter from 3 to 6 inches. Fresh jicama tastes a lot like water chestnuts. In fact, many economy-minded cooks use it as a substitute for water chestnuts in oriental stir-fried dishes. Primarily eaten raw, jicama is rich in vitamins A, B, and C, as well as in calcium and phosphorus.

Chayote—
by Every Other Name

Q. I cannot find information on raising mirlitons, also referred to as vegetable pear.

A. You might have better luck if you look for information on chayote, a more common name. But besides the two names you mentioned, it's also known as mango squash, christophine, and chocho—not to mention its other names outside North America.

Chayote is a tender plant requiring full sun, warmth, moisture, well-drained soil, and lots of space. It's best propagated from shoots taken from a crown division. Plant in hills and give it climbing space. It will reward you with shoots, fruits, and tubers that have many uses in the kitchen. Gardeners in Louisiana, Mississippi, and the southern areas of Florida, California, and Oklahoma have the right climate for chayote, and greenhouse growers farther north can consider giving it a try.

Starting Salsify

Q. I can't get salsify to germinate. Covering the seed with compost and potting soil hasn't helped. How can I get it to come up?

A. Start with fresh seed; salsify seed loses viability after one year. Salsify germinates best under fairly cool conditions. (The optimum germinating temperature is 65° to 70°F, the same as for peas.) Hot weather inhibits germination. Sow seed ½ inch deep any time from six weeks before until two weeks after the last frost. Even under ideal conditions, the seed may take from 7 to 20 days to sprout. Be careful when cultivating—young salsify looks grasslike and can easily be mistaken for weeds, especially if the row germinates unevenly.

If outdoor planting fails, try germinating the seed indoors using the following method: Soak the seeds in cold water for 48 hours, changing the water once. Drain the seeds, then layer them between wet paper towels in a saucer or a plastic bag. Keep the seeds at room temperature during the day and in the refrigerator at night. Check them daily. The alternating temperatures should induce germination in four to five days. Be careful not to break the roots when planting.

Humbug?
No, Hamburg Parsley

Q. I saw a plant in my seed catalog listed as "Hamburg parsley." Is this an herb or a vegetable?

A. Hamburg parsley is a variety of parsley, *Petroselinum crispum*, which is considered a vegetable and is grown for its parsniplike root (thus its varietal name, *tuberosum*). Known also as turnip-rooted parsley, the plant has a smooth-skinned, fleshy white root and flat, parsleylike leaves, which are also edible. As soon as the ground can be worked in spring, plant Hamburg parsley in soil that has been manured and deeply cultivated the fall before. Sow seeds ¼ inch deep in rows 12 to 18 inches apart, and thin the seedlings to stand 6 to 9 inches apart. Germination is slow, so you may want to mix the parsley seeds with radish seeds to mark the rows. To speed germination, soak the parsley seeds overnight before planting. The roots will be ready to harvest in the fall. A frost makes Hamburg parsley sweeter. Five- to seven-inch-long roots are most tender. The roots can be cooked and mashed, sliced and fried, grated in a salad, added to soups and stews, or roasted with meat. They taste like a mild parsnip or like parsley-flavored celeriac.

A Second Salsify

Q. A stand at a farmers' market here recently offered a plant called "black salsify." It looked intriguing. Is it a kind of salsify? What do I do with it?

A. Black salsify, more properly called scorzonera (*Scorzonera hispanica*), is not a kind of salsify (*Tragopogon porrifolius*), although it is also a root and has a similar oyster flavor. To use the roots, steam or boil them until tender—about 45 minutes—and drain. Then, rub off the black or charcoal-gray skin. Serve the roots hot with melted butter or a mushroom or cream sauce. You can also bake or fry them or use them in soup. If you must wait before using cooked roots, put them in water with lemon juice or vinegar to prevent discoloration.

Scorzonera is easy to grow from seed. It does best in a loose, sandy loam that has been cultivated 12 to 18 inches deep. Add compost or well-rotted manure to the soil for larger, straighter roots, but avoid high-nitrogen materials, which encourage the roots to fork and become hairy. Harvest at the end of the growing season. Dig carefully and handle gently: The roots can be brittle and may break easily.

You *Can* Grow Great Fruit

Garden-Fresh Fruit
Strawberries, Grapes, and Bush Fruits

Strawberry Worries

A Berry Poor Crop

Q. My strawberry plants are a beautiful dark green, but the few berries I get are small and puckered. What's wrong?

A. The problem could be excess nitrogen, which stimulates lush leaf growth and inhibits flower production. Fruits that form inside the overfed canopy may be misshapen because the dense leaves interfere with wind pollination. Heavy foliage also stays wet, favoring the development of diseases such as botrytis, which can infect flowers and deform fruits.

If your plants bloom normally, the problem could be late frosts. Open flowers exposed to temperatures below 30°F become blackened and die. Closed flowers may be partly damaged and later produce malformed berries. Cover your plants if frost is predicted during bloom, or grow them under polyester row covers until frost danger is past. Even if temperatures stay above freezing, cold, rainy weather at bloom time can inhibit pollination, producing small, knobby fruits.

A third possibility is insect damage. When they're abundant, mites and sucking insects such as tarnished plant bugs and thrips can damage flowers and fruits. You'll have to examine the plants closely to find these small pests. Flat, seedy brown tips on berries are a symptom of tarnished plant bug damage. If necessary, apply insecticidal soap or a botanical insecticide such as pyrethrum, rotenone, or sabadilla.

Sloping Strawberries

Q. **I grow strawberries in a 35-by-6-foot plot on a fairly steep slope behind my garden. I can't work nutrients into the soil because of severe erosion. Will this keep me from gardening organically?**

A. Because strawberries like sun, moisture, good drainage, and soil loaded with organic matter, we suggest that you terrace your slope to make adding that organic matter easier. Try creating a semipermanent bed by alternating rows each year. Let runners get established in rows next to the mother plants, then remove these. Work organic matter into empty rows and mulch to prevent erosion. By rotating your strawberry plants this way, you'll prevent the weeds and diseases that plague plots used for the same crops year after year.

Wedge-Shaped Strawberries

Q. **This is the second year for my 'Sure Crop' and 'Ozark Beauty' strawberries. The problem is that they are not shaped like strawberries; they are flat on the opposite end of the stem instead of pointed. Can you tell me what the problem is?**

A. Most bigger strawberries are "flat" rather than pointed. Wedge-shaped would be a better description. As long as the berries taste good, ripen well, and size up decently, don't worry about how they look. If all your berries are wedge-shaped, even the little ones, then possibly a mild freeze at blossom time may have injured the fruit so that it did not form correctly.

*Training
Strawberry
Runners*

Outrunning
Strawberry Runners

Q. **Keeping strawberry runners under control is a lot of work. Can I keep the plants from forming runners, or must I cut each one off?**

A. There are a few strawberry cultivars like 'Tioga' and 'Redglow' that don't set many runners. These, however, aren't necessarily desirable, since runners produce next year's berries, increasing the yield for your planting. Everbearing strawberries also tend to produce few runners.

To control varieties that *do* form runners, try the hill system, which allows easy removal. Set the plants 1 foot apart each way in twin or triple rows. Remove *all* runners from the mother plants with a tiller or hoe. (Space the rows according to the tool you'll use.) Plants grown in the hill system become quite large and produce more berries than those grown in the matted-row system.

Thinning Everbearers

Q. **When is the best time to thin everbearing strawberries?**

A. Thin everbearers in late fall after the last harvest or in early spring before growth begins. Since the plants you remove will have initiated flower buds, you will lose some fruit, but the remaining plants will make up for the loss by bearing more and larger berries. When you thin, take out old and diseased plants first.

Everbearers Don't

Q. **My everbearing strawberries produce a strong June crop but nothing in August or September. How can I get them to live up to their name?**

A. Try a different variety, suggests Dr. Gene Galletta, director of the U.S. Department of Agriculture (USDA) Fruit Laboratory in Beltsville, Maryland. Many older everbearing varieties won't flower during the summer heat. However, newer, day-neutral strawberries such as 'Tribute', 'Tristar', 'Hecker', 'Brighton', 'Aptos', and 'Fern' produce a spring crop followed by lighter but steady production during the summer and a second heavy crop in fall. To fruit well in hot weather, strawberries need large amounts of water and a steady supply of nutrients within easy reach of their shallow roots. Lay soaker hoses in the beds and mulch the plants to keep the soil moist. Apply a balanced organic fertilizer such as fish emulsion lightly and often, rather than in one or two heavy feedings, and maintain a soil pH of about 6.0.

Strawberry Barrel Blues

Q. Last year we started a strawberry barrel. We used a wooden whiskey barrel, drilled 3-inch holes 10 inches apart, and planted a tube with holes in the middle for watering. Only 3 plants out of 50 lived. Why?

A. We can't find fault with your construction. Maybe your growing techniques were to blame. Here's a checklist of best techniques for barrel planting: Make drainage holes and place broken crockery, gravel, or brick on the bottom. Be sure all plants get plenty of sunshine. A rich mix of loam and compost or rotted manure—slightly acid, fertile, and loose—is the best soil for strawberries. Keep the soil wet but not waterlogged. Runnerless everbearing varieties are best for barrels. Choose varieties that are recommended for your area. Finally, strawberries are very particular about planting depth. Cover all of the roots right up to the shoulder, with the crown neither completely under nor completely above the soil level.

Beetled Berries

Q. What can be done about the little black beetles that eat holes in our strawberries?

A. The pests are sap beetles, which feed and lay eggs on ripe and fermenting fruit. You can reduce their numbers by keeping the berries picked and promptly composting overripe fruit in a hot pile or burying it at a spade's depth. Thin your plants, if necessary, so you don't overlook berries that could become breeding sites for the beetles.

Strawberry High Rollers

Q. Strawberry leaf rollers attacked my strawberries last spring and fall. Can you suggest a control?

A. *Bacillus thuringiensis* (Bt) sprays will control strawberry leaf rollers, but timing is critical. First-generation caterpillars hatch in May, usually on the underside of leaves. They soon move to the upper leaf surface, where each caterpillar bends a leaflet at the midrib and ties it with silk, forming a protective fold in which to feed and pupate. The caterpillars eat only the outer leaf surface, not the entire leaf, but their feeding causes leaves to turn brown and die. Reddish-brown moths with a ¼-inch wingspan emerge from pupae about 54 days after eggs are laid. These moths produce a second generation, which appears in late August and September. The caterpillars are most vulnerable to Bt between hatching and the time they fold the leaves. Young leaf roller caterpillars are hard to see because they are pale green and less than ½ inch long. Ask your county agent or state university entomology department when hatching occurs in your area, and then apply Bt two or three times at weekly intervals. Bt has the advantage of being harmless to the parasitic wasps and flies that normally keep strawberry leaf rollers in check.

Sudden Strawberry Death

Q. I have grown strawberries for several years with very good luck, but last year the leaves turned yellow, then brown, and most of the plants died. What can I do?

A. Move your patch. Verticillium wilt (*Verticillium* spp.), rhizoctonia root rot (*Rhizoctonia* spp.), and anthracnose (*Colletotrichum* spp.) are diseases that can cause strawberry plants to die suddenly. Dr. John Maas, a pathologist at the USDA Fruit Laboratory in Beltsville, Maryland, suggests that you have the disease identified through your county or state Extension Service. Some strawberry cultivars, such as 'Illinois', are resistant to verticillium wilt, and the Extension Service can recommend the best ones for your area. If it's found to be rhizoctonia root rot, rotation is the only control. If the disease is diagnosed as anthracnose, a common problem on strawberries grown in California and the Southeast, try purchasing berry plants from another region of the country. But no matter what the disease, Maas recommends moving the strawberry bed to another area, preferably one that has not been used to grow strawberries or vegetables recently.

Strawberry Mold

Q. Last year, quite a few of my strawberries were covered with a fuzzy gray mold. What can I do to reduce or eliminate this problem?

A. Your strawberries are infected with gray mold (*Botrytis cinerea*). It is usually worst during a cool, wet spring. You may not be able to eliminate the disease, but you can curb its damage and get a good crop. The most important control is site selection. Choose a location that gets full sun all day. Make sure it isn't in a low spot where cold air tends to collect. A raised bed helps ensure good air drainage. Space the mother plants and their runners no closer than 12 inches apart. Don't use the matted-row system, which crowds the foliage and prevents good air circulation. Too much nitrogen can lead to gray mold by creating a thick leaf canopy and a cool, moist microclimate. Mulch the plants and water early enough in the day so the fruit and foliage can dry before dusk. Pick off and destroy all infected fruit and leaves to reduce the amount of fungus that will overwinter. Cultivars that are resistant to gray mold are 'Catskill', 'Fletcher', and 'Tioga'; 'Dixieland', 'Midway', and 'Sparkle' have intermediate resistance.

Grape Expectations

Concord Cuttings

Q. How can I root 'Concord' grape cuttings?

A. In late winter, take cuttings from healthy one-year-old canes that have fairly short internodes (the distance between buds). Each cutting should be ¼ to ½ inch thick and 12 to 18 inches long, with four to six buds. If you can't plant them immediately, store the cuttings in the refrigerator in a plastic bag filled with damp peat moss. As soon as the soil is workable, plant the cuttings in a trench in the garden, covering all but one or two buds. Be sure the buds are not at or just below ground level—they will produce suckers later. Keep the cuttings moist and weed-free. Transplant them the following spring. You can also root cuttings indoors in individual half-gallon milk cartons or cans with drainage holes. Use a fast-draining potting mix. Cover the containers with plastic and place them in a warm room or on a heating cable. When the cuttings sprout, remove the plastic and grow them in a sunny window or a coldframe. Plant them outside when they're well-rooted and danger of frost is past.

Name Brands Are Best

Q. I have a 20-year-old grapevine that I sprouted from a store-bought blue-black grape. It has never produced fruit, even though it is covered with blossoms in the spring. My other vines give good yields. Is there any way to make it produce grapes?

A. While cultivated grape varieties are monoecious, with both sexes on the same plant, many wild grapes and some seedlings are dioecious, each having only male or female flowers. Since yours produces flowers and no fruit, even though there are other grapes flowering nearby, it is undoubtedly a male plant, and there is no way to make it produce fruit. But even if the plant were a female, the chances of it producing good-quality grapes are extremely slim compared with other fruits started from seed, according to University of California extension viticulturist Fred Jensen. Unless you want vines for ornamental purposes, you're better off sticking with named varieties.

Concord Discord

Q. Could you tell me why my 'Concord' grapes don't ripen all at the same time? There will be a few ripe grapes in a bunch, but most will be half-ripe and some still green.

A. Although uneven ripening of grapes is a somewhat mysterious disorder, it is usually caused by inadequate sunlight, too heavy a crop load on the vine, or in some cases, a potassium deficiency in the soil. Proper pruning will solve the problem of inadequate sunlight. Prune to distribute the foliage evenly along the trellis, spacing the buds out so that all the new growth gets plenty of sunlight. Most growers either prune too severely or don't prune their vines enough, which produces too many clusters. Next, thin the remaining grape clusters by 15 to 20 percent. It's best to do that just before or after the clusters have flowered. If you're still getting small clusters with small berries that don't ripen at the same time, your soil may lack potassium. A soil test will tell you for certain. To correct the problem, spread as much as 1 pound of wood ashes or ½ cup of kelp meal at the base of each vine. Grape roots are shallow, so just sprinkle it over the top of the soil, then water the ground heavily and mulch.

Thompson Grapeless

Q. Last year my 'Thompson Seedless' grapes didn't produce even one bunch, while a 'Concord' vine a few feet away was loaded. Can you tell me how to remedy this problem for this year's crop?

A. Proper pruning should solve the problem. Most grape varieties (including 'Concord') form fruit on the buds nearest the main stem. A popular pruning technique for these grapes is spur-pruning—pruning all canes back to 2 buds. Spur-pruning gives good production with these varieties but removes all fruiting buds on 'Thompson Seedless'. 'Thompson Seedless' forms fruit only on canes arising from the middle 4 or 5 buds on each one-year-old cane. The buds nearest the main stem and those near the tip of the cane produce fruitless canes. So for this variety, try cane-pruning instead. Select two long shoots on the vine, each with 10 to 15 buds. Before the plant leafs out in the spring, prune all other shoots close to the main stem, leaving only short spurs with 2 buds each. Those two canes will bear grapes. Next winter, cut the two canes flush with the trunk. Then select two new canes with 10 to 15 buds and cut all the other shoots back to short spurs, just as you did this year. Cane-pruning can be used for all grape varieties and often yields larger crops than spur-pruning.

Raising Raisins

Q. How can we dry grapes at home to make raisins? Are there any special problems we should watch out for?

A. Dry grapes for raisins in a food dehydrator or an oven for about 14 to 20 hours at 95° to 120°F. The raisins will be lighter in color and slightly plumper than those you find in the store. Grapes usually can't be sun-dried because that technique requires two weeks of dry, bright weather. Choose sweet, fully ripe grapes that still have stems attached, advises Linda Wood of the California Raisin Advisory Board. Discard bruised or moldy grapes. Split the grapes before drying either by blanching for one minute in boiling water or by slicing the skin with a knife. Otherwise drying can take longer than the normal time. After the grapes have dried, remove their stems by rolling a handful of raisins between your palms. Four and one-half pounds of grapes will yield 1 pound of raisins. To retain the color and nutrients for up to 15 months, store at 40° to 50°F. Raisins freeze well, too. Seedless varieties are best, but seeded varieties of table (not wine) grapes are fine if you cut out the seeds afterward.

Routing Elm Sprouts

Q. We've recently purchased an old farm with a nice row of grapevines along the garden plot. Our problem is that there are elm sprouts growing from old stumps in the grapevines. Is there any way we can stop these from growing without hurting the grapes?

A. Short of pulling up the stumps, there's no easy way to stop the sprouts. Just plan to spend a little time cutting the new sprouts off each year in early spring.

Sparrows Are Pests of Grapes

Fowl Play

Q. Last season my five vines were loaded with grapes. The sparrows had a feast, but I didn't get any. What can I do?

A. Since you have only a few vines, you can cover individual grape clusters with pieces of netting or paper bags. Don't use plastic—it heats up too much. Early in the season, thin the clusters to encourage fewer but larger bunches rather than many small ones. Then cut out the end of each bag to provide ventilation, slip it over the grapes, and tie around the base of the cluster. The opening isn't a problem because "birds don't bother anything they can't see," according to A. N. Kasimatis, grape specialist at the University of California at Davis. You may, however, find it simpler to cover the vines with bird netting. Be sure the netting contains an ultraviolet absorber, which will slow down the sun's deteriorating action. You can get up to 11 years of life out of treated netting, compared with about two if it's untreated. A 14-foot width is adequate for most vines, but if you have *vinifera* grapes or use the Geneva double curtain training method, you'll need a width of 17 feet. Don't skimp on the size—pulling the netting too tightly will reduce photosynthesis. And if the net doesn't reach the ground, birds will get caught underneath. Secure the edges to the ground with U-shaped pieces of wire, or weigh it down with boards or rocks. Clip ends together or staple them to the posts.

Wormy Grapes

Q. My grapes have little worms in them. What are they, and how can I keep them from ruining future crops?

A. The worms are probably larvae of the grape-berry moth. Adult moths are brown and gray and have a ½-inch wingspan. They're native to the northeastern United States and usually have two generations a year. First-generation caterpillars hatch on grape flower stems and young fruits in spring and spin webs in the fruit clusters as they move from grape to grape. After about a month, they form a cocoon on a leaf and pupate. Moths begin to emerge and lay eggs in late July. This second group hatches in August and bores into ripening grapes. When mature, they drop to the ground and overwinter as pupae on fallen grape leaves.

The key to control is good timing. Insecticides are effective only before the larvae enter the grapes. Starting immediately after bloom, spray the clusters every seven days with rotenone or every three days with *Bacillus thuringiensis* (Bt), continuing for two weeks. You may have to spray again in summer if the second generation is large. Contact your state agricultural experiment station for second-generation emergence dates to time sprays effectively. In summer, handpick and bury or burn webbed bunches and leaves bearing cocoons. Rake and burn all fallen leaves in autumn or bury them by cultivating in early spring. Be on the lookout for reinfestation from nearby wild and cultivated grapes.

Powdered Grapes

Q. The blossoms of my seedless grapes growing in Iowa turned brown and dried up. Are they diseased?

A. Yes. Several diseases produce these symptoms, but by far the most common one in your area is grape powdery mildew (*Uncinula necator*), according to Dr. Robert Pool, a viticulturist at the New York State Agricultural Experiment Station in Geneva. Powdery mildew also covers leaves, canes, and young fruit with white patches. You can control the fungus with a sulfur dust or spray. Make the first application when new shoots are 6 to 8 inches long, the second about two weeks later when shoots are 12 to 16 inches long, and the third at early bloom stage. If mildew symptoms continue to appear, spray or dust when the fruit is half-grown and again when it begins to ripen.

Blueberry Blues
and Currant Problems

Making More Blueberries

Q.How can I propagate blueberries?

A. The most common method is by rooting cuttings. Take soft-wood cuttings from new shoots in the spring after the leaves have fully expanded. Prune the shoots to 3½ inches long, avoiding those with flower buds, which are fat and round. Pinch off all the leaves except the two at the top. Fill a flat with equal parts of peat and perlite. Stick the cuttings into the rooting medium, 2 inches apart each way, allowing only the growing tip to protrude. Place the flat in a partially shaded area and keep the medium well watered. Cover with a tent of plastic for humidity and water-retention, but remove it for at least an hour every other day to allow air to circulate. Roots will form in a few weeks. Then pot up the newly rooted plants in a soil mix containing some leaf mold or other acidic material. Pinch off all flower buds and the following spring, transplant to a permanent location. Remove flowers then, too, and the next year you may get a small harvest.

Mounding is another way to start new plants. Build a wooden frame about 1 foot high and 3 feet square around the blueberry bush. Fill this structure with a mixture of moist peat moss and rotted sawdust, mounding the medium around the canes of the bush. They will form roots beneath the surface of the medium. The canes can then be cut off below the roots and planted. Both cuttings and mounding will reproduce the parent plant exactly, so you'll get more plants of a specific cultivar.

Blueberry Blues

Q. Though they're planted in some of Minnesota's finest acid soil and mulched with oak leaves, pine needles, and manure, our blueberries haven't fruited in six years. Why?

A. If you planted highbush varieties, and if winter temperatures in your area drop to −31°F, the problem may be lack of hardiness, says Dr. Jim Luby, a fruit breeder at the University of Minnesota. Though the bushes survive these low temperatures, the flower buds and often the branch tips are killed. Three blueberry varieties hardy to between −30° and −35°F are 'Northblue',

'Northsky', and 'Northcountry', developed by Luby and his colleagues at the Minnesota Agricultural Experiment Station. Though these varieties may sustain some injury in the coldest winters, they will produce reliable crops, says Luby. The bushes are lower-growing than highbush varieties, so they're better protected by snow cover.

Slow Down for Sweetness

Q. **I have several varieties of blueberry and they bear large, plentiful fruit, but the berries are very tart. How can I grow sweeter blueberries?**

A. You may be picking the berries too soon. Blueberries need about five days after they turn blue to reach maximum sugar content, says Dr. P. Eck, a pomologist at Rutgers University. Timing the harvest properly is important because blueberries don't ripen off the bush—if you pick them sour, they stay sour. Cover the bushes with netting when the fruit colors up, advises Eck, or birds may beat you to the ripe berries. If your berries are sweeter in some years than in others, the weather may be partly to blame. A long period of rainy or cloudy weather during the ripening period can cut down sugar production by the leaves, resulting in sour, watery fruit.

A Web of Trouble

Q. **My blueberries attract a pest that spins webs around the fruit clusters and shrivels the berries. What is it?**

A. Webbed berries are a sign of the cranberry fruitworm, a green caterpillar. The adult is a moth that lays its eggs on the fruit when the largest berries on early varieties have reached about one-quarter of their maturity. After hatching, the caterpillars bore into and hollow out the berries, leaving them shrivelled and filled with sawdust-like frass. They move into adjoining berries as they grow, each caterpillar eating as many as four fruits. After about 24 days, the caterpillars crawl to the ground and pupate in mulch or beneath about ½ inch of soil, emerging as adults the following spring. Handpick and destroy fruit clusters as soon as you notice webbing. In early spring, rake up and burn the old mulch and shallowly cultivate the soil under the bushes to destroy overwintering pupae. Fertilize if necessary and put down a fresh layer of mulch.

Mummified Blueberries

Q. Could you tell me what's wrong with our blueberries? We mulch and fertilize them. The bushes look healthy, but the berries turn hard and red instead of blue. Even the birds reject them, so we know they are inedible.

A. Your blueberries have "mummy berry," a disease caused by the fungus *Monilinia vaccinii-corymbosi*. It is quite common in the North. Spores of the fungus infect the developing berries at flowering time. The diseased berries appear to grow normally at first, but instead of ripening, they first turn a reddish-tan color and then become the gray, hard, shriveled mummies that give the disease its name. The fungus overwinters in the mummies, most of which fall to the ground. Spores released by the mummies the following spring are blown to the newly opened buds and perpetuate the cycle.

You can break this cycle and control the fungus by removing the mummified berries. Clean up and discard all the mummies you can find in fall. Before the bushes break dormancy next spring, rake up and discard mulch residues and cultivate shallowly around the bushes to bury any mummies you might have missed. Fertilize if necessary and apply a fresh layer of mulch 2 to 4 inches deep. If there are no other diseased blueberries nearby to reinfect your bushes, you should be able to eradicate the fungus in one or two seasons.

Currant Affairs

Q. Our currant bushes no longer bear well. How should they be pruned and fertilized?

A. Currants fruit best on one- to three-year-old wood. Remove older canes and all weak, diseased, and broken shoots. Thin the remaining growth so that every bush has three or four each of one-, two-, and three-year-old canes. Prune the oldest canes every year and leave just enough young shoots to replace them. For maximum yield, currants need cool, moist soil rich in nitrogen. Top-dress annually with an inch of manure or compost or scratch in about ½ pound of cottonseed meal around each bush in early spring. Apply about 2 inches of mulch, and water during drought.

Cutting Down
on Currantworms

Q. **Inch-long green worms with black spots stripped most of the leaves off my currant bushes last year. What were they, and how can I prevent injury next year?**

A. Imported currantworms, larvae of the currant sawfly, defoliated your bushes. They hatch about the time the leaves reach full size and usually start feeding near the center of the bush. The ⅓-inch-long, wasplike adults are black with yellow markings on the abdomen. Females lay shiny white eggs in rows on the underside of the leaf veins in late spring. After feeding for two to three weeks, the larvae crawl to the ground and pupate. A smaller second generation emerges in June or July. These overwinter as pupae. Handpick the worms or treat with rotenone or pyrethrum as soon as they appear.

Puny Gooseberries

Q. **My gooseberries bear well, but the berries are very small. How can I get bigger fruit?**

A. Watering, feeding, and pruning should help increase fruit size. Gooseberries need cool, moist soil, especially in a warm climate such as yours. Maintain at least 2 inches of mulch under the plants, and make sure they get an inch of water a week during the growing season. In early spring, feed with a complete granular organic fertilizer or top-dress with about an inch of rotted manure or compost. Bushes crowded with canes more than three years old often bear poor-quality fruit. Cut out older canes and weak or diseased younger growth, leaving the bushes with three or four canes each of one-, two-, and three-year-old wood. Remove the oldest canes each year and leave enough new shoots to replace them.

Getting the Worms
Out of Gooseberries

Q. **Some of my gooseberries had a brown spot on the skin and a small white worm inside. Can you identify the insect and suggest a control?**

A. Maggots of the currant fruit fly were feeding on your gooseberries. Infested berries ripen prematurely, and many fall to the ground. When full grown, the maggots leave the fruits and crawl 1 to 2 inches underground, where they overwinter as pupae. The housefly-size adults, yellow-bodied with dark bars on the wings, emerge during bloom. Within a week, the females begin laying eggs in the developing fruits. To kill the flies before they can lay eggs, apply rotenone two or three times at weekly intervals, starting as soon as the flowers fade. Destroy infested fruit.

Thorny Problems
with Blackberries and Raspberries

Polar Berries

Q. I raise bush fruits in Wisconsin. Every year my blackberries have a profusion of blossoms, but once the developing fruits reach the size of peas, they just dry up. Why do I have this problem when I've had such healthy bushes and blossoms?

A. Blackberries aren't reliably hardy in Wisconsin. Thornless varieties are only hardy to about 0°F, and the thorny types will be injured below −5° to −10°F. If the canes have been damaged by very cold temperatures, plants may look normal and will flower as usual; however, once the berries begin to form, the damaged canes can't supply enough water to the fruits, and they dry up. To check for winter injury, scrape the outer skin off part of a cane. Damaged canes will be brown on the inside rather than green. You may be able to prevent winter injury if you lay down the canes and cover them with a thick layer of mulch in late fall. The plants will also overwinter better with a continuous snow cover.

If you can't find any evidence of winter injury, look near the base of the stems for brown or white lesions 1 to 6 inches long. These lesions are caused by a fungus, and canes should be pruned off and burned. Dust sulfur on the crowns before plants emerge in spring and again after the canes come up. Sterility, or sterile-plant virus, is also a common problem in northern blackberry areas, according to Dr. Robert Skirvin of the University of Illinois. Afflicted plants look deceptively healthy and bloom profusely, but the berries never develop beyond nubbins (a common name for this disorder). There is no cure for sterility, so the plants should be dug up and destroyed. Dig out any suckers that might appear later in the season from pieces of root left in the ground. Grow a different crop there for at least one year before planting blackberries again. Buy only plants that the nursery can assure you have been propagated from proven bearing stock that is virus-free.

Second Spring for Blackberries

Q. This fall my blackberries are greening and putting out buds. So far they haven't bloomed, but I'm afraid they'll be damaged by cold. Will they bloom next year?

A. The phenomenon you've described is fairly common and has been nicknamed "November bloom," according to Dr. Owen Rogers, ornamentals specialist at the University of New Hampshire. It's nothing to worry about, Rogers says, because usually no more than 1 percent of the flower buds open, leaving plenty for spring.

Cutting Off the Raspberry Crop

Q. Three years ago I planted 'Blackhawk' black raspberries that still have not produced any flowers or fruit. I fertilize the plants well and prune the canes to 6 inches high each fall. What can I do?

A. Don't prune black raspberries until after they have fruited for the first time. Like red raspberries, they produce fruit on two-year-old wood—that is, canes that grew for a full season the previous year. As soon as you've harvested the crop, cut all canes that bore fruit to the ground, and thin the remaining canes to stand 8 to 10 inches apart.

Relocating Raspberries

Q. When is the best time of the year to transplant raspberries? Mine have gotten so thick that my neat rows have all but disappeared.

A. You have a choice: Transplant in the fall, after a killing frost when all the leaves have fallen from your plants, or in the early spring, when you can get a shovel in the ground but before the beds have leafed out. Pick a new cane (the bark on old canes hangs in tatters) and spade around it until you can lift out the soil and roots in a large shovelful. After you set it in a predug hole, cut back the cane to 6 inches or so. If you have black raspberries, it's safer to transplant them in the spring—they are not as cold-hardy and vigorous as the reds.

Netting a Good Crop

Q. **How can I keep the birds out of my black raspberries? I've tried nets, pie pans, and so forth, but nothing seems to stop them.**

A. Netting is the only way to keep them out, but it must be held away from the bushes so the birds can't reach through. The quickest solution is a frame made from arched PVC pipes or poles lashed to form a teepee. Cover the supports with netting. For a more permanent screen, we recommend that you set 8-foot-tall posts (or higher than your bushes and with enough room to work in) 8 feet apart around the edge of your patch and in rows through the patch 8 feet apart. Nail framing along the top of the posts, connecting one post to the other. Some good framing materials are 2-by-4s or even 2-by-3s. Next, nail wire screening (of a mesh small enough to keep out birds) all around the outside posts as if you were putting up a fence. Be sure to allow space for a gate of some kind. Then fasten screening over the top of the framing to form a "roof" over the bushes. Planting elderberries and mulberries may also protect your fruit. Given the choice, birds prefer these berries over raspberries and blackberries.

Bugged by
Black Raspberries

Q. **This year many of my black raspberries had dry, red to brown spots on them. What was the problem?**

A. The problem may have been feeding injury caused by wasps, hornets, stinkbugs, or other plant bugs. These insects pierce individual drupelets and suck out the juice, leaving dry spots on the berries. If damage is intolerable, protect the fruit with fine netting. Reduce stinkbug numbers by cleaning up weeds and plant debris to deprive the pests of alternate hosts and overwintering sites.

Raspberry Beetles

Q. **I found worms in my red raspberries this year and couldn't use the fruit. What are they, and how can I keep them out of the berries?**

A. The pests are raspberry fruitworms, the larvae of ⅛-inch-long, light brown beetles that emerge from the soil in early spring to feed on unfolding leaves and flower buds. The females lay eggs on on the flowers and young fruits, and the larvae bore into the berries after hatching. They mature as the berries ripen, drop to the ground, and pupate in the soil. You can kill the beetles before they lay eggs by spraying with rotenone when the flower buds appear and again just before they open. Make sure the spray penetrates the blossom clusters and covers all leaf surfaces.

Gray Raspberries

Q. **My raspberry bushes produce mostly small, knobby gray fruits that are inedible. What's the problem?**

A. Your problem may be caused by stamen blight (*Haplosphaera deformans*), according to Dr. Ralph Garren, extension specialist in small fruits at Oregon State University. This fairly widespread fungal disease interferes with proper fertilization of the flowers because it affects the stamens and sometimes the pistils. Since stamen blight is spread by pollen, you can reduce its severity by cutting out all bearing canes for one season, a cultural practice called alternate-year cropping. Without flowers or pollen, the fungus will not be able to effectively reproduce or spread. Garren cautions that it is difficult to identify bramble diseases accurately without having a sample of the affected plant analyzed by a pathologist. Plant disease identification services are available through many universities. Contact your county extension agent for more information.

Chapter 13

Trouble-Free Fruit and Nut Trees

Fruit without Fear

For Fruitful Soil

Q. How should I get my soil ready for a small organic orchard?

A. If you're anxious to get started quickly, simply apply half a wheelbarrow of compost, natural rock fertilizers, and humus-rich soil to each new tree-planting hole. This method is particularly convenient in small city plots. A more time-consuming but excellent soil-building technique is the cover-crop system. To covercrop, plant soybeans in the spring. When they bloom, turn them under with a tiller or disk. Then plant a mixture of hairy vetch (15 pounds per acre) and rye (3 pecks per acre). When these bloom in the spring, work them into the soil and plant soybeans, cowpeas, or a combination of both. When flowers appear again, usually in early August, turn the cover crop under and let the land rest. After fall frost—in most areas about Thanksgiving—you're ready to set the trees.

Exposing Graft

Q. I'm planting grafted fruit trees. Should the graft be buried or left above the ground?

A. The graft should remain just above the soilline. If the tree is set deeper, the scion (or top part) may root, taking over and killing the rootstock. In addition to dwarfing the tree, a rootstock brings it into production earlier and helps prevent biennial bearing. However, it's all right to plant the tree a little deeper than it was grown in the nursery. Fruit trees are usually grafted 6 to 10 inches above the ground. This is done so more of the rootstock can be buried, giving the tree better anchorage and support.

First-Year Feeding

Q. I planted fruit trees with manure and compost. Do they need additional feeding the first year?

A. The normal advice when planting a new tree is not to add fertilizer to the planting hole. However, well-rotted compost could be mixed with the soil tamped around the roots. A mulch of rotted manure, compost, old hay, or leaves on top of the ground around the tree will add nutrients slowly. More important, mulch will preserve moisture during that first critical summer when the tree is getting established. If soil tests indicate an inadequate amount of any necessary trace element or phosphorus, these could be applied the first year under the mulch. But avoid high-nitrogen fertilizers. And don't heap mulch, especially fresh manure, right against the trunk of the tree; this could kill it.

How Much Mulch?

Q. Can I leave a year-round mulch under fruit trees without encouraging insects, as long as I remove fallen fruit and branches?

A. No. A permanent mulch encourages insects. To make matters worse, mice occasionally nest in thick mulch for the winter and girdle the tree during their stay. Instead, renew your mulches every year by turning them into the top 2 inches of soil and using new material. Keep the ground within a foot of the tree clean. Use pH-neutral mulches like hay and straw; avoid acidic mulches such as pine needles, oak leaves, and sawdust.

Mix-and-Match Fruit

Q. Is there any advantage to interplanting different varieties of fruit trees—for example, mixing apples, pears, and peaches in the same block?

A. Yes. Just as in a companion-planted vegetable garden, interplanted fruit trees form natural barriers that block the spread of insects and diseases. And a varied environment encourages natural predators, including pest-hungry birds. Less insect damage also means fewer diseases. Interplanting prevents the spread of disease in another way, too. Some virus diseases, especially those of cherry and apple trees, can be spread through natural root grafting, when the roots of two adjacent trees grow together. If trees of the same species are planted next to one another, their roots are more likely to become grafted and transfer the virus. Interplanting prevents trees of the same species from making root contact. By the way, interplanting will *not* reduce pollination. Honeybees generally harvest nectar from one species of tree at a time, pollinating as they go. Since cherries, peaches, pears, and apples bloom at different times, pollination of interplanted trees should be complete and fruitful.

Water Sprouts

Q. What is a water sprout? Should they be pruned off?

A. Quick-growing, upright shoots on tree branches are called water sprouts. If allowed to grow, the sprouts will crowd the tree and cut off light. They should be pruned off, except when one is needed to fill in a gap. The shoots are usually caused by improper pruning techniques such as overpruning, says Dr. Alex Shigo of the U.S. Department of Agriculture (USDA) Forest Research Lab in New Hampshire. He suggests pruning fruit trees in the late winter, making cuts just above the slight ridge at the branch base. But even properly pruned trees will occasionally put up a water sprout. Simply cut them off with clippers.

This Budstick's for You

Q. I've seen references to something called a budstick. What exactly is it?

A. A budstick is a piece of branch with buds. It's often called a scion, and you can use its buds in a method of grafting fruit and nut trees called budding. For spring budding, budsticks are cut in fall or early spring when the tree is still dormant. To keep the budstick in storage, place it inside a plastic bag that is not completely airtight but is kept moist, and store in the refrigerator.

Frosted Fruit

Q. **Here in Cornville, Arizona, folks say, "five peach trees, five peaches." We live at the bottom of the few miles of geographical declivity that separates Arizona's northern forest from its southern deserts. The desert spring in February and March is followed by forest-country freezes in April and May. How can we retard our trees' early blossoming or ward off the subsequent frost kill?**

A. We contacted Robert Kurle of the North American Fruit Explorers for advice concerning your area. He answers: "We certainly would not recommend your area for fruit growing, but since you are so determined, here are some recommendations. For apples, try grafting on the 'Court Pendu Plat' variety, known as the 'wise old apple' because it blooms several weeks later than other late apples. Another solution is to grow dwarf trees that can be covered if it freezes. Good candidates for your specialized conditions are apples on Malling IX stock, pears on quince C stock, genetic dwarf peaches and nectarines that bear when 15 inches tall, apricot on *Prunus besseyi* rootstock, and the compact 'Lambert' cherry that grows to one-fifth the size of a normal sweet cherry. Overhead sprinkling systems and heaters can also be of value. Try other late-blooming tree and fruit crops like Chinese chestnuts, persimmons, beach plums, suda cherries, and fall-bearing raspberries. Another approach is to grow fruit trees in pots that can be moved under shelter or easily covered in case of frost."

Oiling Up the Orchard

Q. **When is the best time to spray dormant oil on fruit trees?**

A. Spray in late winter, before any leaf buds begin to open. A light film of dormant oil sprayed on fruit trees will cover aphids, thrips, mealybugs, whitefly, pear psylla, scale, and spider mites that are clinging to the bark. It suffocates them. The treatment will also destroy the eggs of codling moths, oriental fruit moths, and assorted leaf rollers and cankerworms. But if the buds have burst, the coating of oil will also smother the emerging plant tissue. Don't spray before late winter for two reasons. First, it's the time when insects and their eggs are coming out of dormancy; their shells and protective coverings are softer and more porous then, so they're vulnerable to the effects of the oil. Second, the oil/water mixture should not freeze on the tree; when you spray, the temperature should be above 40°F. Delay spraying if freezing night temperatures are predicted. Choose a calm day. Spray the whole tree at one time, concentrating on the trunk, large branches, and crotches, rather than spraying down a whole row of trees at one pass. If you've experienced extremely bad infestations of these insects, you might treat your orchard a second time. Dormant oil can also be used after the leaves have dropped in the fall. Never spray when any foliage or fruit is on the trees.

No Browsing, Please

Q. What's the best way to keep deer out of my orchard, short of shooting them?

A. The only method known to be 100 percent effective in keeping hungry deer out of orchards and fields is an 8-foot-tall woven wire fence. Electrified fences also seem to work well but are quite expensive. Scare devices and repellents have produced mixed results. Foxglove and castor beans have been reported to repel deer. Trap crops such as soybeans and corn planted around the perimeter of the orchard or garden often keep deer from venturing farther onto your land for food. Of the repellents, human hair wrapped in cheesecloth and hung from the lowest branches of trees and bloodmeal or human urine sprinkled around the base of trees are the most popular. But famished deer will often gnaw the bark off fruit trees despite these repellents. To discourage deer from "tip-pruning," wrap wire around the shoots in a spiral and extend the straight tip of the wire just beyond the end of the shoots. Thin iron-based wire will rust off in about a year, so you don't have to remove it before it interferes with the next season's growth.

About Apples and Pears

Apple branches:
Standard (top),
Spur-Type (bottom)

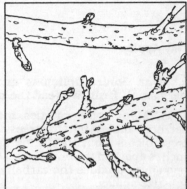

Winning Your Spurs

Q. How are spur-type apple trees produced? How do nurseries propagate these trees, and how big can I expect them to grow?

A. All spur-type fruit trees are developed from natural mutations with more than the average number of spurs—the short growths on the stems. These unusual trees were first grown in the late 1950s in Washington State from sprouts of trees that had died back to the roots after an exceptionally cold winter. The spur types on the market usually have a compact growth habit roughly equivalent to that of trees on semidwarfing rootstocks. A spur-type cultivar is grafted onto a standard rootstock, which is more vigorous and more extensive than a dwarfing rootstock, creating a stronger tree. Yields are high, since each spur is capable of producing an apple. (Production begins two to three years after planting, about the same as with dwarf apples.) Fruit thinning is especially important with spur-type trees, as overloaded branches can easily break.

Restoring Old Apple Trees

Q. We bought a small farm recently with about a dozen neglected mature apple trees. We plan to prune them and apply a dormant oil spray. Is it safe to scrape the outer layer of bark to dislodge insect breeding grounds and diseased patches?

A. Scraping the outer bark of your apple trees and using a dormant oil spray are excellent techniques. Pruning is usually best if done over a period of several years. Too much hard pruning in one year can cause excessive sucker growth and delay fruiting. Rotten knotholes in the trunk can be chiseled or trimmed to solid wood. But if they are deep enough to weaken the tree, it might be better to replace the tree with a dwarf interstem tree from a reliable nursery.

Tiny Apples

Q. Our 'Golden Delicious' and 'Red Delicious' apple trees bear very small fruit. We feed the trees. What is wrong?

A. Many apple varieties, including the ones you grow, tend to set more apples than the trees can handle. Several weeks after the trees bloom, thin the young apples until they are about 6 to 8 inches apart on the branches. This allows about 50 leaves per fruit, enough to produce the carbohydrates needed to mature a crop of full-size apples.

Drop Everything

Q. I know trees are supposed to have some fruit drop, but last year my 'Rome' apple tree had June drop, July drop, August drop, and so on until there was no harvest. Can I do something now to prevent this next year?

A. Several conditions can contribute to premature fruit drop just before harvest time. A tree often drops fruit because it is unable to support a large load. Many trees bear a heavy crop every other year rather than a crop of moderate size every year. To promote the annual bearing of a moderate crop, prune carefully and thin the fruit each year. Good soil fertility is essential, because a tree is prone to dump fruit if it runs out of fertilizer in late summer. Compost is an excellent source of nutrients. Sometimes too much or too little lime in the soil can cut off the nourishment just when the tree needs it badly, so check your pH and adjust it if it's very far off neutral (7.0). Lack of adequate rain during the summer and early fall can also keep vital nutrients from reaching your tree. Keep a thick organic mulch over the roots to retain moisture.

Unfortunately, some of the best late-maturing apples are prone to drop before they are ripe. 'Macintosh' apples are especially likely to drop early, as are many other members of its large family, including 'Early Mac', 'Macoun', 'Milton', 'Puritan', and 'Spartan'. Other apple favorites that are often early droppers are 'Earlyblaze', 'Niagra', 'Northern Spy', 'Red Astrachan', 'Rhode Island Greening', 'Rome', and 'Twenty Ounce'. Varieties more likely to stick to the tree until maturity are 'Cortland', 'Delicious', 'Empire', 'Holly', 'Honeygold', 'Idared', 'Lobo', 'Monroe', 'Mutsu', 'Spijon', and 'Stayman'.

Slow Summer Pruning

Q. I summer-pruned my apple trees last July. In September the 'Cortland' bloomed heavily but later produced a very light crop. None of the other trees had this problem. What went wrong?

A. July is a little early to prune, according to Dr. Alan Lakso, a plant physiologist at Cornell University, but it depends on the variety and climatic conditions. The rule of thumb is to wait until the shoots have stopped growing and terminal buds have formed (they'll look plump and dormant). 'Cortland' is a fairly vigorous variety and may have been induced to bloom if it was still actively growing when pruned.

Potato/Apple Problems

Q. Some people say that as apples ripen, they release ethylene gas, which causes potatoes to sprout. To avoid this, you shouldn't store them together. But other people claim that the ethylene gas released by apples acts as a natural sprout inhibitor. Who's right?

A. Both are right. Ethylene, a plant hormone given off by apples as they mature, can stimulate potato sprouting *and* inhibit it. Under warm conditions, the gas may encourage sprouting. However, if the area in which they are stored does not have good ventilation, enough ethylene gas may accumulate to inhibit sprouting. To prevent sprouting when apples and potatoes are stored together, make sure that temperatures never go above 45°F. Above that point, ethylene is released more rapidly. But the best advice is to store potatoes and apples apart.

Blistering Trees

Q. **What causes the blisters on the trunk of my apple trees? Recently, they burst and secreted a brownish liquid. What's wrong?**

A. Water blisters on the outer bark of the trunk are caused by the uptake of excess manganese from very acid soils. It's normal for them to burst, releasing a brown liquid that streaks down the bark. The blisters do not penetrate to the cambium. Manganese itself won't hurt the tree, but the low pH it indicates leads to reduced growth and yield. To control the problem, raise the soil pH by adding crushed limestone to the soil. Wood ashes, marl, and ground oyster shells are also very helpful and may be added to the compost pile.

The Tender Trap

Q. **I would like to make moth traps for our apple trees. Can you tell me how?**

A. Traps can take any form as long as they catch the pest in either the moth or larval stage. For flying insects, the easiest trap is to coat any type of surface with a sticky medium (Tanglefoot, pine tar, or anything similar) and hang it in the tree. Research indicates that moths are attracted to circles as opposed to squares, and the color orange seems to be an especially effective attractant—as are red and blue—while yellow is not very effective. Because insects follow a scent upward, traps do best when positioned on the windward side of a tree. Hang these traps at blossom time to catch the emerging moths at a young stage. Another effective form of hanging traps is nothing more than an attractive mixture placed in small containers of water. The moths are drawn to it and drown. You can successfully trap codling moths (the "worm in the apple") by pouring a mixture of molasses, water, and a little sugar into buckets. Codling moths are also sometimes attracted to sassafras oil. Try making a solid bait for codling moths by filling a small ice-cream cup two-thirds full of sawdust, stirring in a teaspoon of sassafras oil and a tablespoon of glacial acetic acid, and then adding enough liquid glue to saturate the sawdust thoroughly. When the cup is dry, suspend it in a mason jar partly filled with water.

To trap gypsy moth larvae, wrap several layers of burlap around the trunk and fold the top over to form a good shelter. Worms will be attracted to the burlap when they feel it is time to pupate. You can then crush the caterpillars inside the band or remove the band and shake them into a pail of water and kerosene. You can also apply bands of sticky material around the trees to foul up the pests as they travel up and down the tree. Inspect the bands every few days to kill any insects and reapply the sticky material.

Tanglefoot Tangles

Q. **We have several dwarf fruit trees. For the past five years, we've applied tree Tanglefoot to control gypsy moths. This week, we noticed the bands were dry and cracked. As we scraped, we found small white worms under the Tanglefoot, and the bark appeared to be rotted away. Will we lose the trees?**

A. Tanglefoot is used to control ants, gypsy moth caterpillars, cutworms, and other insects that tend to crawl up a tree. Heavy or careless applications can damage the bark. If you use a narrow band on a bearing tree for a season, you shouldn't have any problem, but avoid continuous applications. For extra protection on smooth-barked trees, put the Tanglefoot over a paper wrap. On rough-barked trees, cotton batting can be placed under the paper wrap to prevent bugs from climbing through crevices. On young fruit trees, always apply Tanglefoot over paper. The small white worms you noticed were probably feeding on the dead bark under the Tanglefoot. Carefully scrape the dead bark and old Tanglefoot from the area and determine the degree of damage. If your trees are seriously injured, a plastic wrap may prevent dehydration and help heal the damage.

Scabby Apples

Q. **I planted two 'Haralson' apple trees five years ago, and I manure them each fall in an area equal to the spread of their branches. Why are they producing only a few flowers and fewer scabby apples?**

A. "Your five-year-old apple trees should be producing abundant yields, especially with the manure applications. They may have poor drainage or be too close to large trees that shade them or rob their roots of nutrients, or they may have scab," explains Robert Kurle of the North American Fruit Explorers. "For scab control, use a spray of a handful of wood ashes and ground limestone to 2 gallons of water. We recommend that scab-resistant apple varieties like 'Prima' and 'Priscilla' be planted. Using dormant oil spray in early spring and giving your trees a mild pruning to let the sun through should also help."

Blotched-Up Apples

Q. **My 'Yellow Delicious' apples were covered with black mildew. It scrubbed off in a bleach/detergent solution, but could you tell me what caused it and how to prevent it without spraying?**

A. If the apples felt sticky, the discoloration may have been caused by sooty mold. The mold colonizes honeydew that drips onto fruit from colonies of aphids feeding on nearby leaves and shoots. Aphids can be washed off with a high-pressure spray from the garden hose or killed with insecticidal soap. Apples can also be discolored by sooty blotch, a minor fungal disease that leaves an olive-green to brown or blackish stain on the skins. Sooty blotch often occurs with another minor fungal disease called flyspeck. Flyspeck creates circular patches of raised, shiny black dots on the fruit. These fungi infect apples during cool, wet weather in spring and fall. Since these diseases are skin-deep and don't spoil the flavor of the fruit, scrubbing or peeling the apples is probably the best way of dealing with them. If you can't stand the appearance, the sulfur sprays used to control apple scab should also control these fungi.

Cedar-Apple Rust

Q. **We have cedar galls on our cedar and arborvitae trees, and we're wondering whether our nearby apple trees will be harmed. Is there anything that can be done about the galls?**

A. Your apple trees will certainly be harmed! What your trees have is a curious disease called cedar-apple rust. It starts when spores are blown from infected cedars to apple trees, where they cause bright orange spots on the foliage and to a lesser degree on the fruit. The infections on apple foliage produce another spore stage that reinfects the cedar and keeps the vicious cycle going. The best control is to remove all red cedars, wild apples, and crabapples within a radius of one to two miles of the orchard. If this is impractical, you may want to cut down your apple trees and plant resistant varieties to break the destructive cedar-apple cycle.

Resistant varieties recommended by the USDA include 'Baldwin', 'Delicious', 'Rhode Island', 'Northwestern Greening', 'Franklin', 'Melrose', 'Red Astrachan', 'Stayman', 'Transparent', 'Golden Delicious', 'Winesap', 'Grimes Golden', and 'Duchess'.

Quince Rust Carryover

Q. I have a small quince bush in my yard, and I recently read that it can carry quince rust disease. Are my apples in danger?

A. Not unless there are junipers in the area. Like cedar-apple rust, quince rust requires red cedars or junipers to complete its life cycle, and it can't spread directly from quince to apple. The disease is relatively uncommon, so even if you have both junipers and an alternate host like quince, apple, pear, or hawthorn, you won't necessarily have a problem. Quince rust usually causes distorted fruit and sometimes affects twigs and buds, but it seldom spreads to the leaves. 'Red Delicious' apples are quite susceptible; varieties such as 'Rome' and 'Jonathan' are resistant. Control the fungus by pruning and burning diseased parts or by spraying with wettable sulfur.

Attack of the Pear Killers

Q. My pear trees are being injured by an insect or parasite that seems to enter the tree at or below ground level. I've never seen it. The bark splits and dries out. The wood under the bark is hard and dry, and the cambium layer is gone. The condition creeps up the trunk to the limbs. What is this?

A. From the brief description of the situation, it's hard to diagnose the problem. It could be damage from lawnmowers. It might be a bacterial root canker or type of root injury. If it is a canker, we suggest you remove any dirt from the infected area, trim away dead bark and limbs, and paint the infection with a brown creosote made from wood. Recovery is usually slow. If the trees have to be completely removed, don't plant other pear trees in the same location. Trim back the entire tree to compensate for root damage and fertilize the tree well. You might stake the tree to prevent wobbling until new roots grow. Contact your county extension agent if several trees have the same symptoms.

Cracked-Up Pears

Q. **Why do my pears develop deep cracks that make them inedible?**

A. Deep cracks, unnaturally rough, russeted skin, or deep, corky pits are all signs of a boron deficiency. Contact your county extension agent to have your soil or a sample of fruit tested to confirm this diagnosis. One way to correct the problem is to add unprocessed borax, a natural source of very slowly available boron, to your soil. Be sure to use *unprocessed* borax. (*Processed* borax, the kind found in grocery stores, can injure or kill plants.) Use borax sparingly. An excess of boron is harmful to soil and plants.

Pear Psylla

Sooty Pears

Q. **My three dwarf pear trees are covered with soot. Will it harm them?**

A. The "soot" on your trees, called sooty mold, won't hurt them, because it's not a disease. It's a saprophytic fungus that lives on the sticky honeydew secreted by small ($\frac{1}{10}$-inch-long) insect pests called pear psyllas. They rarely do serious damage, but if you find the sooty mold unsightly, spray the trees with a dormant oil in early to mid-April, before the psyllas lay their eggs on spurs and branches. Repeat seven to ten days later. If psyllas and sooty mold are a problem later in the season, dust trees with diatomaceous earth or ground limestone.

Stone Fruits: Peaches, Plums, Apricots, and Cherries

Plucky Peach Tree

Q. A year ago, my parents planted a peach tree in their back-yard. The snow that winter broke off the main trunk. This year, the tree developed leaves, but it's getting wider, not higher. Can it be saved?

A. There's a good chance the tree will grow. Prune to one vigorous central leader. Cut off low side branches to force growth into this upward-growing leader, which will become the new trunk. One caution: Make sure the growing shoots have not come from below the graft (the swollen part that is usually right above the ground); if shoots are that low, you've lost the variety you started with and should buy a new tree.

Frost Fighters

Q. I live in a mountain valley of Kentucky. Every year we have about three weeks of warm weather, which puts every peach tree in bloom. This is followed by several nights of frost, leaving us without any peaches. I have considered using smudge pots but cannot find them anywhere. What do you advise?

A. Smudge pots are actually outlawed in some states. If yours is not one of them, you can use an empty tar barrel with one end cut out to burn charcoal on frosty nights. Place a barrel near enough to a tree that the heat can help it but far enough away that it won't burn the blossoms. If only one or two trees are involved, covering them with sheets or blankets takes only a few seconds and will save the buds. Another trick for the home gardener is to put an electric fan under the tree so that it forces air up and into the branches or to the side of the tree. The fan creates air currents that prevent frost from settling long enough to injure buds or blooms.

Protecting Fruit
Tree Trunks

Winter in the Southwest

Q. Last spring I noticed a deep vertical split in the trunk of one of my peach trees. What caused it? Is there a way to protect my other trees?

A. The problem may be southwest injury, which occurs in midwinter when the temperature drops rapidly on clear nights following sunny days. The low winter sun shines directly on the trunk all day and can raise the bark temperature on the southwest side more than 60 degrees higher than the air temperature by midafternoon. Snow aggravates the problem by reflecting more light onto the trunk. When temperatures plummet after sundown, rapid freezing of water in the trunk causes the bark to split. Tissue around the split dries out and dies, weakening the tree. Research on winter injury to peach trees conducted at the Georgia Experiment Station by Dr. R. A. Hayden showed that three- to seven-year-old trees are most vulnerable to southwest injury. The trunks of younger trees are too thin to absorb much heat, and the older trees are insulated by corky bark. To prevent this injury, keep the sun from warming the trunk. You can do this by leaning boards against the trees for shade, but the standard practice is to coat the trunks up to the scaffold limbs with white latex paint. The paint reflects sunlight and keeps the cambium temperature from rising more than about 10 degrees above air temperature. Use paint that doesn't contain mildew-killing compounds and apply it in late autumn after leaf fall.

Bitter Split Pits

Q. Our 'Elberta' peaches develop split pits, gumming, and a bitter aftertaste, and often one side of the fruit ripens while the other side remains green. Is this a blight?

A. Split pit and lopsidedness are physiological disorders, not diseases. Split pits occur under conditions that stimulate rapid growth of the fruit while the pit is hardening, such as warm weather, high rainfall or heavy irrigation (especially after a drought), or heavy feeding with nitrogen. This disorder is most common in years when fruits are large and the crop is light. Split pits, like other wounds in peaches, often exude bubbles of gum. The bitterness is thought to be caused by ethylene released by the pit. Lopsidedness is fairly common in peaches, plums, and cherries. Their flowers have two ovules, but one usually withers before bloom. The other ovule goes on to produce a seed, and that side of the fruit is often larger, sweeter, more colorful, and sometimes earlier-ripening than the other side. This is caused by uneven concentration of growth hormones. To help control these disorders, keep the soil evenly moist, especially during the early stages of fruit development. Don't overfeed with nitrogen and try not to overthin the fruit.

Rotten Luck

Q. **How is peach brown rot transmitted from year to year, and how can I control it? My early peach is not affected, while a nearby late peach is hit badly every year.**

A. Peach brown rot is a fungal disease that overwinters as cankers on twigs and infected shrunken fruit (mummies) on the tree and ground. In spring, the spores germinate during moist, warm weather above 70°F. They infect the blossoms, which turn brown and rot. The resulting fungus spreads to the fruit, and the peach develops a brown, mushy spot that may become covered with a gray powder of spores. Your early peach tree may escape because warm, moist weather occurs after the tree blossoms, or that variety may be less susceptible to brown rot. 'Baby Gold', 'Goldhaven', and 'Elberta' are among the most resistant peaches; 'Mayflower', 'Red Bird', 'Hale Haven', 'Summer Crest', and 'South Haven' are among the most susceptible.

Your best bet against peach brown rot is sanitation. In the fall, pick up and burn or bury all fallen mummies. Prune out any badly cankered twigs before leaf fall. During early spring pruning, thin the trees to encourage rapid drying after rains. Peaches are more likely to become infected if they're punctured by insects, so control of pests like plum curculio is important. If the problem persists, spray with a wettable sulfur powder at blossoming and after rains.

Consult your county agent for the best timing of the spray in your region. Dip freshly picked peaches into 120°F water for approximately seven minutes. This won't harm the peaches, but the heat will kill the fungi.

Plum Disappointed

Q. I have a prune-type plum that was loaded with fruit last year. However, as they started to ripen, brown spots appeared on all the plums, and they either rotted or shriveled up. How can I control this problem organically?

A. What you describe is undoubtedly brown rot (*Monilinia fructicola*), one of the most common and serious fungal diseases of stone fruits. The first symptoms usually appear on the flowers as brown spots, followed by a gray fuzz in humid weather. The rotten flowers may cling to the twigs for some time. Frequently, the infection travels to the twigs, where a depressed, reddish-brown, shield-shaped canker forms. Because the fruits' main source of infection comes from these flowers and twigs, the best time to control brown rot is when your plum tree is in bloom. Dust or spray with sulfur two to four times after the blossom buds show pink until the petals fall. Sanitation is also very important. Twig cankers and rotted, shriveled fruit are the primary overwintering sites for spores, which infect the flowers the following spring. Remove and burn all infected fruit and twigs.

A Knotty Problem

Q. Many branches on our plum tree have developed rough, woody swellings, but the tree is still growing and bearing well. What causes this disease, and will it eventually kill the tree?

A. Your tree has black knot, a fungal disease that also attacks cherries. The fungus elongates the knots from year to year, stunting and gradually killing the branches by reducing the flow of water and nutrients. Black knot is spread by spores released during wet, warm spring weather. The spores infect new growth, producing olive-green swellings by late summer or the following spring. The swellings become black and warty and usually begin producing spores of their own the second spring after they appear. Cut down badly infected trees with many dead branches and remove knotted wild plums and cherries within 500 feet of trees under cultivation. If you feel you must keep infected trees, cut off all infected twigs and branches at least 4 inches below the knots and burn them. Do this in early spring while the trees are still dormant. Cut out knots on the trunk or scaffold limbs along with an inch of surrounding healthy wood. Coat the wounds with tree-wound dressing. The plum cultivars 'Formosa', 'Santa Rosa', and 'Shiro' are only slightly susceptible to black knot, and 'President' is resistant.

Spurring On Apricots

Q. **Our three-year-old apricot trees are producing numerous short spurs on the branches. How do we prune the trees? Should we cut these spurs off?**

A. Prune young apricot trees lightly, just enough to shape them. You can either train apricots like peaches, which have three main limbs, or like apple trees, which have scaffold branches on a single trunk. (This method is called the modified leader system.) Since the fruit buds are produced on one-year-old shoot tips and spurs, don't remove them this year unless the trees have set such a heavy crop that branches might break. After about three years, these spurs and shoots will stop producing. When the trees are dormant, cut back the nonproductive branches to stimulate new growth.

Birds and Bees
and Cherry Trees

Q. **I have one tart and one sweet cherry tree, both self-fertile. For the past three years, most of the cherries have fallen off both trees when only ⅛ to ¼ inch long. The trees aren't bothered by insects or diseases, but sometimes we get bad weather when they bloom. Why don't the cherries ripen, and is there anything we can do about it?**

A. Young, vigorously growing trees sometimes invest their energy in vegetative growth at the expense of fruit production. If this is the problem, your trees will outgrow it and ripen their fruit when they become more mature. Bad weather at flowering time can prevent pollination, causing a crop loss. Cherry flowers are most receptive to pollen the first two days they're open. If cold, damp weather keeps bees away, most of the flowers won't be pollinated. If you consistently get unfavorable weather when your cherries bloom, you might have to pollinate them by hand or keep a beehive near the trees. Bees will be more likely to visit the flowers if they don't have far to fly. Beekeepers will usually rent you a hive during bloom season.

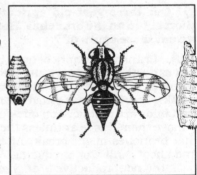

Cherry Fruit Fly:
Pupa (left),
Adult (center),
Maggot (right)

Cherry Fly Traps

Q. Every year there are little white worms in my cherries. How can I keep them out?

A. The worms are cherry fruit fly maggots. The only way to keep them out is to trap or spray the flies before they can lay eggs in the cherries. Adult cherry fruit flies are two-thirds the size of houseflies and have yellow marks on the thorax, four narrow, white bands on the abdomen, and black bars on their clear wings. To trap them, coat two or three bright yellow 10-by-10-inch boards with Tack Trap or Tanglefoot. Hang these boards in the tree about three weeks after bloom, just after the flies emerge from the ground. The boards will be even more attractive if you attach a small jar containing a solution of equal parts household ammonia and water. When the female flies are ready to lay eggs, they can be attracted to sticky, red, apple-size plastic (or wooden) balls. Hang six balls in the tree when you begin to catch flies on the yellow boards. The traps alone might catch enough flies so that you get an acceptable cherry crop. If you find that they don't, spray with rotenone as soon as you see flies on the red balls, and repeat at weekly intervals if trap counts warrant it. Two or three applications should be enough.

Citrus and Other Tropical Treats

Grappling with Grapefruit

Q. We have a 20-year-old grapefruit tree that's taking over the yard. When and how can we prune it?

A. In citrus trees, flushes of growth alternate with periods of rest throughout the year. Prune during any of the rest periods, but preferably in winter. Pick a time when most of the fruit has been harvested. Unless you need to remove diseased, competing, or crossed and rubbing branches, try to avoid opening the canopy of the tree. Letting sunlight in can stimulate a jungle of water sprouts and cause burning of the exposed bark. Instead, head back branches to strong lateral shoots, trying to maintain the natural shape of the tree. If you need to remove lower branches, paint the exposed trunk and bases of scaffold limbs with whitewash or a half-and-half solution of water and white latex paint (without fungicide) to protect against sunscald. Citrus trees can also be sheared into formal or semiformal shapes, but this reduces fruit production. Your county extension agent will have more information on pruning citrus.

Whitefly Attack

Q. There has been an outbreak of citrus whitefly in this area, and garden centers prescribe malathion. Is there an organic alternative?

A. Like greenhouse whiteflies, citrus whiteflies feed on the undersides of leaves, scattering like flying dandruff when disturbed. The adults and their scalelike nymphs suck sap and excrete honeydew, which becomes covered with sooty mold. Horticultural oil sprays used against scale insects will also control citrus whitefly. Follow dilution directions on the label. Oil sprays may cause some cosmetic damage to fruits and can make the trees more susceptible to winter injury if applied in late fall. If you must spray in late fall, use commercial insecticidal soap, which is known to control greenhouse whitefly and related insects.

Bringing Up Kiwi

Q. I tried to start kiwifruit from seed but it didn't germinate. What went wrong? Also, will the vine be hardy in my area— Oregon?

A. Kiwi seed germinates best when sown immediately after removing it from the fruit. It takes three weeks at 65° to 75°F for it to sprout. When the seedlings are 3 inches high, transfer them to 3- or 4-inch pots. Plant outside after the danger of frost is past. The vines will flower within several years, but since they are dioecious (sexes on separate plants), you'll need a male and a female plant (or at least one male for every eight females) for fruit to be produced. You can also graft a male branch on a female vine. Fruit quality will be unpredictable because you started with seed. For more certain results, grow the named varieties available from nurseries. The vines of *Actinida chinensis* are hardy to 10°F (0°F if well mulched) and should survive in your area. As a rule, they can be grown wherever wine grapes are found. Hardy kiwis (*A. arguta*) are hardy to −25°F.

Fruitless Figs

Q. My fig tree is loaded with fruit every year in late summer, but only a handful ripen. I don't feed the tree, but I do keep it watered. What else should I do?

A. Figs need warm weather to ripen. If the fruit is almost ripe when cool fall weather comes, try covering the tree with a clear plastic tarp to raise temperatures and extend the season. If that doesn't work, transplant the tree to a warmer microclimate, such as against the south wall of a house. Even if they're not fertilized, figs growing in rich soils can produce lush new growth that doesn't set fruit until late in the season. To induce earlier fruit set, limit new growth to a few well-spaced stems so sunlight can reach the center of the tree. Root pruning in spring or early summer can also control topgrowth and stimulate fruiting. Cut roots by repeatedly driving a spade into the soil all around the dripline. A good way both to control growth and protect the plant in winter is to grow it in a 30-gallon container that can be moved indoors. If none of these techniques works, try planting a shorter-season variety, such as 'Osborne Prolific' or 'Hardy Chicago'.

The Wild Bunch: Mulberries, Pawpaws, and Persimmons

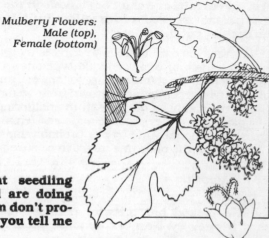

Mulberry Flowers:
Male (top),
Female (bottom)

Mum Mulberries

Q. I planted eight seedling mulberry trees. All are doing well, but half of them don't produce any fruit. Can you tell me why?

A. Mulberry trees are usually either exclusively male or female. Occasionally a tree will grow that has both male and female flowers. Trees that produce only male flowers will never have berries. However, female trees will often set fruit without the benefit of pollen. Mulberry flowers, both male and female, are catkins. The male catkins are longer. Viewed through a magnifying glass, male florets will show four stamens. If your nonproductive trees have female flowers, chances are the plants haven't yet come of age. Mulberry seedlings tend to be quite variable, and bearing age can differ widely from tree to tree.

Pawpawless Westerners

Q. I'm curious about pawpaw trees. Can I grow the fruit in my La Mesa, California, climate?

A. Probably not. Pawpaws need a winter chill to break dormancy in the spring. They do best in areas with cold winters, humid summers, and 30 inches or more of rain a year, most of it falling during the growing season. Pawpaws are hardy to −30°F and thrive in USDA Hardiness Zones 5 through 9.

Persistent Persimmons

Q. I have two American persimmon trees that I raised from seed. One tree never bears fruit; the other bears heavily, but the fruit never falls and can't be shaken off the tree, even in winter. The parent tree produces excellent fruit. Is there anything I can do besides cut them down?

A. Yes, you can improve your trees by grafting scionwood of a named variety or of a good wild type onto the branches. Use the same techniques you would use to topwork an apple tree. As is true of most fruits, persimmons grown from seed rarely produce fruit of the same quality as the parent. In addition, persimmons are usually dioecious—they produce male and female flowers on separate trees. Your nonbearing tree is probably male. Leave some of the branches on the male tree intact to be sure pollination occurs.

All Puckered Up

Q. We picked our oriental persimmons a little early and they're puckery. How can we make them edible?

A. A time-tested way to remove astringency is to tightly seal firm-ripe persimmons in a plastic bag with a few ripe apples. Leave them alone for a few days at room temperature. Ethylene gas given off by the apples ripens the persimmons, which are ready to eat when soft. Researchers in Israel recently found that bagged persimmons ripened just as well without the apples. They attributed ripening, which occurred in three or four days, to low oxygen levels in the tightly sealed bags. Persimmons will keep in the bags for about ten days at room temperature.

Mixed Nuts and Maple Syrup

Unripe Almonds

Q. Last year, my 'Hall's Hardy' almond trees finally bore a crop, but half the kernels were nothing more than dry husks. The trees weren't affected by insects or disease. Can you suggest a reason?

A. The withered nut meats indicate that the trees didn't receive enough heat units to mature. (Heat units, or growing degree-days, are a measurement of temperatures accumulated over the growing season.) Just prior to ripening, the kernels resemble a milky liquid. If the nuts fall from the tree too soon, the liquid just dries up instead of solidifying. There's really nothing you can do except hope for a longer stretch of warm weather. Planting on the south side of a building or wall isn't recommended, as it increases the risk of frost damage to the blossoms.

Grubby Chestnuts

Q. Last fall two-thirds of my Chinese chestnuts had worms. Is there a way to control them?

A. You can control chestnut-weevil grubs by picking up all nuts that fall to the ground every day, according to Dr. Warren Johnson, an entomologist at Cornell University. Store the nuts in tightly sealed containers and destroy any grubs that emerge. Since the weevils overwinter in the ground, in three to four years you will greatly reduce the number of infested nuts if you follow this practice every season.

Pruning for Plenty

Q. I planted two American filberts this spring. How should I prune them for best nut production?

A. American filberts grow naturally as freely suckering shrubs. Prune them to five or six main stems, and if necessary, thin the tops so that light can reach all the branches. Cut out the older stems when they become unproductive and train some of the suckers as replacements. Vigorous suckers with strong roots make good transplants if you want to start new bushes. For better pollination, many experts recommend growing three different varieties, so consider planting one more.

Jet-Setting Filberts

Q. Eight years ago we planted one European and one American filbert, but so far only the American bush has produced a few small nuts. Aren't they supposed to pollinate each other?

A. The European filbert will pollinate the American but not vice versa, says Douglas Campbell, filbert grower and member of the Northern Nut Growers Association. However, bloom times must overlap for pollination to be successful, and this rarely happens when only two plants are grown. To ensure a bountiful supply of nuts, you should have at least three—preferably four or five—different varieties of each species. Most American filberts offered for sale are close to the wild state and are not very productive. Campbell recommends planting European filberts or Euro-American hybrids instead, since Europeans and hybrids pollinate each other if enough varieties are planted. The hybrids combine the hardiness and filbert-blight resistance of the American filbert with the large, thin-shelled, flavorful nuts of the European species and are three to four times more productive than ordinary strains.

Stratified Seed

Q. I want to plant hickory nuts for rootstocks. I've been told that the seed should be stratified. What does this mean?

A. Stratification (also called moist-chilling) is a technique to break seed dormancy by reproducing winter conditions. Trees and shrubs with a hard seed coat must be soaked two to four days before chilling. Then put the seeds in a moist medium such as sphagnum moss, vermiculite, or old sawdust. Mix the seeds with one to three times their volume of medium, or alternate layers of seeds and medium. Put the mixture or layers in a container that will allow aeration, such as a polyethylene bag, tin, or jar with a perforated lid. Store at temperatures just above freezing (35° to 45°F) for one to six months, depending on the species. Hickories should be stored for three to four months before planting. Storage time and temperature recommendations for most trees and shrubs can be found in *Seeds of Woody Plants in the United States* (USDA Forest Service, Agriculture Handbook #450). Check with your local public or university library.

Hickory Headaches

Q. My hickory nuts, especially those still in the green shucks, often contain small, brown-headed worms. How can I get rid of them?

A. The pests could be pecan weevils or hickory shuckworms. Adult pecan weevils are ¾-inch-long, brown, long-snouted beetles that emerge from the ground in August or September and crawl up hickory or pecan trees. They feed on the shucks and nuts before the shells harden (often causing the nuts to drop prematurely) and lay eggs in nearly mature nuts. The creamy white, brown-headed grubs feed on the kernels till they mature, then cut round ⅛-inch exit holes and enter the soil to pupate for two or three years. Pecan weevils usually don't move far from the tree where they hatched, so if your trees are isolated, you should be able to reduce the population without spraying. You can monitor weevil emergence and intercept many of the adults by tying skirts of burlap around the trunks by August 1. Those that avoid the burlap can be caught by spreading sheets under the trees and jarring the limbs with a padded pole. Pecan weevils drop to the ground when disturbed. If you still get too many wormy nuts, try a botanical spray such as rotenone.

The hickory shuckworm, a brown-headed, off-white caterpillar under an inch long, is the larva of a moth that may produce up to four generations a year. The caterpillars bore into pecans and hickory nuts before the shells harden (causing premature drop) or feed in the shucks of older nuts, which fail to fill out properly and develop stained shells. Because it is highly mobile and can produce several generations each year, this pest is hard to control. The caterpillars overwinter in shucks both on the ground and in the trees. You can reduce the population by cleaning up and burning all the old shucks in fall. If you need to spray, apply a botanical insecticide three times at two-week intervals, starting in August when the shells begin to harden.

Twig Girdler

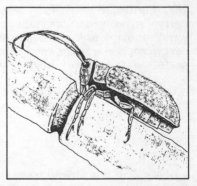

That's Some Girdle

Q. A bug girdles the small branches of my hickories and pecans, causing them to break off. What control do you suggest?

A. Your trees are host to the twig girdler, which lays eggs in the girdled twigs in late summer and fall. The grubs feed in the wood until the following August, when they change into adults. Gather and burn girdled twigs of domestic and nearby wild trees in late fall and winter to kill the eggs and young grubs.

No Better Nutcracker

Q. I hate to crack hickory nuts one by one. Is there an easier way? I tried a pressure cooker method, but it did not work.

A. Sorry—as far as we know, hickory nuts need to be cracked one by one. The task is easier if you use a nutcracker designed specifically for tough nuts like black walnuts, hickory nuts, and butternuts, but the 16-ounce hammer is still the preferred tool of many nut enthusiasts. To make cracking easier with whatever tool you use, don't let the nuts dry out and plant varieties known to be good crackers, such as 'Porter', 'Walters', 'Weschcke', 'Fayette', or 'Henry'.

Stop Those Stinkbugs!

Q. My pecans become partly black and bitter. I was told this is caused by a virus transmitted by a bug. Can you give me more details and a remedy?

A. Your pecans have kernel spot, which isn't a virus but a feeding injury caused by stinkbugs, leaf-footed bugs, or related species. The bugs pierce the shells of the maturing nuts and inject saliva that partly dissolves and discolors the kernel. The adults are ½-inch-long, green or brown, shield-shaped insects. They winter in plant debris, emerging to lay eggs in early spring. The young bugs feed on weeds, vegetables, and field and cover crops, then fly to trees when full grown. There may be up to four generations a year. Control these pests by reducing their breeding areas, says Dr. Jerry Payne, pecan specialist at the University of Georgia. Keep weeds mowed and avoid planting summer cover crops. (Winter cover crops like hairy vetch and crimson clover don't harbor the pests.) Watch for the bugs on your vegetables and handpick or spray with soap, pyrethrum, rotenone, or sabadilla if they become numerous. Clean up dead plants—the pests' winter quarters—in fall.

Walnutless

Q. My English walnut trees refuse to set fruit. One set two nuts three years after I transplanted it, but it hasn't set a crop since. What can I do?

A. Walnut trees take from 4 to 12 years after transplanting to begin producing nuts. Your trees may simply be too young. A problem with pollination could also be contributing to lack of nut set.

This often happens when only one walnut cultivar is planted. Many times, the pollen and the pistils on a tree mature at different times, so pollination does not occur. Planting another variety usually solves this problem. Contact a local nut tree association for suggested varieties.

To Prune or Not to Prune?

Q. Should the leaders of newly planted Carpathian walnuts be cut back or left unpruned?

A. Cut them back to 24 to 30 inches above the bud union, advise nut researchers Bill Reid of Kansas State University and Loy Shreve of Texas A&M. Taprooted trees such as Carpathian walnuts and other nuts suffer massive root loss with even the most careful transplanting. If the top isn't pruned, more buds will sprout than the reduced root system can support, resulting in weak growth that may not survive such stresses as drought, disease, and winter temperatures. Pruning channels the tree's limited resources into fewer buds, which should produce a strong new leader.

Tents in Walnut Trees

Q. Every year, fuzzy, yellow-brown caterpillars about an inch long make webs in our English walnut tree. How can we stop them?

A. The caterpillars are fall webworms, which spin loose tents on the ends of branches and skeletonize the foliage inside. The dirty white tents are unsightly, but there are seldom enough caterpillars to injure the tree. When the tents begin to appear in early summer, prune infested branches or spray with *Bacillus thuringiensis* (Bt).

A Boring Subject

Q. I was disappointed when I found worms in my walnut harvest this year. Is there any way to avoid an infestation of them in the future? What are they?

A. Most likely, they are filbert worms. Filbert worms bore into nuts, including acorns, filberts (hazelnuts), chestnuts, and walnuts. They look like small, pinkish caterpillars about ¾ inch long while they're feeding in the nuts. In their adult stage, they turn into moths with a wingspread of about ½ inch and two golden bands across each forewing. They lay their eggs singly on top of leaves. Filbert worms overwinter in silken cocoons found in the soil, leaves, and debris on the ground, so fall cleanup and mulches are useful. Adult moths usually begin to emerge in early July, and may continue to appear through late August and early September, at which time their egg laying begins. The eggs hatch in about eight or nine days, and the new larvae go hunting for nuts. In the future, avoid this pest by practicing good sanitation under the trees. Harvest nuts as early as possible and dry them immediately.

Rotten Walnuts

Q. **Last year a disease rotted the hulls of all my Carpathian walnuts and turned the kernels black. How can I combat this problem?**

A. Your nuts were spoiled by walnut anthracnose, a fungal disease that also causes spotting and yellowing of leaves. Anthracnose can defoliate trees by midsummer, which saps the energy of a tree so it can't fill out its nuts properly. Infected nuts often drop prematurely and have dark, shriveled kernels. The fungus spreads fastest in wet summer weather, when the brown spots characteristic of the disease become a common sight on leaves of wild trees. You may be able to reduce infection by raking and burning all leaves and diseased nuts in fall. However, the most effective control is to replace or topwork susceptible trees with resistant varieties like 'Reda', which is hardy to central Kansas.

Sweet Trees

Q. **I just moved to Vermont and would like to experiment with making my own maple syrup this winter. Although I have my pick of trees, I don't know which ones are best for tapping. Any suggestions?**

A. You're in prime territory for making your own maple syrup! But don't attempt to tap your trees until the sap rises—when daytime temperatures reach above freezing but nights are still below freezing. Try any or all maple species that are available. The sugar maple, *Acer saccharum*, and the very closely related black maple, *A. nigrum*, are best for sugar content and taste. Coming in a close third is the Norway maple, *A. platanoides*, followed by the common box elder, *A. negundo*. Next in quality is the red or swamp maple, *A. rubrum,* and the silver maple, *A. saccharinum.* Bear in mind that the sugar content of maple sap also differs widely from tree to tree, even in the same species.

Spigots for Sugaring

Q. **After tapping trees for maple sugaring, what do I do with the spigots? Should the holes be plugged after they are removed?**

A. Robert Foulds, an extension forester in Vermont, tells us the tapholes should not necessarily be plugged when the spout is removed. He knows people who tap maples and have fitted dowels in the holes, but it does not seem to make a difference. The wood in the immediate area of the taphole is dead, and the bark around the hole might be stained. However, a hardy tree will heal in two years, so the emphasis is on keeping your trees as healthy as possible. The following year, tap no closer than 16 inches above or below the old taphole and ½ inch to either side. It's also important to wash the spouts, then sanitize (in a solution of 1 part liquid bleach to 20 parts water), drain, and store them in a covered container for the winter.

FOUR

Beautify Your Home

Chapter 14

Growing First-Rate Flowers

Annual Mysteries

Seed-Saving Savvy

Q. I have tried to save seeds from flowers such as marigolds and zinnias but have had no luck getting them to come up. How should I collect and store the seeds?

A. If you collect the seeds too early, they won't be fully mature and won't germinate next spring. Wait until the flower head is completely dead and dry. As you gather them, the seeds will almost fall into your hand. Spread the seeds in a warm place for a few days to be sure they are free of moisture. Store in closed glass jars in the dark at about 50°F.

Head Start for Annuals

Q. Can seedlings of hardy annuals started indoors be planted outside before the last spring frost?

A. If the plants have been hardened off, such cold-tolerant annuals as bachelor's button, calendula, larkspur, California poppy, baby's breath, sweet alyssum, candytuft, China pink, poppy, pansy, snapdragon, and wallflower can be set out about the same time as cold-hardy vegetables like cabbage and leaf lettuce. Acclimate the seedlings for a week before transplanting by keeping them in a coldframe that's vented on mild days or by setting them outside in a sheltered place on days when the temperature stays above freezing. Like the vegetables, these flowers will tolerate light frosts but not hard freezes. Hardy annuals are even more frost-tolerant if sown directly outdoors in fall or as soon as the ground can be worked in spring. Some, like bachelor's button and larkspur, will germinate in fall and survive the winter as seedling rosettes if protected by snow cover or a light mulch. Many hardy annuals will self-sow prolifically; watch for their seedlings when you clean up in fall or begin cultivating in early spring.

Sprouting Small Seeds

Q. I have tried unsuccessfully to germinate the fine seeds of browallia, begonia, calceolaria, and other flowers. Do you have any suggestions?

A. The seeds of all three require light to germinate, so don't cover them after sowing. Use a light medium, such as a 3:1 mixture of peat and vermiculite. Was the soil warm enough? Ideally, the temperature should be 75°F, although tuberous begonia seed will germinate at 65°F. Begonia and browallia seed will sprout in two to three weeks; calceolaria takes five to ten days.

Generating Geraniums

Q. I haven't had any luck starting geraniums from old plants. What's the best technique?

A. Geraniums root best in the spring and summer when they are putting out new growth. If you take cuttings in the late fall or winter, they are more likely to rot than root. For success, take the cuttings from succulent young growth rather than larger, woody stems. Cut 2- to 3-inch pieces from the tips of the stems. Include several nodes (the point where the leaf meets the stem) in each cutting. Take off the lower leaves and stick the bottom part of the stem into a sterile medium of vermiculite and sand. Put in a sunny place and keep the medium evenly moist. In two to three weeks, dig up a cutting to check on its progress. When ¾-inch roots have formed, pot the young plant.

Perpetual Geraniums

Q. I grew over 40 geraniums this summer and hated to let them freeze, but I would have had no place to put them if I had potted them all up. Is there some other way to overwinter the plants?

A. Geraniums, which are treated as annuals but are really tender perennials, can be carried through even northern winters. Choose your nicest plants, cut them back severely, and pot them up to add color to your home in the gray season. Dig up the remaining geraniums and store them without soil in a cool, humid storage area such as an unheated, earth-floored basement or a root cellar. In the spring, prune back to the main stem and replant.

Blackleg Kicks Geraniums

Q. About a week after we transplanted our geranium seedlings into unsterilized soil, the leaves on many of the plants turned red; the stems darkened and the plants died. What killed them, and how can we prevent a recurrence?

A. Your plants had blackleg, a common disease of geranium seedlings and cuttings that is caused by the soilborne fungus pythium. It can be prevented by practicing good sanitation. Pasteurize potting soil by heating it to 160° to 180°F and holding that temperature for 30 minutes. Disinfect pots, flats, and tools by soaking them in a solution of 1 part chlorine bleach to 9 parts water for 10 minutes. Space potted plants so the leaves don't touch, and avoid overwatering.

Doubt about Double Impatiens

Q. I grew double impatiens from seed but was disappointed when many turned out to be single or only semidouble. Did I get ripped off?

A. No. Right now, the best you can expect from double impatiens seed is 40 to 50 percent fully double flowers. Reputable seed dealers indicate this on the package. When double-flowered impatiens first appeared in 1968 as a mutant, propagation was a problem because the plant didn't produce viable pollen. Renowned breeder Claude Hope solved the dilemma by crossing doubles with semidoubles and singles, and seed was made available in 1983. But because of the mixed parentage, the progeny are not all double. New varieties like 'Rosette', 'Duet', and 'Double-Up' are much improved over early strains, with more compact foliage and large, roselike flowers.

Impotent Impatiens

Q. **Three years ago we were given a red-flowered impatiens with variegated leaves. It grows well from stem cuttings, but its seeds won't germinate. Do they need special treatment?**

A. Your impatiens is almost certainly one of the New Guinea hybrids, which generally produce very few, mostly sterile seeds. The only New Guinea hybrid that can be grown from seed is 'Sweet Sue', an orange-flowered variety with bronzy green leaves. Continue to propagate your plant from cuttings—it's the only way to reproduce the other New Guinea varieties.

Statice Symbols

Q. **Can you tell me how to grow annual statice and the best time to pick it for drying?**

A. Statice (*Limonium sinuatum*) needs a long season for profuse bloom. Buy hulled seeds for high germination rates. Sow it in flats indoors at 70°F six to eight weeks before the last frost. Transplant to small pots or other flats when the first true leaves appear. After the last frost, set out the plants about 12 inches apart in fertile, well-drained soil in full sun. Statice tolerates drought but will produce many more flowers if watered in dry weather. Statice produces a flower head crowded with many small, papery, funnel-shaped blooms, not all of which open at the same time. For maximum color, cut the stems when most of the funnels are fully open. If you wait too long, the oldest flowers will begin to brown or fade. Yellow and white varieties sometimes fade faster and may need to be picked sooner than darker colors. Cut the flowers on a clear day and hang them to dry in a well-ventilated place out of direct sunlight.

Strange Sunflower

Q. One of the 'Mammoth' sunflower seeds I planted grew 11 feet tall and produced 32 flower heads, none more than 6 inches across. Is this rare? What caused it?

A. It *is* unusual. Sunflower expert Dr. Charles B. Heiser, Jr., of Indiana University explains why: Giant cultivated sunflowers are descended from the common or wild sunflower *Helianthus annuus*, which is a tall, branching plant that produces many small flower heads. Native Americans domesticated this species, selecting and propagating mutants that produced unbranched plants with single heads. Modern plant breeders have reinforced this characteristic in varieties like 'Mammoth', but occasionally the ancestral branching habit comes through, producing a plant like yours.

Less-Sweet Peas

Q. I saved my own sweet pea seed for many years but last year was unable to do so. None of the varieties I've grown this year have that good old-fashioned fragrance. Can you help?

A. The original strains of sweet pea were extremely fragrant—they were said to have one of the most delicious scents in the plant kingdom. Their sweet odor and masses of colorful blossoms made them the most popular flowers at the turn of the century. But because these older types languished in the heat, which shortened their bloom time, breeders worked to replace them with more heat-tolerant varieties. Unfortunately, much of the distinctive fragrance was sacrificed in the process. More recently, breeding efforts have been made to regain the scent. Some recent cultivars to try are 'Snoopea', 'Rosy Frills', 'Leamington', and 'Royal Wedding'. Old-fashioned varieties once again available are 'Antique Fantasy' and 'Painted Lady'.

Mildewproof Zinnias

Q. My zinnias produce only one flush of bloom before mildew spoils the leaves and flowers, even though I grow them in full sun with wide spacing. Can you recommend disease-resistant varieties?

A. Yes. Of more than 40 zinnia cultivars grown in ten years at the Rodale Research Center, Kutztown, Pennsylvania, the 'Ruffles' series (especially 'Scarlet Ruffles') has been outstanding for disease resistance and flower production, even under crowded conditions in less than full sun. 'Chippendale', 'State Fair', 'Yellow Marvel', 'Small World Cherry', and the 'Border Beauty' series are tolerant of powdery mildew.

Puzzling Perennials and Biennials

Divide and Multiply

Q. When is the best time to divide my perennials?

A. Many perennials die down by themselves in the fall, making this a good season to dig up the plants (very carefully!) to divide them. The advantage of dividing perennials in the fall is that they can get established before the next season. Established plants will be less likely than spring-divided plants to have a setback, which can cause reduction or loss of bloom for a year. The disadvantage is that the looseness of the soil around the transplanted perennial may cause heaving during the soil's alternating freezing and thawing in winter and spring. A thick mulch will help keep the division's roots underground.

Feeding Perennials

Q. I recently moved to a house that has a perennial flower border. What's the best way to fertilize it?

A. In general, perennials don't need heavy doses of fertilizer, since they produce only flowers and not fruit. (The practice of dead-heading—removing faded flowers—prevents seed-head formation.) Most herbaceous perennials can be maintained from year to year by mulching with compost, grass clippings, leaves, pine needles, or straw. You can top this with wood chips or pine bark if you prefer their textures, but they decompose too slowly to be of nutritional value. Perennials like astilbe, bleeding-heart, delphinium, and Shasta daisy, which are heavy feeders, should receive several summer applications of manure tea or fish emulsion. On the other hand, keep high-nutrient mulches away from species such as yarrow and butterfly weed, which grow best in a relatively infertile soil.

Bringing Up Baby

Q. I've been unable to grow baby's breath—either perennial or annual—from seed. Can you suggest a successful technique?

A. Sow seed of perennial baby's breath (*Gypsophila paniculata*) indoors in flats of light, porous potting mix in late winter or early spring. Barely cover the seed. At 70°F, the seeds will germinate in one to two weeks. The seedlings quickly develop heavy roots. Transplant them into 2¼- or 3-inch peat pots as soon as the first true leaves appear, and grow them in a cool, bright window or a frost-free coldframe. After frost, set the plants in well-drained, deeply dug flowerbeds in full sun. Baby's breath is a lime-lover: Add ground limestone as needed to maintain a pH of 7.0 to 7.5. Annual baby's breath (*G. elegans*) doesn't transplant well and blooms for only about six weeks even if faded flowers are removed. Direct-seed in spring (pH requirement is the same as for the perennial type), and make successive sowings every two weeks until hot weather if you want to prolong its season. Alternatively, sow pinches of seed in 3-inch peat pots two or three weeks before the last frost. Set these out about 8 inches apart before the pots check growth and stimulate premature flowering.

Crown Rot in Canterbury

Q. My Canterbury bells (*Campanula medium*) develop a type of rot that turns the base of the plant to mush. How can I prevent it?

A. Canterbury bells are very susceptible to crown rot, which is caused by two soilborne fungi, *Sclerotium rolfsi* (Southern blight) and *Sclerotinia sclerotiorum* (stem rot). These diseases are most destructive during warm, humid weather when the soil is moist. To prevent the disease, make sure the soil drains well and avoid overwatering. Keep the crowns as dry as possible by setting them at or slightly above soil level when planting. A traditional rot preventive is to fill in around the crowns with coarse sand instead of soil. Space plants so air circulates freely. Feed moderately; too much fertilizer produces lush, succulent leaves that mat over the crown and keep it wet. Well-timed planting of these biennials also helps prevent crown rot. Sow seeds in flats in late June or July, then line out the seedlings about 10 inches apart in a coldframe. Early the next spring, move the mature plants with a ball of earth into your flower beds. Pull and discard after bloom in June, since the fungi overwinter in dead plants and in the soil. If you have infected plants, dig out 6 inches of surrounding soil along with the plants.

Daylilies Get Spring Fever

Q. Several leaves of my daylily (hemerocallis) plants have spots or brown blotches on them, and some plants die from the top down. They don't bloom as heavily as they should. What's wrong?

A. The symptoms you describe are collectively called spring sickness. This is actually cold injury caused by late spring frosts, explains Ned Irish, publicity director of the American Hemerocallis Society. The leaves and flower buds can be damaged before they emerge from the crown of the plant, and symptoms may not show up until weeks later. There's not much you can do to prevent injury, although a heavy mulch of wood chips or pine needles sometimes helps, says Irish. Trim off browning leaves at the base. Some purple and lavender varieties seem to be especially susceptible, he notes, so you may want to try other colors as well as varieties reported to be hardy in colder climates.

Curbing Clematis Wilt

Q. My clematis vine was green as grass and blooming beautifully when suddenly the leaves started dying. What made this happen?

A. Any serious injury to the base of the vine, such as from a lawnmower or rodents, can cause the top to die back. If there is no evidence of such injury, the vine may have clematis wilt, a fungal disease that produces reddish lesions that girdle the stems, causing the foliage above the lesion to suddenly wither. On established plants, the older, woody stems in the upper part of the vine are usually attacked first, says Jim DeRue of D. S. George Nurseries in Fairport, New York, a nursery that specializes in clematis. On young plants, stems may be girdled just above the ground. If unchecked, the fungus moves up and down the stems, eventually killing the plant. Rainy weather and thick, tangled topgrowth that doesn't dry out favor the spread of the disease.

You can save a wilt-infected plant by radical pruning, says DeRue. As soon as you notice topgrowth withering, cut the vine back to 6 inches above the ground, or lower if there are lesions below this point. The vine will usually send up new shoots from the base, though clematis can be slow to resprout. To help prevent reinfection, immediately burn the prunings or dispose of them in a trash bag. Clematis hybrids in the *jackmanii* group are most susceptible to wilt, but no clematis is immune. The best way to keep from losing a plant is to take special steps at planting time, says DeRue. Clematis are fussy about their roots, which need both good drainage and moist soil. Choose a well-drained site and dig the planting hole 12 inches wide and deep. Put 6 inches of gravel in the bottom, then fill the hole with topsoil. Set new plants deeply enough so the lowest pair of buds (they're opposite each other on the stem) is below the soil surface. If the top dies for any reason, these buds will sprout and renew the vine. To help keep the soil moist, mulch the plants or shade the root zone by planting a ground cover.

Boredom Strikes Iris

Q. **I discovered borers in my bearded irises last summer, so I dug them, discarded the infested rhizomes, and reset the healthy ones. How can I keep the plants borer-free?**

A. After frost in fall, remove and compost or burn leaves, stems, and debris of irises and nearby plants to destroy overwintering eggs. In early spring, look for small holes and irregular, water-soaked streaks in the leaves; these are tunnels made by surviving larvae as they bore down toward the rhizome. Squeeze the leaves to crush the pests. Borer damage is easier to detect when the plants aren't overcrowded. Divide the clumps every three to four years in July so that you can find the borers in the rhizomes before they pupate.

Keeping Lily-of-the-Valley Cool

Q. **My lilies-of-the-valley flower well, but by August the leaves develop brown targetlike spots, then yellow and die. Why do they die back so early?**

A. Leaf-spotting fungi and hot, dry weather can cause lily-of-the-valley to die back early. Control the fungal diseases by raking off and burning all the dead foliage every fall or composting it in a hot pile. Lily-of-the-valley is a woodland plant that grows best under cool, moist conditions. To help keep it green all summer, top-dress with leaf mold or compost in fall or early spring and water during hot, dry spells.

No Luck with Lupines

Q. I've had no luck getting lupine seeds to germinate. Can you help?

A. Use fresh seeds to ensure viability. Before sowing, nick the hard seed coats or soak the seeds in warm water overnight. Plant them outdoors in early spring or germinate them indoors at 55° to 70°F. Using another method, place the seed packet in the freezer for 48 hours, then wrap the seeds in a wet paper towel for 24 hours before sowing indoors at about 55°F. With either method, germination may occur irregularly over two to three weeks. To avoid breaking their taproots, transplant seedlings while they're young or avoid transplanting by sowing in peat pots at two seeds per pot, later thinning to the stronger plant.

Patience with Peonies

Q. The peonies I planted last year grew only about a foot tall and produced no blossoms. Why are they so small?

A. The plants need more time to become established. Depending on growing conditions and the size of the divisions, peonies can take three to five years to reach full size after transplanting, and there may be few or no blooms for the first two years. If the plants still fail to grow and flower well after that time, they may be planted too deep. The roots should be set so the buds (called eyes) are no more than 2 inches under the soil surface (1 inch in heavy clay). You can make peonies grow faster by feeding once a year with compost or any complete, granular, organic fertilizer, keeping grass and weeds away from the crowns and watering during summer droughts.

Peonies Nipped in the Bud

Q. For the last three years my peonies have had small, aborted brown buds. How can I correct this condition?

A. First, determine what's causing your problems. Both botrytis blight and bud blast can wither peony buds. Botrytis blight, a fungal disease, also rots the bases of young stems in early spring, causing them to fall over. Wind-borne spores infect buds, flowers, and leaves later in the season. Infected tissue turns soft and brown, then becomes covered with gray mold. Snip off and burn diseased plant parts during the growing season. In fall, cut off the stalks slightly below ground level and burn them along with the old mulch. Avoid mounding moisture-retentive compost or manure around stem bases. If only young buds are affected and there is no sign of disease, your peonies may have had bud blast, a physiological disorder. While its cause is uncertain, it has been attributed to potassium deficiency, poor soil, low spring temperatures, drought, shade, and root-knot nematodes.

Bewildering Bulbs

Forcing the Issue

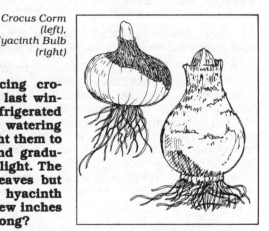

Crocus Corm (left), Hyacinth Bulb (right)

Q. I first tried forcing crocuses and hyacinths last winter. After potting, I refrigerated them for six weeks, watering occasionally. I brought them to room temperature and gradually exposed them to light. The crocuses produced leaves but no flowers, and the hyacinth blooms were only a few inches tall. What did I do wrong?

A. You didn't chill them long enough, says Dr. August De Hertogh, bulb specialist and head of the department of horticulture at North Carolina State University. Crocuses and hyacinths need a minimum of 13 weeks at 40° to 50°F to force successfully. Large-flowered Dutch crocuses, such as 'Remembrance', 'Flower Record', 'Peter Pan', 'Jeanne d'Arc', and 'Pickwick', are much easier to force than species crocuses. Most hyacinth cultivars are suitable for forcing.

It's Transplanting Time

Q. When and how do I transplant hardy bulbs?

A. Dig them up when the foliage is about half yellowed. By then, the bulbs will have ripened but will still be easy to find, and the dying leaves will give you a convenient handle by which to lift the clumps out of the ground. Separate the bulbs and replant them immediately in well-drained soil enriched with compost and a sprinkling of any complete, granular, organic fertilizer. Be careful to set each species at the proper depth and spacing. Small offset bulbs can be planted at the same depth and location as mature ones, but they might reach flowering size sooner if you grow them in a nursery bed or garden row.

Bulbs

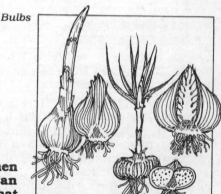

Menu for Bulbs

Q. I didn't add fertilizer when I planted my bulbs last fall. Can I apply it in spring? If so, what should I use?

A. Your bulbs will perform well if you apply a complete fertilizer this spring and a nitrogen supplement in the fall. Bulbs produce new roots in fall and actively absorb nutrients throughout the winter and spring. In a field study of the nutritional needs of bulbs conducted at North Carolina State University, Dr. Paul Nelson found that bulbs need more nitrogen than was previously thought. Based on his study, Nelson recommends an annual application of a slow-release fertilizer that will supply 5 ounces of nitrogen, 5 ounces of phosphoric acid (P_2O_5), and 3½ ounces of potassium (K_2O) per 100 square feet. Since nitrogen leaches readily, he recommends applying an additional 5 ounces of nitrogen per 100 square feet the following spring or fall.

Here are three organic fertilizers you can use to satisfy these requirements: (1) Apply 2 pounds of dried blood, 2 pounds of bonemeal, and 3 pounds of greensand or wood ashes per 100 square feet this spring, followed by 2 more pounds of dried blood in early fall. If your soil is acid, wood ashes will help raise the pH, but if the pH is already near neutral, use greensand. (2) Top-dress with ¼ inch of dried manure per 100 square feet (about 2 bushels) in spring and fall. (3) If you apply compost generously in fall, says Nelson, you might get away with just adding nitrogen in spring. Put down 2 bushels of compost in fall and 2 pounds of dried blood in spring.

The best time to apply fertilizer in spring is when the foliage spears have just emerged from the ground. If you apply it after the leaves unfold, be careful not to get any on the plants, or you may burn them. Don't scratch the fertilizer into the soil surface—you might damage the bulbs, and spring rains will wash in the nutrients.

Burned Bulbs in Florida

Q. We recently moved from Wisconsin to central Florida and would like to know if we can grow tulips, hyacinths, and other "northern" bulbs here.

A. You can if you are willing to take some time and trouble. In September or October, chill the bulbs in the refrigerator for 12 weeks, then plant them. The bulbs will bloom in midwinter. Because daytime temperatures often reach 80°F even in winter, each flower will last only two to three days, according to Dr. Benny Tjia, an ornamentals specialist at the University of Florida. The bulbs also deteriorate during the summer in the hot, dry soil, so it's best to treat them as annuals and discard them after flowering. If this is more than you want to take on, try some of the many beautiful and exotic tropical bulbs that will thrive in your area. Agapanthus, amaryllis, calla lilies, cannas, and clivias are just a few that are well suited to central Florida's climate.

Cannas from Seeds

Q. How can I sprout canna seed? Are any compact varieties available from seed?

A. Because canna seeds have a very hard seed coat, germination is usually poor unless they are nicked first. Dr. Jim Alston, director of research for Park Seed Company, recommends rubbing each seed on a piece of medium-coarse sandpaper until a small section of the black seed coat has worn away, revealing the white interior. Then germination is easy, he says. Plant the seed vertically ⅜ to ¾ inch deep in a seed-starting medium. At room temperature (70° to 75°F), the seed should germinate within 15 to 25 days. 'Seven Dwarfs Mixed', a relatively new dwarf canna from seed, grows only 18 inches tall. It comes in shades of red, rose, orange, yellow, and salmon.

Dahlia

Dahlia Dilemma

Q. **The garden center where I bought my dahlias last year told me to dig them up after frost and hang them in the basement. I did this, but the roots died. How can I store the roots successfully?**

A. Dahlia tubers need to be kept cold and protected from drying out. Here are some storage techniques recommended by Mark Algers, president of the American Dahlia Society. After frost, cut the tops back to about 5 inches, then lift the clumps gently so that you don't crack the necks of the tubers. Wash the soil off and look for signs of disease or injury. Let the tubers dry under cover for about a week. You can divide the clumps once they've dried or wait until spring. Make sure that each division has a piece of the stem attached; new shoots sprout only from that part of the tuber. Thin or immature tubers will shrivel in storage and should be discarded. Layer the tubers in dry vermiculite, perlite, sphagnum peat, or sawdust in containers that admit air. (Algers has found that tubers kept in plastic tend to rot.) Store the containers in a dark, frostproof place that doesn't get warmer than 45°F. Your dahlias should stay in good condition until spring.

Groundcovers for Daffodils

Q. Last fall I put in a large daffodil planting. Can you suggest a perennial groundcover that will look good, need very little care, and won't compete with the bulbs?

A. Periwinkle or vinca, Baltic ivy, and ajuga (carpet bugle) are evergreen in light shade or sun if sheltered from winter winds. Ivy will need an annual trimming once established. Several species of violet self-sow to form dense colonies in sun or shade. Sweet woodruff and many ferns are fine-textured groundcovers for humus-rich soil in light shade, where lily-of-the-valley also thrives. Strawberries (cultivated, wild, and alpine) are an edible-fruited but higher-maintenance alternative for full sun. Any groundcover will need routine weeding and watering until the plants grow together. After that, an annual application of screened compost, leaf mold, or a complete granular fertilizer and watering in dry spells will help keep both groundcover and daffodils vigorous.

Gladiolus Corms

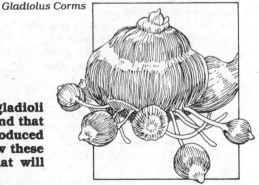

Glad for More Glads

Q. When I dug up my gladioli for winter storage, I found that most of the bulbs had produced bulblets. How can I grow these into good-size bulbs that will produce flowers?

A. Technically, gladioli grow from corms rather than bulbs. The small cormels can be grown into flowering-size (1- to 1¼-inch) corms in two to three years. Once you've dug the corms, cure them by keeping them at 85° to 90°F for 10 to 14 days. After curing, you can separate and grade them. Then store the corms and cormels in a cool, dry place until spring. Plant the cormels in an out-of-the-way spot or the end of a row at the same time you plant the rest of your glads.

Chapter 15

All about Herbs

Queries on Herb Culture

How to Harvest Herbs

Q. We just moved to an old farm with a marvelous herb garden. Could you tell me how to gather herbs and dry them?

A. The timing for harvesting herbs varies according to what you're going after. If you want their seeds, pick them in the early stages of ripening, just as the seeds turn from green to gray or brown. Gather the heads in the morning, preferably just as the dew leaves the plants. Try to maneuver the seed heads into a large paper bag or paper-lined basket and tie the stems in a bunch. Then clip the stems near the neck of the sack so the herbs hang freely within the bag. Hang the bagged herbs in a dark, dry closet for two to three weeks, or until the seeds are perfectly dry. (It takes seed longer to dry than foliage.) This seed-head drying technique works well with such herbs as fennel, coriander, dill, cumin, caraway, and anise.

If you want to gather herb leaves to use in cooking, pick them just before flowering. At this time parsley, sage, chives, thyme, savory, marjoram, mint, and basil are at their peak of flavor, and they're ready for drying and storage. Bunch and hang them in a dark, dry closet where they can dry out slowly. By hanging them upside-down, you allow the essential oils to flow from the stems to the leaves. Ornamental herbs like lavender, borage, valerian, and chicory should also be hung upside-down to dry in a dark, dry closet. Another way to air-dry herbs is to disassemble the herb plants and spread the parts on screens to dry. Window screens work well if they're propped up in some way that allows the air to circulate freely through them. For example, you can set them on bricks. Just remember to keep the screens away from direct sun and dampness.

Care of Contained Herbs

Q. **Can you recommend a feeding program for container-grown herbs?**

A. Pot your herbs in a nutrient-rich mix composed of one-third to one-half porous, fertile soil or compost. One mix that has worked well at the Rodale Research Centers consists of two parts compost-rich soil, one part perlite, and one part vermiculite. Cyrus Hyde of Well-Sweep Herb Farm in Port Murray, New Jersey, uses equal parts of soil, peat, and sand.

When the plants are established, begin supplemental feeding. Organic herb grower Carol Hildebrand of Casa Yerba Gardens in Days Creek, Oregon, applies a seaweed foliar spray every two weeks. To make a concentrate of seaweed, dissolve 10½ to 12 ounces of seaweed powder in 1 gallon of water. Apply this or a commercially bottled concentrate at a dilution of 1 tablespoon per gallon. Feed plants with fish emulsion at 1 tablespoon per gallon every two weeks if herbs are harvested frequently. If they are grown as ornamentals, feed once a month.

Homegrown Pickling Spices

Q. **This spring, I'd like to raise my own pickling spices. Any suggestions?**

A. Garlic, dill, and coriander will start you on your way to all sorts of pickling. You can plant dill directly into the garden as soon as the soil can be worked in the spring. Plant in rows ¼ inch deep, thin from 6 to 12 inches when the plants are 3 inches tall, and harvest the umbels before the heads shatter. You can also plant garlic in early spring. Set cloves 2 inches deep in moist, sandy soil. And coriander, also known as Chinese or Mexican parsley, can be sown directly in late spring. Plant seeds 1 inch deep and thin to 8 inches in rows. You can enjoy these herbs in most of your pickling recipes, as well as with meats, salads, soups, and stews.

Herbs Make Great Mothballs

Q. I've read about an herb that can be stored with woolens to protect them from moths. Can you help me?

A. There are several combinations of herbs that can help prevent moths from feasting on your woolens. And it's easy to sew the dried herbs in small cloth pouches to place among your clothes. Dried rosemary leaves should keep the moths at bay. Other combinations of repellents include equal parts of ground camphor wood and wormwood; southernwood, wormwood, and lavender; or cedar wood shavings and ground sassafras root.

Herbs Up Close

Buggy Basil

Q. Harlequin bugs appeared in my garden around the first of August and ate up my broccoli, then moved on to the basil. What can I do to stop them?

A. Harlequin bugs, which occur in the southern half of the United States, overwinter as adults in garden debris and litter. You can cut down their numbers by thoroughly cleaning your garden every fall. In the spring, check the undersides of plants (especially brassicas) for their distinctive eggs. Look for small white "pegs" attached to black loops, standing on end and lined in double rows. Destroy any you find. Sometimes a trap crop of mustard or turnips will successfully lure the beautiful harlequin bugs away from your other crops. Handpick the bugs from the trap plants, dropping them into a can of water and detergent. Two botanical poisons, pyrethrum and sabadilla, will also control them.

Recharging Chives

Q. **I've been told you can dig up and pot garden chives for winter use, but I've never had any success. Is there some trick to it?**

A. Chives must have a cold rest period. For chives in winter, plant seeds in pots during late summer. Two to three months later you'll have sturdy young plants for winter use. You can also force garden-grown chives for late winter or early spring cutting. Pot some up before the ground freezes in the fall, but leave the pot in the ground for three to four months. Bring the plants inside during a thaw in January or February. The warmth will stimulate new growth.

Lavender Has No Thyme for Mulch

Q. **Should I mulch my lavender and thyme plants this fall for winter protection?**

A. English lavender and thyme are hardy perennials. They don't need to be winter-mulched (completely covered with straw) and should do well in most of the United States, provided they are in a sheltered, well-drained location. You need to take special precautions only where the temperature can go below −30°F. French lavender, however, is not as hardy and should be brought in during the winter where temperatures go below 0°F (north of U.S. Department of Agriculture Plant Hardiness Zone 7). We talked to professional herb growers from Washington, D.C., to southern Michigan, and they all confirmed that their English lavender and thyme do fine without winter mulch. (Most professionals do mulch the plants during the growing season.) M. J. Hampstead of Fox Hill Farm in Parma, Michigan, feels that winter mulch can hold moisture against the plants and cause them to rot.

Oregano's Lost It

Q. **Our seven-year-old oregano plants have lost their pungency. Is this unusual? Can you recommend a flavorful variety to replace them?**

A. Seedlings of a highly flavored plant of common oregano (*Origanum vulgare*) often fail to inherit their parent's pungency. Over the years, your original plants may have died and been replaced by flavorless, self-sown seedlings. To be sure of getting kitchen-worthy replacements, buy seeds of *O. vulgare* subsp. *hirtum* (also called *O. heracleoticum* and simply *O. hirtum*) or *O. vulgare* 'Viride'. If you start plants from seed, grow more than you'll need, then propagate the best-flavored plants from cuttings.

Roots for Soup

Q. I recently bought parsley root at my farmers' market, and it made great soup. How can I grow it?

A. Hamburg or root parsley is grown like common parsley. Harvest the greens as they are ready. But remove only a few sprigs at a time from each plant, so root growth isn't set back. Herbalist Bertha Reppert feels the leaves are much more flavorful than those of common curly-leaf parsley. She grows Hamburg parsley both for the pungent, broad leaves and for the parsniplike roots, which have a strong parsley flavor. The roots can be harvested about three months after planting, though they will continue to grow throughout the season and are sweeter after a frost. Since parsley is a biennial, the plant will sprout back the second spring and the roots will continue to grow. Be sure to harvest the roots before the plant flowers or they will be tough. Hamburg parsley is available from most seed companies.

Sage

Sage Propagating Advice

Q. When I divide old sage plants, the divisions die. How can I divide sage successfully?

A. The woody crowns of old sage plants can seldom be divided successfully. This herb is best propagated from seed or cuttings. Sow seed indoors at 60° to 70°F in late winter or early spring and set out the plants after the last frost. Alternatively, root 3-inch tip cuttings from established plants in late summer, winter them in a sunny window or a protected coldframe, and plant them in the garden by spring.

The Truth about Tarragon

Q. I bought a plant labeled tarragon at a nursery. How can I be sure that it's French and not Russian tarragon?

A. The crush-and-sniff test is the best way to determine if you have the valued culinary herb, French tarragon, or its weedy Russian relative. The leaves of French tarragon have a distinct anise (licorice) scent. The Russian smells more like lawn grass. The plants also look slightly different. French tarragon has long, narrow, glossy leaves and is rarely taller than 2 feet. Russian tarragon is much taller (up to 5 feet) and has lighter green, rough leaves.

Chapter 16

Advice on Lawns, Trees, and Shrubs

Help for Unhappy Lawns

Oaks over Grass

Q. What kind of lawn grass will grow on a dry hilltop shaded by oaks?

A. Improved tall fescue grasses such as 'Rebel', fine-textured ryegrasses like 'Manhattan 2', 'Yorktown 2', and 'Prelude', and fine fescues, including Chewings fescue, creeping red fescue, and hard fescue, should all do well in dry shade, says Dr. H. W. Indyk, extension turf-management specialist at Rutgers University. If you don't mind a coarse-textured lawn, plant a mix containing 60 percent improved tall fescue, 20 percent fine fescue, and 20 percent perennial ryegrass, he advises. Before planting, have the soil tested; if it's acid, add enough lime to raise the pH to 6.5. Sow the grass in spring or fall, when cooler, more moist conditions prevail. Keep the soil moist by watering lightly two or three times a day, if necessary, until the grass is established. Feed the new lawn with organic fertilizer high in nitrogen.

Lone Star Lawn

Q. **Can you recommend one of the newer varieties of grass for my sparse St. Augustine, Texas, lawn? The lawn is shaded by pine and sweet gum trees.**

A. "You need a turf-type, tall fescue, such as 'Falcon', 'Rebel', 'Mustang', or 'Olympic', for your shady southern lawn," says Eliot Roberts of the Lawn Institute. Because of the deep shade cast by the pine and sweet gum trees, he recommends overseeding each spring to keep your lawn thick and healthy.

Buffalo Grass, Won't You Come Out Tonight?

Q. **For our Flagstaff, Arizona, yard, we want a lawn that requires minimal irrigation but still looks nice. We've heard that buffalo grass is drought-tolerant and does well at our altitude of 7,000 feet. Can you tell us more about this grass and how to grow it?**

A. Buffalo grass, native to the Great Plains, is a gray-green, fine-textured grass that spreads by stolons to form a dense turf. Its adaptability to poor, alkaline soil and resistance to cold, heat, and drought make it a good lawn grass for semiarid regions. Once established, it needs only 1 inch of water a month (in areas with a minimum annual rainfall of 15 inches), versus 4 inches for bluegrass. Buffalo grass does have some drawbacks, however: It turns brown with the first frost and stays that way till spring; and in high-rainfall areas, cool-season grasses and weeds can crowd it out.

Depending on competition, buffalo grass takes two to three years to form a dense turf. Till the lawn to get a clean seedbed. Sow after the soil temperature reaches 60°F—about May 15 to June 1 in your area—at the rate of 1 pound of pure, live seed per 1,000 square feet, recommends Dr. E. J. Kinbacher, horticulturist at the University of Nebraska. Cover the seed 1.4 inches deep and keep the area moist. Germination occurs in 14 days. Buffalo grass does well without fertilizer, but an annual application in early to mid-June of 1 pound of nitrogen per 1,000 square feet (about 14 pounds of cottonseed meal or 100 pounds of dried manure at 1 percent nitrogen) makes the turf denser and greener, says Kinbacher. Mow once a month to 2½ inches for a manicured look or let the grass grow to its natural height of 6 to 8 inches.

Zoysia: Everything but Evergreen

Q. The manager of my local garden center advised me to plant a zoysia lawn this spring. What are the advantages of planting zoysia?

A. The big advantage of a zoysia lawn is that it grows slowly, so it needs mowing only every ten days to two weeks. Zoysia makes a tough, cushiony turf. It grows on a wide range of soils, from sandy to heavy loams, if there is good subsoil drainage. It thrives in high summer temperatures as well as in moderate shade. Since zoysias grow densely, a mature turf will crowd out weeds and requires little fertilizer. In addition, these grasses are practically free of diseases and insect pests. It's also a great grass to plant around a swimming pool, because it's salt- and chlorine-tolerant. Now for the drawback: It turns brown with the first frost and is late to green up in the spring.

Zoysia's Not Made for the Shade

Q. Will zoysia grass grow well on a shaded lawn?

A. No, says Dr. Martin Petrovic, a turf specialist at Cornell University, who instead recommends using a fine-leaved fescue mixture if the site is relatively dry. For every 1,000 square feet, sow a mixture of about 3¾ pounds fescue seed with ¾ pound of improved perennial ryegrass and ½ pound of a shade-tolerant cultivar of Kentucky bluegrass, such as 'A-34' or 'Glade'. You can sow a pure stand of Kentucky bluegrass if the area is moist, and if it's very moist, Petrovic recommends 'Sabre' rough bluegrass.

Doggone Dead Spots

Q. My dog's "outings" have resulted in dead spots in my lawn. What can I do?

A. To repair brown spots, dig out the dead grass and roots with a spade, fill the holes with topsoil, and rake smooth. Broadcast seed over the topsoil at the recommended rate, rake it in lightly, and mulch with a thin layer of straw or salt hay. Keep the seeded areas well watered until the turf is thoroughly established (four to six weeks). Because dog wastes are high in salts and urea, occasional spot reseeding will be an ongoing maintenance chore as long as your dog continues to use the lawn. One way to prevent dead spots, suggests Beverly Roberts of the Lawn Institute, is to train your dog to use a specific area of the yard that you have covered with bark mulch, cat litter, or other absorbent material. Change the material as needed. However, since dog manure can contain several internal parasites hazardous to human health, we recommend disposing of it—as well as the clumps of dead grass from lawn repair—rather than composting it (see "Dog Wastes" on page 57).

Choking Out Chinch Bugs

Q. We have chinch bugs in our lawn. What is the least toxic way to eliminate them?

A. You have several nontoxic options. Chinch bugs are ⅛- to ¼-inch, blackish-brown insects with white wing patches. The adults and their reddish nymphs kill grass by sucking out its juices, and they're most likely to damage lawns in hot, dry weather. They rarely feed in shady areas, so one long-term defense is to plant shrubs and shade trees. According to Eliot Roberts, director of the Lawn Institute, the best way to deal with chinch bugs is to let them run their course, rake out any dead turf, and overseed with a resistant perennial ryegrass like 'Repell', 'Pennant', 'Regal', or 'All-Star'. These new ryegrasses are protected by a seed-transmitted symbiotic fungus that makes them repellent to chinch bugs and other insects. The fungus remains viable in the seed for about one year, so check the date on the package before buying. You can also discourage their growth by keeping your soil rich with nitrogen. Tests show that chinch bugs not only live longer but produce more eggs when they eat plants grown in nitrogen-poor soil. Some natural sources of nitrogen are bloodmeal, manure, and sludge. Should the chinch bug infestation get severe, send out their natural predator, the big-eyed bug (*Geocoris pallens*). It won't repair the bare spots in lawns damaged by chinch bugs, but it will control the pests so you can reseed in late summer.

Grub Grabber

Q. Our lawn is crawling with grubs. What can we do to control them?

A. Grubs are beetle larvae that feed on grass roots. The Japanese beetle is the best known, but several other species might also be found in lawns. The best control is milky spore, commercially available as Doom and Japidemic. It's a bacterial disease (*Bacillus popilliae*) that kills only beetle grubs. You can spread the powder anytime the ground isn't frozen. It takes one to three years for the disease to give full control, but it remains effective indefinitely (see "Once and Done" on page 286).

No More Mole Holes

Q. Moles have made unsightly tunnels throughout my lawn. Traps haven't worked. Can you help?

A. The common or eastern mole spends most of its life underground, eating earthworms and the larvae and adults of many kinds of insects. Moles don't feed on plant material, but in making their tunnels they inadvertently sever grass roots, which are concentrated in the top few inches of the soil. The problem is worse in dry weather, when the raised areas of lawn are more likely to turn brown. Field research has shown that after a lawn has been treated for grubs, the mole population usually goes down. Apply milky spore "Grub Grabber," a bacterium that will control grubs permanently (see above). It takes several years to become established in the lawn, so in the meantime you might want to give traps another try.

Traps can be effective, but you have to be persistent. Moles are solitary animals, and it's likely that only one or two are responsible for the damage to your lawn. In its search for food, the mole makes an extensive network of tunnels, many of which are used only once. To find out which runs are used as "travel lanes," Dr. Bob Mormon, an extension wildlife conservationist at the University of Iowa, suggests stepping lightly on small sections of several tunnels so that you disturb them but don't completely collapse them. Mark these sections with stones or garden stakes. After two days, note which ones are raised—those are active runs and are good locations for setting a trap. Moles do not see but are guided by their highly sensitive nose, which leads them to their prey. So to set out traps successfully, sterilize them first to eliminate all human odor. To do this, scorch the trap over a burning newspaper, then use gloves when handling it. You can restore turf over unused tunnels with a lawn roller or by treading on it.

Top Tips for Trees

*Planting a
Christmas Tree*

Keeping the
Christmas Spirit Alive

Q. I'd like to have a live Christmas tree this year. How can I make sure it will survive after the holidays?

A. Consult with your county extension agent to select a species that's suited to your region. Although container-grown trees are more expensive than field-grown ones, they have a better chance of survival. If you live in an area where the ground freezes, be sure to dig a hole *before* the holidays so you can plant the tree. Fill the hole with leaves or mulch so it doesn't freeze, then cover it with a board. Store the soil you've removed from the hole where it won't freeze. After you buy the tree, acclimate it to the house by placing it in a protected place such as an unheated garage or shed for a week. The tree will dry out quickly, so keep the roots moist and the branches well misted. Wrap the roots of a balled-and-burlapped tree in plastic before setting it in a container.

Indoors, keep the tree away from heat. In fact, the cooler the temperatures and the shorter the time indoors, the better. Don't let the room get warmer than 68°F or keep the tree indoors longer than a week. After the holidays, harden-off the tree by returning it to the protected place for a week, then plant it. Fill the hole with the stored soil and tamp it down lightly. Water generously and mulch with 3 to 4 inches of hay out to the dripline. Stake the tree until spring. If the temperature rises above freezing during the winter, check to see if the tree needs water. If you can't dig a hole before the ground freezes, overwinter the tree in a cool place that gets some light. The temperature should be above freezing but below 50°F. (Growth will resume if the temperature climbs over 50°F.) Keep the tree well watered, and plant it as early in the spring as possible.

Getting the Jump on Gypsy Moths

Q. Last year many of our alder and oak trees were completely defoliated by gypsy moths. What can we do to stop them this year?

A. To protect your trees and shrubs, spray *Bacillus thuringiensis* (Bt) as the gypsy moth larvae emerge from their egg clusters in late April and early May. When the caterpillars eat the Bt, its spores paralyze their guts, and the insects starve to death within a few days. Safe for humans, Bt affects only caterpillars like gypsy moths, cabbage loopers, and tomato hornworms. Because it is difficult to cover the leaves of large trees, you might contract with a local landscaper or tree surgeon to spray Bt with a commercial spraying rig. When the caterpillars are active in late May and June, you can trap them. Tie burlap in a skirt around the trunk of each tree. The caterpillars will crawl under the burlap during the day to escape the heat of the sun. After they do, simply remove the skirts and shake them over a bucket of soapy water, where the larvae will drown.

Trying to reduce this year's outbreak by destroying the egg clusters in March and early April—before the hungry larvae start to hatch—is futile and can actually create more problems than it solves. Locating the 1- to 2-inch-long, tan oval egg masses is difficult because they are laid high in tree crotches, under rocks and roof eaves, and in woodpiles and other protected spots. Destroying the egg masses on your property often *helps* the gypsy moth by preventing a starvation-introduced population collapse later in the season. In fact, some biologists say the best thing to do about gypsy moths is nothing at all. The damage they do is unsightly, but few trees are killed. Gypsy moth populations usually diminish naturally after a few years.

Bouncing Birch Aphids

Q. For the past three years, I've had aphids on my white birch trees. Their honeydew drips on everything below. How can I deal with them?

A. In late winter, spray with dormant oil to kill overwintering eggs in bark crevices and twig crotches. If aphids reappear in summer, spray with insecticidal soap, pyrethrum, rotenone, or summer oil—the same oil used in the dormant season but applied at a higher dilution. To prevent foliar damage from summer oil sprays, carefully follow dilution recommendations on the label. Don't spray when shoots are elongating (very young leaves are highly sensitive to oil), when the relative humidity is over 90 percent (high humidity retards oil evaporation), or when the trees are suffering from drought.

Leafminers Lose Out

Q. **Every spring, and again in late June or early July, our white birches are disfigured by the blotchy mines of birch leafminers. How can I control this pest?**

A. There's a new product ready to come to your rescue—neem extract. The birch leafminer is a tiny sawfly whose larvae tunnel into the young leaves of birches, often causing most of the new foliage to turn brown. White-barked birch species are most susceptible. There are two or three generations a year, but the first is the most destructive. Later generations attack only the new leaves at the tips of branches.

In research conducted in New York State, U.S. Department of Agriculture (USDA) entomologist Dr. Hiram G. Larew and two colleagues controlled this pest with an extract of seeds of the neem tree (*Azadirachta indica*). The new commercial neem-derived insecticide Margosan-O will give virtually the same results as the extract, says Larew. Spray the trees when the leaves are half-grown; by then, the adult leafminers will have laid their eggs. Spraying when mines first become visible is equally effective, says Larew, but if the mines are fully developed, it's too late. If you notice some leaf damage developing after you spray, be patient. Though neem is best applied before mines are evident, it doesn't kill the larvae until they're almost grown or have already pupated, according to Larew. He thinks a higher concentration of neem extract might kill the miners more quickly, but he has not tested this hypothesis. Sprays for the second generation, which usually appears in June, are harder to time, but if you knock out the first generation, the second should be much less of a problem, says Larew. If there are infested birches near your treated ones, you'll probably have to spray every year. You can help injured birches recover by mulching them out to the dripline, feeding them in spring with a high-nitrogen fertilizer, and watering deeply during hot weather.

Curbing Dogwood Decline

Q. The lower branches on my dogwoods are dying. A friend told me the disease is dogwood decline and that it will kill the trees. Is there anything I can do?

A. Dogwood decline is a catchall term used to describe several problems. Drought and winter injury also cause branches to die, usually from the top down. According to Margery Daughtrey, a specialist in ornamental diseases at the research laboratory of Cornell University, your trees probably have a fungal disease called anthracnose, which is characterized by lower branch dieback. It affects flowering dogwoods (*Cornus florida*) from Connecticut south to West Virginia and Maryland. You may be able to keep the trees going by preventing other stresses, Daughtrey says. Prune the dead wood and water sprouts, and water during dry spells. Provide full sun if possible, even if it means pruning adjacent trees or shrubbery. Avoid wounding the trunk with a lawnmower or a weed trimmer. Another option is to replace the flowering dogwoods with kousa dogwoods (*Cornus kousa*), which are resistant to anthracnose.

Soaping Down
Hawthorn Lace Bugs

Q. By late summer, the leaves on my Lavalle hawthorn look more yellowish-tan than green, and I've noticed many small black spots on the undersides. If bugs are the problem, what is a safe way to get rid of them?

A. The tree probably has hawthorn lace bugs, which are only about ⅛ inch long and hard to see. The clear wings of the adults are marked with a dark pattern, giving them a lacy look. The bugs feed by sucking sap from the lower leaf surfaces and characteristically leave many small, shiny spots. As their population builds through the summer, the foliage looks more and more stippled and bleached. Adult lace bugs overwinter in bark crevices on their host plants, which include cotoneaster, pyracantha, and quince as well as hawthorn. Control the pests by spraying with insecticidal soap or pyrethrum in late spring when the first signs of damage appear. Aim the spray at the lower leaf surface where the lace bugs feed. Examine the tree each week through the summer and spray again if the pests reappear.

A Honey of a Pest

Q. **I planted a honey locust thinking it would be pest-free, but last summer dark, 1-inch-long caterpillars with light stripes spun webs on the leaves and ate them. How can I control them?**

A. The caterpillars were mimosa webworms, which feed only on mimosa and honey locust trees. This pest has become more widespread as honey locusts have become more popular. The first generation hatches in June. Remove the webs as soon as they appear or spray at high pressure with *Bacillus thuringiensis* (Bt), repeating at weekly intervals until feeding stops. Watch for the larger second generation, which usually appears in August. When it appears, apply the same treatment. In the Southeast and parts of the Southwest, there may be a third generation in September.

Tilting the Scales

Q. **We have a magnolia that is infested with scales, which are tended by ants. How can we get rid of the pests?**

A. The best way to eliminate scale is by spraying with dormant oil in late winter before the buds begin to open. Wait for a calm day when the temperature is 40°F or warmer and no overnight freeze is predicted. A band of Tanglefoot applied near the base of the trunk will keep ants from climbing the tree. Prune any nearby shrub or tree branches that could provide bridges for the ants.

Maple Splits

Q. **What makes the bark on maple trees split, and what can I do to prevent it?**

A. Bark splitting, a vertical crack in a limb or trunk that may extend into the heartwood, is caused by wide temperature fluctuations in winter. Fruit-tree growers know it as sunscald or southwest injury, since the cracks usually appear on the south or west side of the trunk when there is a sudden, extreme drop in temperature after the wood has been warmed by a sunny winter day. Ash, beech, horse chestnut, linden, London plane, and several other common shade trees are also susceptible. Trees standing alone without the shade of the woods and those with trunks 6 to 18 inches in diameter are more likely to crack. Though the tree seals the surface with callus tissue, deep cracks never knit and may reopen in subsequent winters. Besides weakening the tree structurally, they provide an entrance for bacteria and fungi.

Prevent cracking by shading the trunk in winter. Orchardists coat their trees with whitewash or white latex paint that doesn't contain a fungicide. Commercial tree-wrapping paper, plastic tree guards, and burlap are equally effective, as is tying a board to the south side of the trunk. To keep injured trees vigorous, water them deeply during summer dry spells, keep them mulched out to the dripline, and feed them with a high-nitrogen fertilizer in early spring.

Don't Spit on My Pines

Q. I recently discovered spittlebugs on my pine trees. Can you suggest a nonchemical way to control them?

A. Peter Rush, an entomologist for the USDA's Forest Service, recommends that as soon as you see the white masses of spittlebug foam on branches in the spring, spray the trees with a high-pressure jet of water, and repeat spraying a week or so later. Spittlebug foam, formed from plant sap, protects the nymph-stage spittlebugs within, but the insects won't survive once they fall to the ground. Rush says most trees can tolerate some feeding, so it isn't necessary to annihilate the insects. He adds that healthy trees planted in well-drained, fertile soil and watered regularly are less subject to attack.

Spruces from Seed

Q. I've tried growing white spruce and Colorado blue spruce from seed and cuttings with no success. How can I get them to sprout or root?

A. It's much easier to grow spruces from seed than from cuttings. Even so, the seed will need a period of cold temperatures to break dormancy. If you sow seeds in a bed outdoors after you collect them in fall, winter will provide the necessary chilling. Plant the seed ¼ inch deep in soil lightened with peat moss and sand to ensure fast drainage. Cover the bed with wire to keep out rodents, and mulch after the ground freezes. If you have only a few seeds, mix or layer them in a plastic bag with damp peat moss or vermiculite. Store the bag in the refrigerator for at least three months. At the end of the cold period, sow the seeds in containers of your usual seed-starting mix. Spruce seedlings are very susceptible to damping-off, so be sure to pasteurize the soil mix if it's homemade. Transplant the seedlings when they begin to crowd each other.

Colorado blue spruces produce more seedlings that are greenish-blue than bright blue. If you prefer the bluest ones, sow extra seed to be sure of getting some.

Bagging Bagworms

Q. On our Pennsylvania property, we have a Colorado blue spruce that is infested with bagworms. How can we get rid of them?

A. Burn their bags. Bagworms feed on many species of ever-green and deciduous trees and shrubs in the eastern United States. As they feed, the caterpillars spin silken, spindle-shaped bags and disguise them with bits of leaves from the host plant. They feed until late summer, then pupate in their bags. The black male moth, with a wingspread of about 1 inch, emerges and flies to the wing-less female, mating with her through an opening in the bottom of her bag. She lays 500 to 1,000 eggs inside her bag, then crawls out and dies. The eggs overwinter in the bags and hatch in late spring when trees are in full leaf—early June in your area. You can effectively control this pest by picking and burning the bags before the eggs hatch in spring. (You may have to cut the bag off the twigs; the silk is strong and resists pulling.) If you can't reach the bags, spray with *Bacillus thuringiensis* (Bt) at seven- to ten-day intervals from shortly after hatching until you see no further evidence of feeding.

Spruce Gall

A Galling Problem

Q. What causes spruce galls, and how can I prevent them?

A. Spruce galls, conelike swellings of new growth, are caused by the eastern spruce gall aphid, whose galls appear at the base of Norway and white spruce shoots, and the Cooley spruce gall aphid, whose galls kill twig tips on white, Colorado blue, Sitka, and Engelmann spruces. Cooley spruce gall aphids also cause spotted, distorted needles (but no galls) on Douglas fir. Female aphids overwinter at the base of spruce buds and emerge in early spring to lay eggs near branch tips. The eggs hatch in about two weeks, and the nymphs crawl to expanding buds and begin to feed. Saliva injected during feeding causes the galls, which gradually cover the aphids, protecting them from pesticides, predators, and bad weather. In mid- to late summer, the nymphs leave the drying galls and transform into winged adults, which disperse to lay eggs on spruce branches, then die. The eggs hatch about 16 days later, and the young aphids immediately move to bud bases to overwinter.

Correct timing is essential to control these pests. While the galls are green and growing in spring and early summer, cut off and destroy as many as you can reach to kill the nymphs inside. Before buds open in spring, spray with dormant oil to kill overwintering aphids. If trees are heavily infested, spray with pyrethrum, rotenone, or insecticidal soap at bud break to kill nymphs before galls form.

Shrubby Solutions

Superhardy Shrubs

Q. Can you recommend some shrubs that can take our North Dakota winters?

A. There are quite a few superhardy shrubs for your area. Dr. Dale E. Herman, professor of ornamentals at North Dakota State University, has tested many species at sites throughout the state. He recommends the following shrubs. Russian pea shrub (*Caragana frutex* 'Globosa') grows round and compact, to 4 feet wide, without pruning; 'Miniglobe' shrub honeysuckle (*Lonicera* 'Miniglobe') is very hardy; and shrubby cinquefoil (*Potentilla fruticosa* 'Hurstbourne') has golden yellow blooms all season. You might also try some native plants, such as viburnums (*Viburnum trilobum*, *V. lentago*) and sumacs. 'Gro-Low' fragrant sumac (*Rhus aromatica*) forms an 18-inch-tall groundcover, and cut-leaved smooth sumac (*Rhus glabra* 'Laciniata') is a taller form with finely divided foliage.

Keeping Shrubs Evergreen

Q. **What can I do to protect my evergreen shrubs from winter damage?**

A. In winter, evergreens are damaged by wind and sun drying their foliage. To shield them, staple burlap around stakes set about 6 inches away from the shrubs. Put the stakes on the windward side if wind protection is needed and on the southwest side to keep the sun from burning the foliage. Evergreens planted where snow or ice may fall on them need a wooden A-frame or tepee structure for protection. You can prevent sheared yews or hemlocks from spreading under the weight of snow by tying string around them.

The Gall of Those Azaleas!

Q. **Last year my azaleas had ugly, greenish-white galls on some of the leaves. What caused them, and what can I do if they recur?**

A. Azalea leaf gall, also called pinkster apple and honeysuckle apple, is caused by a fungus that overwinters as spores in bud scales of azaleas and rhododendrons. Under moist conditions in early spring, it infects expanding leaves, shoots, and flowers, causing them to form irregular light green or pink galls that later become coated with powdery, white, spore-producing tissue. Infected rhododendron leaves may be yellowed or bleached and slightly thickened, with white fungal tissue underneath. This disease is more conspicuous than serious. Control it by handpicking the galls before they turn white and by pruning low, overhanging tree branches and nearby plants to increase air circulation around azaleas and rhododendrons.

Forsythia Bottom Bloom

Q. **Some years my forsythia blooms only near the bottom, and other years it doesn't bloom at all. Why?**

A. The flower buds are being killed by cold winters or spring frosts. Even though forsythia (*Forsythia intermedia*) is hardy to USDA Hardiness Zone 4, its flower buds are more tender, hardy only to Zone 5 or 6 (about $-10°$ to $-15°$F). Forsythia planted in northern areas often blooms only near the base of the plant, where snow has covered and protected the tender buds. For more reliable flowering, you might want to try *Forsythia ovata*, a similar species with buds that are hardy to −29°F.

Fall-Blooming Forsythia

Q. **This fall my forsythia is greening and putting out buds. So far it hasn't bloomed, but I'm afraid it will be damaged by cold. Will it bloom next year?**

A. Yes. The phenomenon you've described is fairly common, and has been nicknamed "November bloom," although it can happen from August on, according to Dr. Owen Rogers, ornamentals specialist at the University of New Hampshire. It's nothing to worry about, Rogers says, because usually no more than 1 percent of the flower buds open, leaving plenty for spring.

Forsythia Pruning Primer

Q. **When and how should I prune my forsythia bush?**

A. The forsythia, like all spring-flowering shrubs, should be pruned after blooming. Next year's flowers will form on this year's new wood, so summer pruning allows plenty of time for the new wood to grow. Always cut out any dead wood. Then thin your shrub by cutting a third of the older, woodier stems to ground level. Cut back long stems to encourage branching and flower production. If the plant is unsightly, you can rejuvenate the entire shrub by cutting all stems to within 2 inches of the ground. Don't shear your forsythia like a hedge; the result will be compact, top-heavy growth with all the flowers at the top.

Help for Heather

Q. **Will heather grow in Maryland, where I live? If so, what special care does it need?**

A. As long as you have the right conditions or can create them, heather will grow in your area. Scotch heather (*Calluna vulgaris*) is hardy to USDA Hardiness Zone 4, and heath (*Erica carnea*), also occasionally called heather, is hardy to Zone 5. Plant heathers in full sun on an eastern or northeastern slope, away from direct winter winds. They grow best in very well drained, infertile, acid soil (pH 4.5 to 5.0). Double-dig the soil, adding plenty of compost and peat moss, but avoid manure or other nutrient-rich materials. If your soil is heavy clay, fill a raised bed with compost and peat. Space the plants about 3 feet apart and mulch with leaves, pine bark, or pine needles. Although heathers are fairly drought-tolerant once established, water frequently the first season. In early spring, shear the callunas to encourage new growth. Ericas do not need pruning.

Hibiscus No-Show

Q. Our hibiscus plant won't bloom. Any suggestions?

A. Erik Neumann, curator of education at the U.S. National Arboretum, offers two possibilities. You could be fertilizing the hibiscus with too much nitrogen, which causes lush, leafy growth at the expense of flowers. Try a more balanced fertilizer, such as fish emulsion. Or the plant may be growing in too much shade; transplant in spring or fall to an area in full sun.

Hollies Need Food

Q. My Chinese hollies and yaupons are loaded with red berries, but the leaves look yellowish instead of their usual dark green. We have sandy soil and I mulch with pine needles. How can I get the bushes to look healthier?

A. An unusually heavy fruit crop puts a great deal of stress on a plant, especially when the soil is low in nutrients, as sandy soils often are. Your hollies need a balanced fertilizer rich in nitrogen to restore good leaf color and healthy growth. A 1-inch topdressing of compost or rotted manure will feed the plants and provide humus to improve your soil's structure. Cottonseed meal is a good alternative. It won't add much organic matter, but its 7 percent nitrogen content will turn your plants green again. Broadcast it over the mulch at the rate of 4 to 5 pounds per 100 square feet before growth starts in spring.

Hydrangea Blues

Q. I have several hydrangea bushes in my yard. They all have blue flowers, except the two in the front of the house, which have some blue and some pink flowers. Can I do something to get all blue flowers?

A. You can change the color of your hydrangea flowers by altering the soil pH. They will bloom blue or pink depending on the availability of aluminum in the soil, which is determined by pH. (There are also white-blooming varieties, which will never bloom blue or pink regardless of soil conditions.) The blooms in front of your house are being affected by the cement in the foundation. Cement is composed mostly of lime, and some leaches into the ground around the foundation, turning the soil alkaline and the flowers pink. Flowers farther away from the house aren't affected by the lime and remain blue. To get the whole plant to bloom blue, you'll need to lower the pH to between 4.5 and 5.5 near the foundation. Elemental sulfur (also known as flowers of sulfur) will acidify the soil. If, on the other hand, you decide you want pink flowers, raise the pH to between 7.0 and 7.5 by liming the soil. Alkalinity above 7.5 is likely to bring about yellowing and poor growth. The exact amount of sulfur or lime will depend on your soil type, but in general, for every 25 square feet of soil, use ⅓ pound of sulfur to lower the pH one unit or 1 pound of lime to raise it one unit.

Bungled Blooms

Q. I have three blue-flowered hydrangeas, two on the north and one on the east side of my house. Though I prune them to 2 feet each fall and protect them in winter, only the one on the east side produces a few blooms. How can I get more flowers?

A. In this species of hydrangea, the bigleaf hydrangea (*Hydrangea macrophylla*), blooms sprout from terminal buds on the previous season's growth. By pruning in fall, you've been removing most of the following summer's flower buds. The best time to prune these hydrangeas is right after bloom. Continue to protect the plants in winter—low temperatures can nip flower buds as effectively as pruning shears. If the bushes on the north side of the house still fail to bloom, try moving them to a sunnier, warmer location.

Summer Snowberry Cuttings

Q. **Can I root cuttings from a snowberry bush in summer? If so, how?**

A. Yes. Just remember that, as with any leafy cutting, it's most important to keep them from drying out. Take 3- to 5-inch-long tip cuttings in June or July. Pinch off developing fruit and remove the leaves from the bottom half of each cutting. Root the cuttings in pots of moistened, homemade seed-starting mix or use a soilless medium such as one consisting of equal parts of peat and perlite. Insert the cuttings to the level of the lowest leaves, spacing them so the leaves of adjoining cuttings don't touch. To maintain high humidity, place the pot inside a plastic bag, using soda straws or wooden sticks to hold the plastic above the cuttings. Keep the bag in bright light but away from direct sun; open it occasionally to check for drying. Rooting should occur in two to six weeks. Bottom heat of about 70°F speeds the process. When the cuttings are strongly rooted, transplant them to a nursery bed and mulch heavily the first winter.

Scentless Sweet-Shrub

Q. **I have a beautiful sweet-shrub bush, and every year it is full of blooms. Why are the blossoms not fragrant?**

A. There could be two causes. If the shrub was once fragrant, you can try really aerating the soil and working in a good amount of rotted manure. Occasionally revitalizing the bush in this manner will increase the fragrance of the flowers. However, more than likely you have a species of the genus *Calycanthus* that has nonaromatic flowers—*C. fertilis*. If this is the case, there is nothing you can do. You can recognize this type of sweet-shrub by its oblong leaves that are thin and either blunt or tapered. Its leaves are bright green and shiny on both sides or pale underneath. The leaves may be as long as 6 inches and the brown flowers up to 2 inches across. Look for nurseries that carry the fragrant Carolina allspice, *C. floridus*.

What about Weigela?

Q. **How and when should I prune my weigela bushes? They're still young and vigorous.**

A. In northern states, branch tips of weigela often die back in winter; remove this dead wood when the bushes leaf out in spring. It's best to do all other pruning shortly after bloom in June or July. As the plants mature, thin crowded stems to let in light and stimulate vigorous new growth from the base. Cut out spindly stems and old branches that no longer flower well, making the cuts at or near the ground. If the plants grow too tall and leggy, cut back the longest stems to a strong lateral branch, being careful to retain the shrubs' natural shape. By pruning moderately every year, you'll maintain a balance of old and new stems that should keep the bushes growing and flowering well for many years.

Chapter 17

Help for Houseplants

Super Houseplant Hints

Potting Soil Particulars

Q. What's the difference between potting soil and garden soil? Is there any reason why I can't use soil directly from my garden for my houseplants?

A. Yes, there are two reasons. First, garden soil can become waterlogged or dried out in a container. Second, garden soil may contain pathogens that will cause plant diseases. Potting soil includes ingredients such as peat, bark, vermiculite, and perlite. These are blended to hold the right amount of moisture yet also provide good drainage. Also, potting soil should be pasteurized to kill pathogens. Commercial potting soils have a wide range of pH, texture, and fertility. But there are really few differences between general potting soils and those labeled for African violets or cacti. You can have more control over quality and can save money by making your own potting soil mix. Use two parts garden soil, one part compost or leaf mold, and one part sand or perlite. Add 1 tablespoon of bonemeal per quart of mix. Pasteurize the mix before using (see "Pasteurizing Potting Soil" on page 259).

Pasteurizing Potting Soil

Q. **Should I sterilize my homemade potting soil for house-plants?**

A. A lot of people think you should sterilize potting soils, but they're wrong. Sterilizing kills *all* living organisms in the soil, be they good or bad. The way to get around destroying the good guys is to pasteurize the soil. Place the soil in a tray, and water it until it's thoroughly wet for uniform heat conduction. Preheat your oven to the desired temperature. A temperature of 130°F for 25 minutes will kill soil insects, while a temperature of 180°F for 30 minutes will kill plant disease pathogens.

Salty Mushroom Soil

Q. **Is it a good idea to use mushroom soil for houseplants or in the home greenhouse?**

A. No. Spent mushroom soil, a by-product of commercial mush-room cultivation, is very high in soluble salts. High salt levels injure plant roots and interfere with water uptake, causing wilting when the soil is moist, stunted or distorted growth, yellowed leaves, and scorched leaf margins. Leaching—watering heavily enough each time so a significant volume of water runs out of the bottom of the pot—reduces soluble salts to harmless levels, but this can take several weeks. By then, much damage may already have been done to salt-sensitive plants, especially seedlings. Carrying houseplants to a sink or bathtub for a weekly leaching can also be very awk-ward. Because mushroom soil contains a lot of limestone, it can have a pH well above neutral (7.0), which is high enough to cause nutrient imbalances in plants. Fresh mushroom soil shrinks greatly in volume as it breaks down, which can lead to compaction of the potting mix unless it contains equal volumes of more stable materials such as peat and perlite. Aging mushroom soil outdoors helps leach salts and stabilize structure, but the pH usually re-mains high and the piles quickly become weedy. You're better off with soil intended for houseplants.

Old Salts

Q. **All my clay pots have developed a thick white growth on their outer surfaces. I scrub it off, but it grows back. Any suggestions?**

A. The white "growth" is actually accumulated salts, usually caused by improper watering, a saline water supply, or overfertilization. If you have saucers or trays beneath the pots, they are probably holding excess water that drips through the drainage holes. As the water evaporates, some of it is reabsorbed into the pots, and salts of potassium, calcium, magnesium, and nitrates are deposited on the outside of the pots and on the soil surface. Either pour off the overflow water each time or raise the pots on a layer of pebbles to keep them from sitting in water. If salt buildup continues to occur, reduce the amount of fertilizer you use, and flush out the excess salts in the soil.

Beyond Fish Emulsion

Q. **I've been using fish emulsion on my houseplants. I know it is high in nitrogen but low in phosphorus and potassium. Is there a more balanced liquid organic fertilizer I could use?**

A. Fish emulsion has an NPK (nitrogen:phosphorus:potassium) formula of 5:1:1. It's a good fertilizer for foliage plants, which require nitrogen for leaf formation. Flowering houseplants, such as African violets, have a higher potassium requirement. However, the bulk of the nutritional needs for both types can be taken care of by adding amendments to the potting soil when it is prepared, then supplementing with a liquid fertilizer. Veteran greenhouse gardeners Doc and Katy Abraham of Naples, New York, make a soil mix from equal parts of manure-based compost, loam, and sand. They add 1 cup of bloodmeal for nitrogen, 1 cup of bonemeal for phosphorus, and 2 cups of wood ashes for potassium per bushel of soil. "Compost is the backbone of any soil mix," says Doc. The breakdown of organic matter releases humic acids, which make nutrients available to plants. They recommend feeding houseplants once every two to three months with fish emulsion or manure tea (cow manure is 2:0.5:2). Several liquid manure products are also available. Most houseplants aren't heavy feeders, so unless leaves begin to yellow, fertilizing more often isn't necessary.

Nautical Fertilizer

Q. Is there an effective organic fertilizer that can be used on houseplants growing in water? Most result in immediate stagnation.

A. Use the newer deodorized fish emulsions as a source of nitrogen. Pieces of aquarium charcoal (don't use briquettes designed for outdoor barbecuing) can be added to ensure sweetness and prevent stagnation. From time to time, add a little manure tea or liquefied seaweed—the charcoal will help conserve it for plant use. If water becomes covered with algae, change it from time to time.

Houseplant Hunger Signs

Q. The new leaves on our houseplants sometimes stay small and turn light green. What can we do to prevent this?

A. If new leaves are progressively smaller and paler than older foliage, it's a sure sign that fertilizer is needed or that you are overwatering. If you are giving proper amounts of water, try using some fish emulsion, compost, or manure tea. Potted plants should receive only as much fertilizer as they can incorporate into the food manufactured in their leaves—usually no more than three or four feedings a year. During the winter when they get little light, less fertilizer is needed. In the long days of summer, they use more. Young, actively growing houseplants take more feeding than mature plants.

Soap Your Plants

Q. My friend told me that she uses soap flakes to keep the bugs off her houseplants. I would like to use the solution on my own plants. Are soap flakes organic?

A. A solution of detergent-free soap flakes (such as Ivory or Octagon) acts as a mild insecticide against aphids and scale. Because it is mild and will probably not kill all insects on the plant, it can leave just enough pests to feed any beneficial predators and parasites. Soap solutions also wash off dirt, dust, and insect eggs. To make the solution, add 1 or 2 tablespoons of flakes to 1 gallon of tepid (70° to 90°F) water. Apply it to the plants by sponging thoroughly, dipping them into it, or by spraying. Leave the mixture on for one or two hours, and then rinse it off thoroughly with luke-warm water. Don't use soap solution on hairy plants such as African violets and begonias.

A Medley of Houseplants

Leave It to African Violets

Q. **What is the best way to root African violet leaves?**

A. Choose medium-size, healthy leaves. Prepare them by cutting the stems diagonally with a clean razor blade 1½ inches from the leaf base, according to Ronn Nadeau, a commercial grower. Fill a 3½- to 4-inch pot with a soilless mix, such as two parts shredded sphagnum peat moss, one part vermiculite, and one part perlite, and moisten it well. Using a pencil or a wooden stick, make three holes in the mix. Insert the leaf stems to a depth of 1 inch and firm the mix around them. Correctly planted leaves may soften and discolor for a few days, but they usually recover within a week. New shoots should sprout in about two months. When they grow 2 to 3 inches tall, transplant them into 2½- to 3-inch pots. Within five to seven months, you'll have new blooming plants.

Gnats Nab African Violets

Q. **Lately I've seen fungus gnats around my African violets. I've been told they eat organic matter in soil and are harmless to plants. Is that true?**

A. No. When numerous, the larvae of these tiny, highly active black flies feed on plant roots and crowns as well as organic matter. They're especially damaging to young plants, cuttings, and seedlings. To kill the larvae, repot your violets frequently into clean pots and fresh potting soil, and use one of the following three solutions. They're recommended by Bob L. Green, author of "Beginner's Column" in *African Violet Magazine*. To 1 quart of warm water, add 2 drops of dishwashing detergent or 2 tablespoons of Safer's Insecticidal Soap or 1 tablespoon of household bleach. Drench the soil with the solution, discard the runoff, and drench again. Use the bleach solution once a month or one of the other solutions every two months until you no longer see adult gnats.

Violets Fight Fungus

Q. My African violets have a very contagious soil fungus that has spread to my other houseplants. A white mold forms on the top of the soil, which has a very vinegary odor. What can I do to control this disease? It is stunting my plants.

A. Fungus likes a damp, dark area to grow in. To control it, move your plants into good light and fresh air, and give them proper drainage. Wash the infected plants and change the soil mixture to a light, airy soil with sufficient nutrients. If the plant itself looks like it has been afflicted with disease, destroy it. Otherwise, the disease spores will be blown all through the house, and you'll be fighting a losing battle. Use sterile media like perlite, vermiculite, washed sand, and peat moss to start seeds. When you water, don't wet the foliage. Water early in the day so leaves can dry in the sun, and never crowd the plants.

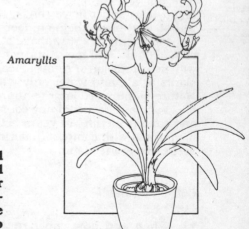

Amaryllis

Amaryllis Again

Q. Last Christmas I received an amaryllis that bloomed beautifully. It was outside for the summer, rested in the garage, and was repotted in late fall. How can I get it to rebloom?

A. Amaryllis bulbs often don't bloom the year after purchase while they produce new roots and rebuild their nutrient reserves. To ensure bloom in future years, grow your bulb in bright light and a rich, porous potting mix, such as equal parts of topsoil, compost, and sand or perlite. Move the plant to a sunny spot outdoors for the summer, and feed twice a month with fish emulsion (1 tablespoon per gallon) or compost tea. The roots will stay cooler and dry out less quickly if you sink the pot to its rim in well-drained soil or nestle it among the leaves of a groundcover. Taper off watering in September so the bulb will go dormant, then store it dry in a cool, frost-free place for 60 to 90 days. At the end of the dormant period, replace the top 1 to 2 inches of soil with compost. Water thoroughly and bring the pot to room temperature. Your amaryllis should bloom in six to eight weeks. Repot the bulb in fresh soil every two or three years. Use a clay pot that is 2 inches wider than the bulb. The weight of the pot will balance the top-heaviness of an amaryllis in full bloom, and its porosity will keep the soil from becoming water-logged.

Bloomless Birds

Q. **My bird-of-paradise plants are thriving, but they haven't flowered in six years. How can I stimulate them to bloom?**

A. Bird-of-paradise (*Strelitzia reginae*) is slow to reach blooming size when grown as a houseplant. Depending on conditions, seedlings may take five to ten years to flower, and divisions may take four years or more. Once they're mature, the plants need very bright light to set flower buds. Keep them in a south window in winter, and move them outdoors to a sunny spot in spring once night temperatures stay above 50°F. During active growth in summer, keep the soil moist but not soggy, and feed every two weeks with fish emulsion or compost tea. During the winter, don't feed the plants at all, and water only when the top ½ inch of soil is dry. Mature plants need large containers. Grow them in a rich potting mix, such as one containing equal parts soil, leaf mold or compost, and sand or perlite. In years between repottings, replace the top inch of soil with compost in spring, being careful not to injure the fleshy, rot-prone plants.

Cutting Up Cacti

Q. **When and how can I root cuttings of Thanksgiving and Christmas cacti?**

A. Cuttings can be taken anytime the plants aren't in flower, but if you root them in late winter or early spring, they may grow enough to bloom the first year. Take tip cuttings two or three segments in length; longer ones tend to fall over in the rooting medium. Two- or three-branched cuttings will produce fuller, more symmetrical plants than unbranched cuttings. Allow the cut ends to callous for a day or two before sticking them into the medium. You can start the cuttings in containers of moist vermiculite or a 50–50 mix of peat and perlite and repot them when rooted. Alternatively, you can root them directly in 3- or 4-inch pots of a pasteurized, coarse potting mix such as equal parts of garden soil or bagged houseplant soil, peat, and perlite. To get full plants fast, use three cuttings per pot. Place the containers of cuttings in sealed plastic bags propped up with wooden sticks or soda straws and set them in a warm, bright place shaded from direct sun. When the cuttings have rooted strongly enough to resist a gentle pull (usually in two or three weeks), remove the plants. After rooting, water only when the soil surface feels dry.

Christmas Chameleon Cactus

Q. **When I bought my Christmas cactus, it had white flowers. But every year since, the flowers have been pink. What happened?**

A. The flower color of a Christmas cactus can be affected by its environment. The environment in your home is probably different from that of the greenhouse where the cactus was grown. For white flowers, the night temperature should remain as close to 60°F as possible. If it's much lower or higher, the white variety sometimes blooms pink. An acid or alkaline soil can also cause pinkness, so test the pH of the potting mix and of the water you're using. Both should be near neutral (pH 7.0).

Rooting Out the Problem

Q. **After blooming profusely, my Christmas cacti changed from a healthy green to a sickly reddish shade. One of the plants died, and the other hasn't recovered its green color, though it continues to bloom. What went wrong?**

A. Most likely, your plants sustained root injury, which often does not become apparent until flowering or some other stress places a heavy demand for water on the reduced root system. When that happens, the topgrowth may wilt, discolor, or try to compensate by producing many aerial roots. The most common cause of root injury is overwatering, though fertilizer overdose and feeding by fungus gnat larvae can also result in severe root loss. Excess fertilizer (one sign is salt deposits on the pot or soil surface) can be removed by leaching. To help an overwatered or overfed plant recover, place it in a cool room out of direct sunlight and keep the soil barely moist. If you see adult fungus gnats—tiny, nervous black flies—flitting about the soil surface, drench the soil with insecticidal soap (see "Soap Your Plants" on page 261) until no more appear or take cuttings and discard the plant.

When repotting is necessary, use a sterile, acid mix of three parts porous, humus-rich soil and one part perlite, says Dolly Kolli, a member of the Epiphyllum Society of America and a Christmas cactus hobbyist and hybridizer from Mashpee, Massachusetts. Add 1 teaspoon of bonemeal per 6-inch pot, and feed every two weeks with compost tea from late winter until Labor Day. Keep the soil moist, especially when humidity is low, but don't let it get soggy.

Cymbidium Solutions

Q. I haven't had a bloom spike on my cymbidium orchids in more than five years. What am I doing wrong?

A. The most common causes of nonflowering in cymbidiums are low light, insufficient nutrients, and lack of a drop in night temperature, says American Orchid Society probationary judge C. Robert Phillips of Bethlehem, Pennsylvania. During the growing season (April to October), give the plants full sun with shading only at midday. Apply liquid fertilizer, such as fish emulsion, at every other watering. If you've had your plants for five years, they may need repotting. Use medium-grade Douglas fir bark and give the plants plenty of nitrogen. Cymbidiums need a 15-degree drop in night temperature to set buds. This should occur naturally if you grow your plants outdoors. "Cymbidiums will tolerate, and even enjoy, a degree or two of frost," says Phillips. If you follow this regimen for a couple of seasons and your plants still don't flower, you may have clones that are naturally reluctant bloomers. In that case, consider buying miniature cymbidiums, which are easier to flower than standards.

Boston Fern Basics

Q. What's the best care for my Boston fern?

A. Don't overwater or repot your Boston fern too frequently. Let the soil dry out slightly between thorough waterings. Mist the leaves twice a day, especially in winter when the air is dry. To clean the fronds, gently sponge with a solution of 1 tablespoon of white vinegar per cup of warm water. When fronds turn yellow, trim them close to the soil level. Pot up only when the roots occupy over three-fourths of the pot space. Boston ferns like to be potbound. Potting soils should be well drained. One composed of four parts sandy loam, one part sand, and one part manure will suit your fern. Side-dress with fish emulsion every third watering during its growing season. The plant grows best in indirect sunlight. It needs 68° to 75°F daytime temperatures, 50° to 60°F nighttime temperatures, and 50 to 80 percent humidity. Keep your Boston fern out of drafts. From fall through winter, the plant stops growing. Keep it at 50°F, reduce watering so the soil is barely moist, and stop fertilizing.

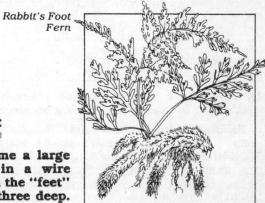

Rabbit's Foot Fern

Rabbit's Foot Replant

Q. **A friend gave me a large rabbit's foot fern in a wire hanging basket with the "feet" wrapped around it three deep. How can I repot it?**

A. A rabbit's foot fern with "feet" or rhizomes growing through the sides of the wire basket isn't necessarily rootbound. A plant that needs repotting will produce small fronds, grow slowly, and need frequent watering, and its lower leaves will turn yellow. If this fern needs repotting, there are two ways to replant it. Cut the rhizomes off the sides and bottom of the basket and transplant the fern to a new basket lined with 2 inches of unmilled sphagnum moss. Or cut away the old basket, removing the fern in pieces. Then replant the healthiest rhizomes in a new basket or several baskets, using standard potting mix. Small rhizomes can be poked through the sides and held in place with wire. Water thoroughly after planting. To revitalize a large fern without removing it from the basket, cut out the central portion, fill the space with potting soil, and cover with sphagnum moss. If the rhizomes surrounding the sides of the basket are growing too thickly and lack vigor, thin them by pruning some off.

Stressed-Out Gardenia

Q. Most of the older leaves on my gardenia are yellowing and falling. I keep it 3 feet below a 75-watt plant light that burns eight hours a day. Why is it declining?

A. Gardenias react to several kinds of stress by dropping their leaves. Your plant may not be getting enough light. Try moving it closer to the lamp, but be careful that it doesn't get too hot. Burning the light a few hours longer can help offset low light intensity. If your plant is potbound and hasn't been fed regularly, the yellowing leaves could indicate nitrogen deficiency. Feed every two weeks with fish emulsion. In early spring, repot if necessary into a well-drained, acidic, peaty soil. Cold or wet soil can also cause blotchy yellowing of leaves. Grow the plant at 60°F or higher and don't overwater.

No Goldfish

Q. How can I get my goldfish plant (*Columnea*) to bloom again? The foliage is healthy, but blossoms never appear.

A. Inadequate light can cause blossom failure. *Columnea* is a gesneriad and must be treated like its relative, the African violet. Try giving your plant indirect but bright light, 10 to 12 hours per day, perhaps by setting the plant in an east window. You may also be overfertilizing. Remove the plant from its pot and rinse the soil ball in water to flush out the excess nitrogen. Repot the plant in a soil mix to which you have added a sprinkling of bonemeal (use 1 tablespoon for a 5-inch pot). Phosphorus, the major nutrient in bonemeal, is required for strong, healthy blossoms and often stimulates the blooming of potted plants.

Never-Blooming Hoyas

Q. I have some four-year-old variegated hoyas that are growing nicely but have never bloomed. Why don't they flower?

A. Hoya, also called porcelain-flower or wax plant, is a genus of tropical vines, some of which are grown as houseplants on trellises or in hanging baskets. The thick leaves may be flecked with silver or variegated pink and white. The clusters of fragrant, waxy, white-and-pink flowers are carried on woody, leafless spurs that grow from the leaf axils; be careful not to prune the spurs when grooming the plants. Variegated cultivars are much slower to bloom than green types, says Jerry Williams of Rainbow Gardens Nursery, La Habra, California, which sells hoyas. To induce flowering in any hoya, grow it in very bright light and allow it to become potbound, advises Williams. Indoors, give hoyas full sun in an east or west window and light shade in a south window. If possible, summer the plants outdoors in bright shade. If they still don't bloom, hold back on nitrogen and substitute fertilizers rich in phosphorus (bonemeal) and potassium (seaweed extract or kelp meal), both of which stimulate flowering.

Punctual Poinsettia

Q. How can I get my poinsettia to bloom for the holiday season?

A. You can force the blossoms for Christmas by giving them 12 hours of darkness and keeping night temperatures between 60° and 68°F. Keep the plants under these conditions until the buds develop or the bracts ("petals") begin to color. When they bloom, take them into a sunny, draft-free room. Poinsettias' bracts will color up within six to ten weeks and can continue to bloom from December through Easter.

Chapter 18

Growing
in Greenhouses

Good Houses Make Good Gardens

Glazing for a Grow-Frame

Q. I want to build a solar grow-frame and would like to know
the best glazing material to use. Are glass panels better
insulators than acrylic or fiberglass?

A. Glass, acrylic, and fiberglass are all good light transmitters.
However, a single sheet of each has an R-value of about 1, meaning
that none of these materials offers much insulation. To reduce heat
loss, cover the inside of the glazing at night with some type of
movable insulation such as rigid foam or an insulating window
shade. For maximum efficiency, the cover material should fit as
tightly as possible against the glazing.

A Black-and-White Issue

Q. I built a lean-to greenhouse that is attached to the south side
of my house in Iowa. Should the back wall be painted white to
reflect light to the plants, or black to absorb heat?

A. If you want healthy plants, you should paint the north wall
of your greenhouse white, since light levels can be critical during

Iowa winters. If your plants lean toward the south, you may have to add fluorescent lights. Rather than using heat storage to moderate temperature extremes, we suggest that you install an exhaust fan with an automatic thermostat in the north wall. Put it 2 feet or less below the juncture of the greenhouse roof and the house wall. The fan will automatically draw excess heat into the house during the day and will return heat to the greenhouse at night. You will probably want to cover the glazing with an insulating curtain at night to prevent excessive heat loss. During the summer, block off the fan. Install vents on each endwall of the greenhouse, a louvered intake vent low on the east wall to draw in cool air, and a fan exhaust vent high on the west wall to draw hot air out.

A Lot of Hot Air

Q. We plan to grow herbs in a solar greenhouse next year and have been exploring different ways of providing inexpensive supplemental heat. Would composting sawdust and chicken manure in 25-gallon plastic garbage cans increase the temperature in our greenhouse?

A. Composting sawdust and chicken manure will add additional heat to the greenhouse, but don't use cans. By using closed containers for composting, you run the risk of encouraging the slow, cold decay produced by anaerobic bacteria. This will make your greenhouse smell more like a sewer than a warm, plant-growing place. For fast, hot, odorless compost, you need to encourage aerobic, oxygen-loving bacteria. Instead of cans, use open bins to store compost, and keep the piles supplied with plenty of air by turning their contents frequently. After a few days the steam will start to rise. Steam from the compost will condense on the glass or plastic and then drop down to the soil and plants, keeping things moist and green. When the sun comes up, the rapid heating of the inside air will accelerate the condensation, providing lots of moisture and heat, as well as extra carbon dioxide, to plants. After three weeks or so, the biological fire of the composting process will die down, and you'll have to start new piles with fresh sawdust and manure.

Cooling the Hothouse

Q. **In our Florida summers, the temperature in my attached solar greenhouse is higher than outdoors. It often soars past 100°F, even though a ¼-horsepower exhaust fan high in the west wall draws in cooler air through a low vent in the east wall. The roof and walls are insulated to R-19. Any suggestions?**

A. There are a number of options that will help lower summer temperatures in your greenhouse. First, the ventilation system should allow at least one air exchange to occur every two minutes. Check the cubic feet per minute (cfm) rating of the fan. Then calculate the area of the greenhouse to see if the fan is powerful enough to provide adequate ventilation. Second, frequent misting of walls, floors, and plants provides some evaporative cooling. Third, shadecloth, on either the inside or outside of the glazing, reduces heat transmission by 50 to 70 percent. Keep in mind that it reduces light by about the same amount, and plant growth may be affected. Another option, which depends on the kinds of plants you raise, is to move the plants to a lath house for the summer. Before returning these plants to the greenhouse, inspect them carefully to avoid introducing pest problems.

Polyethylene Policy

Q. **We've been wondering about using polyethylene glazing for greenhouses. Isn't it harmful?**

A. We don't feel there is any danger using polyethylene in greenhouses. It would take temperatures of 300° to 400°F to release potentially harmful factors in the plastic. In fact, we recommend polyethylene for the inner glazing of greenhouses. It is inexpensive and durable. However, ultraviolet light will degrade it within a year if it is used as outer glazing. We feel replacing it yearly would be wasteful.

Kerosene Kickback

Q. **I have a 14-by-40-foot poly-covered greenhouse and wonder if it's safe to heat with a portable kerosene heater.**

A. Although you can safely use an unvented kerosene heater for several hours in an emergency situation, it is generally not safe to use one as the main heat source for a greenhouse. Burning an unvented heater for several hours depletes oxygen from the air and also causes potentially harmful levels of combustion gases such as sulfur dioxide to build up. If your greenhouse is attached to the house, you can heat it by drawing in warm air from the house with fans. To heat a freestanding greenhouse, install a heater vented to the outside. Companies specializing in florist and nursery supplies offer several types of greenhouse systems, including hot air, hot water, and steam units. These are fueled by oil, kerosene, or natural or liquefied petroleum (LP) gas. These companies can help you design a heating system that suits your needs.

Not Just Hot Air

Q. **Would it be safe to vent the hot air from my gas-powered clothes dryer into my greenhouse?**

A. Yes, but there are drawbacks. The exhaust from your gas dryer will contain a lot of carbon dioxide and small amounts of polluting gases like carbon monoxide, nitrous oxide, and sulfur dioxide. However, in your greenhouse, the harmful gases should dissipate. The carbon dioxide will enhance growth. Gas flames, when ignited and extinguished or when improperly adjusted, can also give off ethylene. While it is a common plant hormone, it will cause some plants, especially tomatoes, to droop. The biggest problem with dryer exhaust is moisture. A load of wet clothes contains a gallon or more of water, all of which gets carried off in the exhaust as water vapor. The resulting high humidity in a greenhouse could cause excess condensation and outbreaks of disease.

Indoor Gardening Tips

Lethargic Ladybugs

Q. **Last December, I ordered 500 ladybugs to control aphids in my greenhouse. The greenhouse has a night temperature of 50°F and a day temperature of 75° to 80°F. When I released the bugs, they seemed lethargic, and almost all died within a week. Was my greenhouse too cold for them?**

A. No. The beetles should feed readily within a temperature range of 65° to 100°F. Ladybugs that seem lethargic upon release have probably suffered from cold in transit. (Temperatures below

30°F will injure them.) They could also have been weakened if they weren't given water while being stored at the insectary. The common ladybug (*Hippodamia convergens*) is often recommended as a biological control, but because of its fairly complex life cycle, even researchers have trouble getting consistent results. You'll have greater success controlling aphids with green lacewings. But order them in the fall, since they are more sensitive to the freezing temperatures they might experience during winter shipping.

Whitefly Woes

Q. **We have whiteflies in our greenhouse. So far we have tried a number of controls, including vacuuming them, dusting them with tobacco dust, spraying them with a solution of water and lime sulfate, and hanging sticky yellow cards to attract flying adults. Nothing has worked. What should we do now?**

A. In the greenhouse at the Rodale Research Center, whiteflies aren't a problem until late spring and summer. The greenhouse has no supplemental heat supply, and in winter it gets quite cool. This may be why the pest isn't much of a pest problem. We do have a whitefly population in our heated Quonset-type greenhouse, which we use for some winter research activities. We have had luck using potted tomatoes as "trap" plants for the whiteflies. We then periodically spray or remove leaves or entire plants. Occasionally on a mild day, we take the trap plants outside to prune them, removing many of the pests in the immature stages of growth. Shaking off the adults in the wind is also helpful. Also, many of the strong herb sprays that we've tried have killed adult whiteflies. Some of the herbs we've had luck with are eucalyptus (*Eucalyptus globulus*), rue (*Ruta graveolens*), and santolina (*Santolina chamaecyparissus*).

Hanging sticky flypaper around the infested plants works well to nab the adults. The flypaper must be replaced regularly, since the stickiness wears off. Hang it rather low around the pots for the low-flying whiteflies. We have also had success using the sticky yellow cards you mentioned. We use ¼-inch plywood sprayed with Rustoleum orange and topped with a mineral oil coating. When the trapped whiteflies cover the square too thickly, we wipe it clean and apply fresh oil. Also, proper air circulation helps to keep the populations from booming.

Greenhouse-Grown Problems

Spindly Sprouts

Q. I'm trying to grow tomatoes, lettuce, and Chinese cabbage in our solar greenhouse, but everything stays thin and spindly. Is there something I can add to the soil?

A. There's an easy way to learn if soil fertility is the problem. Feed your plants a nutrient tea, and if they respond with vigorous growth, you're on your way to successful crops. In wintertime gardening tests at the Rodale Research Center, we compared teas made with chicken and cow manures, bloodmeal, fish emulsion, and Fertrell. The chicken manure and fish emulsion teas promoted the best growth, although we don't recommend fish emulsion in greenhouses because of the possible salt buildup. The other organic materials are suitable if you can obtain them more readily than chicken manure. We use about 6 ounces of dried chicken manure per gallon of water. Don't expect tomatoes to grow as well in the cold months as lettuce and Chinese cabbage.

Cucurbit Flower: Unpollinated (top), Pollinated (bottom)

Hand Pollination

Q. We are about to add a solar greenhouse to our home so we can grow vegetables year-round. Can you tell me which vegetables need to be hand-pollinated and how to do it?

A. Cucumbers, melons, and squash (cucurbits), and tomatoes, eggplant, and peppers (nightshades) must be hand-pollinated. Pollinate the plants in the tomato family by gently flicking the blooms. That will jostle the pollen from the male part of the flower to the female. In the cucumber family, the male and female flowers are separate. You'll have to transfer the pollen from a male to a female flower with a small paintbrush. Pollinate in the early morning while temperatures are cool. At temperatures above 90°F, the pollen may dry out before pollination occurs.

Rotten Lettuce

Q. Last winter several large heads of my greenhouse lettuce rotted. How can I prevent this next year?

A. The spoiler of your lettuce was probably botrytis (gray mold), the same fungus that spoils lettuce in the refrigerator. Botrytis is mainly a disease of old, dying, or injured leaves and soft tissue such as flower petals. Infected areas first look soft, water-soaked, and discolored; the gray mold doesn't appear until decay is advanced. Botrytis spores need humidity levels close to 90 percent to germinate—conditions often found in a closed greenhouse on a cloudy day in winter. Botrytis usually attacks lettuce after it has passed its prime. To keep it from getting a foothold, make small plantings every two weeks so you can use the heads as soon as they mature. Improve air circulation by spacing plants so they won't touch at maturity or gradually thin them by harvesting alternate plants before they crowd each other. Vent the greenhouse on warm days, and run a fan to keep the air moving. Clean up dead leaves and fading flowers to help keep spore counts down. Don't splash water on the leaves.

Wilting Tomatoes

Q. I believe my greenhouse tomato plants have bacterial wilt. How can I control it?

A. To eliminate bacterial wilt (*Pseudomonas solanacearum*) from your greenhouse, remove all the soil and heat it to 120° to 125°F for ten minutes. That's a big job! An easier method is to compost the infested soil in a hot compost pile, which creates fresh, uncontaminated soil. An even easier method is to just replace the soil with new, clean soil. Clean all benches, growing beds, and pots with a mild bleach solution. The first symptoms of bacterial wilt are slight yellowing of the lower leaves or wilting of the younger leaves. If you pull a plant from the soil and cut open a root, it will be brown just inside the stem and look water-soaked.

Figs Indoors and Out

Q. I plan to grow a fig tree in a container outdoors during the summer and bring it into my greenhouse each winter. Do you think the tree will continue to ripen its fruit?

A. As long as it is given adequate drainage, a fig tree will do quite well in a container. Bringing it indoors in the fall should extend the ripening period. The main criterion for growing sweet figs in a greenhouse is lots of direct sunlight. In fact, depending on the variety, you may get a bonus second crop in early spring.

FIVE

Keeping the Garden Healthy

Chapter 19

Protecting
Your Garden

Cautions on Chemicals

The Wrong "Organic"

Q. I've seen the following chemicals referred to as "organic" pesticides: carbaryl, diazinon, and malathion. Can I use these and still sell my produce as organically grown?

A. No! The word organic has more than one meaning. Organic gardening is based on working with nature, returning *organic* (from *living*) materials to the land, and enriching the organisms in the soil. Chemical fertilizers and pesticides only disrupt nature's cycles. The highly toxic pesticides you named are part of a branch of chemistry related to hydrocarbon compounds (organic chemistry) and are considered "organic" only because they contain carbon compounds.

Cleaning Out Chemicals

Q. When I first started gardening, I used the chemicals many books suggested. Now that I'm an organic gardener, my problem is disposing of these chemicals I've been holding for years. What do you suggest?

A. One solution is to return them to the manufacturer. They can be sent through the mail, but use great care to ensure that any container is padded and wrapped securely, with its contents clearly marked on the package. If you choose to dispose of chemicals locally, certain pesticide containers can be buried, burned, or chemically degraded. Check with your extension agent, an Environmental Protection Agency representative, or a specialist at your state college of agriculture for accepted disposal methods. Products containing mercury, lead, cadmium, arsenic, or inorganic pesticides must be specially handled and are usually disposed of by encapsulation. However, even this sealing of the pesticide and container in sturdy, waterproof cartons does not always prevent leakage, as we are now finding. Never dispose of pesticides or their "empty" containers in an open environment such as a landfill or dumping ground, or by burning.

Captan Kills Inoculants

Q. What is captan? Does it interfere with nitrogen-fixing inoculants?

A. Captan, a complex fungicide, is a chlorinated hydrocarbon compound that belongs to the same group of compounds as DDT. It's used to coat seeds to prevent rotting before germination. Because captan is antifungal and antibacterial by nature, it will kill the beneficial bacterial inoculants that encourage nitrogen-fixing nodule growth in peas, beans, and other legumes. And fungicides can harm many of the other beneficial organisms in your soil. Ask for untreated seed when you order seeds—many companies provide them (see "Giving Treated Seeds the Treatment" on page 92).

Organic Alternatives

Right On Ryania

Q. **You've mentioned ryania as a control for codling moths. What is ryania, how does it work, and where can I get it?**

A. Ryania is a botanical insecticide made from the ground stems of *Ryania speciosa*, a shrub native to Trinidad. It contains the alkaloid ryanodine, a stomach and contact poison that kills by causing muscle paralysis. Ryania is especially useful for controlling codling moths and certain other orchard pests because, unlike rotenone and pyrethrum, it kills target insects without eliminating beneficials. It is also effective against European corn borers, leaf rollers and other caterpillars, citrus thrips, sawfly larvae, and some beetles. It is ineffective against sweet-potato weevils, cabbage maggots, Japanese beetle larvae, plum curculios, and spider mites. Because of its fairly low toxicity to humans, ryania is cleared for use within one day of harvest. It retains its potency for several years if stored cool and dry and is highly stable when exposed to light.

Keep Your Powder Dry

Q. **What is the storage life of powder made from dried pyrethrum flowers?**

A. If the powder is fresh when you get it and you store it properly, it should last for at least ten years with little decline in potency, according to Dr. Cecil Still, a pyrethrum researcher at Rutgers University. "Oxygen and light are the major causes of pyrethrin breakdown," says Still. "Store the powder in tightly closed, lightproof containers in a cool, dry place. I have ground pyrethrum flowers dating back to the 1930s that have been stored this way in my lab, and they still show full insecticidal activity."

Marigold Mystery

Q. **Are the new "scentless" varieties of marigold effective pest repellents?**

A. Although marigolds are said to repel many types of garden pests, only their effectiveness against nematodes has been proven in tests. The new "scentless" marigolds are a type of African marigold (*Tagetes erecta*), which is *not* effective for nematode control. The kind that *will* control nematodes are French marigolds (*Tagetes patula*). However, scent has nothing to do with how well marigolds control root-knot nematodes, the most destructive garden nematode. Scientists really aren't sure how marigolds repel root-knot nematodes. One theory is that the plant's roots exude substances that kill the pests. But another theory gaining wide acceptance says that as long as there are no host plants in the area (a not-too-common circumstance, since nematodes will feed on almost any vegetable, weed, or grass), the nematodes eventually die. The French marigolds do not serve as a host. To control root-knot nematodes in your garden, plant the entire infested area with French marigolds for a full season. Spot plantings are not effective against them, although a heavy interplanting (four or five marigolds around one tomato plant) may provide some protection. Researchers at the University of Georgia found that the French marigold variety 'Tangerine' gave the best control, while 'Goldie', 'Petite Gold', and 'Petite Harmony' also showed good repellent qualities.

The Rundown on Rotenone

Q. Is it safe to spray rotenone in my garden?

A. Rotenone is a plant-derived insecticide that is considered organic because it is made from the roots of tropical plants, particularly derris. It poisons many kinds of insects and will suffocate fish, but it has proven to be harmless to warm-blooded animals. Rotenone has little residual effect, but its active period is rather short. When buying rotenone, read the labels carefully to be sure it hasn't been fortified with chemical toxins. Because rotenone is lethal to beneficial insects like bees, use it only as a last resort. A heavy dusting of rotenone will severely upset the natural insect balance of your garden. If you use it once, you may have to use it again that year, since the insect populations will be out of balance. If you must use rotenone, we recommend using the kind you can mix with water. The water aerosol seems to settle more quickly than the dry dust, and it sticks better. Wear a protective face mask to avoid inhaling the spray. Although the label warns against using rotenone within one day of harvest, two Canadian researchers found that residues are still present after a week. To avoid eating traces, pick a week's worth of vegetables before you spray. When you start picking again, wash everything carefully. If you spray your beans for beetles, remember that lettuce in an adjacent bed will catch some of the rotenone. And never spray near a body of water, since you kill the fish in it.

Giving Your Garden the Nicotine Habit

Q. What are the advantages and disadvantages of using tobacco dust as an insecticide?

A. Nicotine, the active ingredient in tobacco dust, is by far the most toxic of the botanical insecticides. Acting as a contact and stomach poison, it kills a very wide range of pests. Gardeners have used tobacco dust or an extract made by soaking tobacco in water mainly against piercing/sucking insects such as aphids, leafhoppers, and true bugs. The dust is effective against hard-to-combat ground-dwelling pests such as root aphids. It has also been used as a dog, cat, rabbit, and insect repellent. Tobacco dust is indiscriminate, killing beneficial insects and earthworms as well as pests. But the very high toxicity of nicotine to humans is its chief disadvantage. Smoking tobacco contains about 3 percent nicotine, and some samples of tobacco dust have been found to contain ½ percent—enough to be concerned about. But perhaps because of the casual way in which smoking tobacco is handled, people don't treat the dust with the respect it deserves, according to Bill Wolf of the Necessary Trading Company. "They dust it liberally around and inhale it," he says. The fine dust is very irritating to mucous membranes and eyes, and nicotine can be absorbed this way. If you use it, wear protective clothing and a mask. If applied heavily, tobacco dust can burn small seedlings and new leaves. It can also carry tobacco mosaic virus (TMV), a serious disease of tomatoes and other vegetables. Once introduced, TMV can survive in weeds and be carried back to crops by aphids and other insects.

Bee Wary

Q. Will the use of an organic insecticide (such as diatomaceous earth or rotenone) on my vegetables and fruits hamper pollination by bees?

A. It depends on the insecticide and how it's applied. Diatomaceous earth is lethal to bees—its sharp crystals pierce their bodies, causing them to dehydrate and die. If you must use an insecticide while bees are pollinating, bee specialist Dr. Philip Torchio of the U.S. Department of Agriculture recommends pyrethrum rather than rotenone. Even though it's more toxic to bees, pyrethrum breaks down faster—within six hours if the temperature is 55°F or higher. As a general rule, don't spray anything on your plants or trees while they are in flower. If you must spray, use a liquid formulation of pyrethrum or ryania—another botanical insecticide that is only slightly toxic to bees and other beneficials. *Bacillus thuringiensis* (Bt) is also safe, since it affects only caterpillars. Spray at dusk, when bees are least active. If the weather forecast predicts a heavy dew, don't use pyrethrum—it won't break down before the bees begin feeding in the morning.

All That Glitters

Q. Is it true that aluminum foil is effective for insect control and as a mulching material? I can't understand how it would be beneficial.

A. It seems unlikely, but it is true. This unusual mulching material serves three purposes—it retains moisture in the ground, reflects an extra dose of light onto the plants, and repels aphids. When aphids take off to fly, they head directly for the sky, and when they decide to land again, they reverse their direction. The reflection of the sky on the aluminum foil probably confuses the insects so that they are constantly reversing their direction. That means they never can land on plants. Tests also show that aluminum foil is most effective for only the first foot or so of space above the ground. Therefore, controlling pests on tall plants, like roses, may require structures to hold the foil aboveground. You can use all types of aluminum foil for insect control, but a special paper-backed kind, sold in many lumberyards as insulation material, will do the best job of mulching directly on the ground.

Bring Back Bt

Q. I used *Bacillus thuringiensis* (Bt) last year. Will these bacteria, like milky spore, overwinter and be effective this year?

A. No. Unlike milky spore disease (*B. popillae*), Bt doesn't reproduce or overwinter. Because it breaks down in sunlight, it remains viable for only seven days after application. You'll need to reapply as usual this year. If you stored your Bt in its container in a cool, dark place, it will remain stable for at least three years in wettable powder form and for one year in the liquid formulation. You can use it indefinitely when stored at 40° to 50°F. Don't keep Bt in a hot garage—at temperatures above 90°F, its shelf life drops to one month.

Once and Done

Q. **Every summer we've had the same problem—Japanese beetles. Last year we treated our lawn with milky spore disease. Must we apply more powder this spring?**

A. One application of milky spore normally is all you need. Although it may take 3 years for the disease spores to spread throughout your lawn, once established, the disease remains effective for 15 to 20 years because the spores stay in the soil. The disease is harmless to humans, warm-blooded animals, plants, and beneficial insects. Inoculating sod with milky spore disease halts the development of the overwintering Japanese beetle grub into an adult bug. As each infected grub dies off, its normally clear blood becomes creamy white with disease spores, which multiply and spread in the soil. That leads to a considerable reduction in the number of beetles emerging from the pupal stage—and fewer eggs laid, of course. This spring, you might try to convince your neighbors to treat their lawns with the disease, too. Community-wide application of milky spore is definitely the best defense against Japanese beetles.

Bring On the Beneficials

Bug Lights vs. Beneficials

Q. **What is your opinion of bug-light traps? Don't they kill beneficial insects as well as pests?**

A. These traps primarily attract moths and butterflies. While some of these moths are the adults of common garden pests such as cutworms, the traps won't provide effective control of garden insects. That's because many of them will have already laid their eggs, says Dr. Michael Peters, who has studied ultraviolet (UV) light traps for several years at the University of Massachusetts. Most beneficial insects like ladybugs and parasitic wasps are active only during the day, so black light traps don't affect them. Hover and tachinid flies aren't attracted to a light trap, either, says Peters: "For the most part, it's not knocking out a lot of beneficials." He adds that some helpful insects, such as the trichogramma wasp, are simply too small to be electrocuted by a bug zapper because of the spacing of the wires. On the other hand, Peters has observed significant numbers of a parasitic wasp called the ichneumon wasp, as well as the predatory rove beetle, that have been caught by UV traps. UV bug-killers do catch a fair number of night-flying mosquitoes, but many species of mosquitoes are day-fliers and aren't drawn to black light.

Ladybug:
Larva (top),
Adult (bottom left),
Eggs (bottom right)

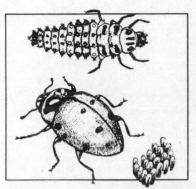

Looking for Ladybugs

Q. What do the eggs, larvae, and adults of the ladybug look like? We handpick a lot of bugs and don't want to destroy this beneficial insect.

A. The ladybug usually lays its bright orange eggs in vertical clusters on leaves and stems. They're so similar to the eggs of the Colorado potato beetle and the Mexican bean beetle that you should wait until the larvae start emerging before you squash any eggs. Fully mature ladybug larvae are ½ inch long and black with orange spots. The ¼-inch-long, rounded adult beetle can be orange, red, pink, yellow, or even gray and may have black spots or be solidly colored. Don't confuse the adult ladybug with the Mexican bean beetle, which is the same size but has a golden lustre and brown spots.

Heave-Ho for Hoppers

Q. Will *Nosema lucustae* work against grasshoppers in my backyard?

A. If you are looking for a quick solution, *N. lucustae* will disappoint you. On the average, this protozoan disease of grasshoppers and Mormon crickets takes 21 days to establish itself in the guts of grasshoppers. On less than an acre of land, grasshoppers spread faster than the spores can kill them—and you'll feel as if you've wasted your money. If you want to use *N. lucustae*, the best bet is to get together with your neighbors and buy enough of the product for a large area. To control grasshoppers before they have the chance to become a problem, till the soil right after harvest. The most harmful grasshopper species spend six to eight months of the year as eggs in the surface layer of the soil. Tilling makes the soil unattractive to egg-laying females and helps destroy the eggs already laid.

Praying Mantis

Mantis Methods

Q. We would like to get praying mantids, but last year we had terrible luck. Is it possible to raise mantids here in Indiana? How should we start them?

A. Praying mantids can be raised anywhere in the United States if there is a sufficient supply of insects for food. The common large Chinese mantis is winter-hardy, and mantis eggs can survive freezing temperatures. Remember that birds and ants are natural enemies of the mantis and will take their toll of egg cases and newly hatched mantids. Keep egg cases collected in the fall or purchased commercially in cold storage through the winter for protection. One method to ensure undisturbed spring hatching is to suspend an egg case in a large jar. (Use a thin needle to attach a thread through the outer top edge of each case.) Secure the thread to the jar top, allowing the case to hang freely, and cover the jar with net or nylon. Place the jar in a warm spot, out of direct sun, and the mantids can hatch undisturbed. Once the shells of the baby mantids dry and harden, they are safe from ants, and you can release the hatchlings into your garden. It might take a few years to build up a concentration of praying mantids, especially if neighbors spray chemicals near your property. Collect cases each fall and release more mantids each spring to replenish your supply.

Mighty Mites

Q. **Will predatory mites control spider mites on vegetables and ornamentals in my San Diego, California, garden? If so, when should I order them, and how many should I release?**

A. A carefully timed release of predatory mites will provide control against spider mites, according to Jeff Hadden of Natural Pest Controls, Orangevale, California. As a rule of thumb, Hadden advises ordering predators six weeks before the date on which you first noticed pest infestation the previous year. Begin looking for mites with a hand lens early in the year. Look for them on the undersides of leaves of susceptible plants. If you wait to order predators until you see mite damage such as webbing, stippling, and graying or yellowing of the foliage, the pest population may be too large for the predators to control in time to save the plant. Weekly soap sprays will help keep pest numbers low until help arrives, but don't spray after you release the predatory mites—the soap will kill them as well as the pests. The best way to deal with plants that are heavily infested each year is to replace them with more tolerant species, says Hadden. Predatory mites are usually released at the rate of 25 mites per 2 feet of plant height. Of the several species available, the best for your situation is probably *Metaseiulus occidentalis*, sold as PMO, advises Hadden. PMO is the most general predator and is very tolerant of heat and dryness. If cover and prey are available, PMO should overwinter in your climate. To help PMO overwinter in the vegetable garden, plant a cover crop such as crimson clover, fava beans, or hairy vetch.

Trichogramma Turnaround

Q. **Last year I purchased some trichogramma wasps and released them into my garden. They did an excellent job of protecting my crops from cabbage loopers. Are these wasps hardy enough to survive the winter, or should I purchase another supply this year?**

A. To be safe, make a fresh release of the parasitic wasps each year. Although some trichogramma wasp species are capable of overwintering as eggs in their host's eggs, those effective against cabbage loopers are not. Cabbage loopers overwinter as pupae on leaves or on the soil rather than as eggs. It is possible that your trichogramma wasps could locate alternative hosts to parasitize and overwinter in, especially if you live near a wild area, but you shouldn't rely on that. Instead, make a new wasp release this coming summer.

Toad Tactics

Q. What can I do to entice the toads to stay in my garden? Since I don't have access to marshy areas, they're hard to come by.

A. Once you've acquired a few toads, cater to them by providing them with some moist, dark shelters located throughout the garden. Toads need to be kept moist because they're amphibians. During the day, they usually seek out cool hiding places beneath loose boards, under garden mulch, or in the shade of low-growing shrubbery. At night, they brave the darkness in search of cutworms, potato beetles, chinch bugs, ants, slugs, and other pests. Keep your toads happy by wetting down the shrubbery on a hot day. Make a little niche for them by cutting a small entrance in a box or by chipping out a small opening in the side of a flowerpot and burying it a few inches into the ground. Place the pot in the shade of a tree or shrub for added comfort. Since toads must have access to water, set out a shallow pan in the garden or in the box or flowerpot. The toad drinks through its skin, so the pan should be large enough for him to sit in. Look for a new supply of toads after a good rainfall, when they'll be hopping across roads, lawns, and pastures. It's worth the search when you consider that just one toad can eat up to 15,000 insects during one active season. If the weather is moderate, toads will watch out for your garden from March to mid-November.

Chapter 20

A Rogues' Gallery of Garden Pests

About Insects and Diseases

Tracking the Enemy

Q. **I always make a valiant effort to identify insects and diseases with the help of reference books and fellow gardeners. However, there are times when I just can't seem to pinpoint the culprits that are harming my plants. What can I do when I'm left in the dark?**

A. When all else fails, contact your local county agricultural agent or the extension specialists who are located at your state's land-grant universities and colleges. If you want to send them specimens through the mail, follow this procedure: Wrap insect pests, including immature stages if possible, carefully in soft tissue paper. Preserve soft-bodied insects in a 70 percent alcohol solution. Package all insects in a small can, plastic box, or other strong container, and send them by first-class mail to the extension entomologist. Plant disease specimens should include entire plants, when possible, with the roots wrapped in moist soil, peat moss, or sawdust. Send these to the extension plant pathologist. Since it's not always easy for the specialist to identify problems, include a letter describing the crop, area, and pest- or disease-control history, as well as the location and type of damage.

Sunning Fungi

Q. I live in Miami, Florida. Because of the hot, humid climate here, I have found it extremely difficult to grow tomatoes and cucurbits. But it is an ideal climate for fungi. How can I grow these vegetables successfully without resorting to using a fungicide?

A. Growing tomatoes, squash, and cucumbers organically in South Florida depends primarily on meeting two conditions: The plants need full sunlight, and they require extremely fertile soil. Full sun is no problem if vegetables are field-grown or if your garden is not shaded. For shaded areas, we recommend "pot-planting." One Florida gardener has had great success using a few old plastic wastepaper baskets as containers. She fills the baskets with perlite and potting soil, then puts two or three plants in each. She reports that three wastepaper baskets supply her family with all the tomatoes and zucchini they can eat, with some to give away. She has no fungus problems.

Most organic gardeners in South Florida battle fungus with good soil. Compost, table scraps, and manure are all good for the garden. The plants that grow in many waterways and canals in Florida are a wonderful source of free enriching material. Seaweed, which is washed up on the beaches, is also a top-notch soil amendment. These plants concentrate nutrients and break down quickly in the garden. But be sure to wash salt from seaweed before using. Begin conditioning the soil in early summer, as soon as the previous year's garden is finished. Dig in table scraps, compost, waterweeds—whatever is available. Sheet-composting with any organic material helps keep heavy summer rains from washing away the nutrients you are adding to your garden. Although you can see improvement in your garden after a single summer of heavy mulching and fertilizing, it takes about three years to get the soil rich enough so diseases just can't keep up with the plants' growth. Don't try to get an early start by planting before the middle of September. It takes cool nights to set fruit, and during winter months the humidity isn't much of a problem.

Wilted Tomato Woes

Q. If my tomatoes were infected with fusarium wilt one year, will it affect anything else planted the next year in that spot?

A. No. Although *Fusarium oxysporum* affects certain other crops, including spinach, peas, radishes, cabbages, watermelons, and cantaloupes, and flowers such as dahlias and carnations, each is attacked by a different strain. (*F. oxysporum lycopersici,* for example, is specific to tomatoes.) To control fusarium, rotate susceptible plants on a three- to four-year schedule and grow resistant varieties.

Insects' Winter Wonders

Q. How do most insects manage to live through the winter in cold or freezing sections of the country?

A. There are few bugs that can migrate to warmer climates, so these cold-blooded creatures are forced to adjust to freezing temperatures. Chinch bugs are lucky; they produce an antifreeze chemical that keeps their insides from turning to ice. Others freeze without injury and await the spring thaw. Many species overwinter as eggs. The cecropia silkworm moth actually spins an insulating cocoon that traps air between double walls for maximum insulation. Some insects burrow their way down below the frost line and sleep away the winter.

Insects sense the approach of winter with a built-in clock that is geared to seasonal variations in darkness and light. This unique characteristic is known as photoperiodism. It serves as a vital early-warning system. For example, long before winter, the female grasshopper buries a mass of eggs wrapped in a gluelike jacket. Nature does not allow warmth to hatch the eggs unless they have been frozen *first*. In this way, it is impossible for a late warm spell in autumn to bring out baby grasshoppers to starve. In autumn, winged ants and ladybugs in California fly up into the mountains to spend the winter huddled by the tens of thousands. Many mosquitoes pass the winter as larvae frozen in ponds. When spring comes, they thaw out, metamorphose, and buzz off. Probably the most coddled of all wintering bugs is the corn-root aphid. Its eggs are carefully collected by a species of ant and carried to nests below the frost line. In spring the eggs are taken to the roots of early weeds to hatch.

Insects A to W

Aphid

Action against Aphids

Q. **Last year we had terrible trouble with aphids and ants in our garden. They were on everything, and my tomato plants developed mosaic from them. What can I do to keep this from happening again this year?**

A. To control aphids, you must attack them on two fronts. First, develop a very fertile soil to produce healthy plants, which aphids have shown a tendency to dislike; and second, to battle peak populations, use one or more of the many controls available. Aphids, or plant lice, are small, soft-bodied insects distinguished by their pearlike shape, long antennae, and twin, tubelike appendages that project from the back end. There are dozens of species, many named for their favorite food preference. Aphids suck plant sap and cause withering of foliage and a loss of plant vigor. Excess sugars and sap are emitted from the insect's anus and are known as honeydew. Ants feed on honeydew and will tend aphids as men do cows. The ants distribute the aphids from plant to plant, quickly spreading any plant diseases with the aphids. In fall, ants carry aphid eggs into their nests to be carried back out in spring and set on plants, making control very difficult. There are two or three generations of aphids a season.

The simplest remedy is to gently rub leaves, crushing the aphids. Aphids can also be washed from plants with a forceful spray of water. A stronger control is an insecticidal soap spray (see "Soap Your Plants" on page 261). In some cases, aphids can be controlled by growing nasturtiums as a trap crop. Wait until the nasturtiums are infested, then pull them from the garden and destroy them, aphids and all. Repellent companion plants include garlic, chives and other alliums, coriander, anise, and petunias. The best-known predator of aphids is the ladybug. Other predators include soldier bugs, damsel bugs, big-eyed bugs, pirate bugs, spiders, assassin bugs, syrphid flies, and lacewings. Ladybugs and lacewings are commercially available. Since ants are often the major cause of aphid problems, you should also try to control them. Keep them away from your plants with barrier strips of small amounts of bonemeal or powdered charcoal. You can also wrap a band of cotton smeared with Tanglefoot or Stikem around the base of larger plants to catch the ants. Good garden sanitation and quick removal and composting of plant debris will help cut down both aphid and ant populations.

Rhubarb Remedy

Q. **A few years ago, I took the advice of a friend and boiled some rhubarb leaves, saving the reddish-green water. Then I used the solution as a spray to control aphids. Surprisingly, it worked. But why?**

A. Oxalic acid kills aphids. Found in spinach, rhubarb, and many leafy vegetables, oxalic acid is poisonous in high concentrations. Although rhubarb contains negligible amounts of oxalates in its edible stems, its leaves are rich in the soluble substances and should not be eaten. The oxalates in the leaves make aphids sick, too. You can mix a simple rhubarb spray by cutting up 1 pound of leaves and boiling them in 1 quart of water for 30 minutes. Then strain and bottle the liquid. To help it stick to leaves, squeeze in a dab of liquid soap when the solution has cooled.

Blister Beetle Blues

Q. **My tomatoes and potatoes have what I think are blister beetles. They resemble potato beetles except they are long and slender, and they make my hands burn when I try to handpick them. How can I get rid of them?**

A. You are right. They are blister beetles. Because these insects contain an oil that will blister your skin if you crush them between your fingers, be sure to wear gloves when handpicking. The beetles are ½ to 1 inch long and about four times as long as they are wide. They are black or grayish and may have yellow or gray stripes or a gray margin. The larvae overwinter in the soil. In the spring they burrow through the soil until they find a grasshopper egg mass to feed on. Although the larvae can be considered beneficial, even where there are a lot of them, they don't consume more than 25 percent of the grasshopper eggs. The best control, short of draping your plants with a protective cover such as spunbonded row cover or screen, is to handpick the adult blister beetles.

Cutworm Capers

Q. I have been mulching my garden with grass clippings. Although they do a good job of keeping moisture in, the clippings make my cutworm problems worse. Should I give up mulching?

A. No. Just change your mulch. A clean garden is your best defense against cutworms. Grass clippings, other organic mulches, and weeds provide them with food, shelter, and egg-laying sites. Switch to black plastic, the only mulch that doesn't encourage cutworms. Black plastic doesn't shelter cutworms, and it prevents young cutworms from entering the soil. Save your organic mulches for the compost pile.

Cutworms, the larvae of many species of moths, cut off young plants at ground level. There are also climbing cutworms that eat the leaves, buds, and fruits of vegetables, trees, and vines. Cutworms can be gray, brown, black, or mottled and are about 1½ inches long. They are active at night and hide in garden litter by day. Cultivate in the early spring to disturb and kill larvae that have overwintered in the soil and to remove weed seedlings before hatching larvae can eat them. Protect individual plants by putting a 3-inch collar made of stiff paper or plastic around them. Push the collar an inch or so into the ground. For serious infestations, you may want to try the nematode *Neoaplectana carpocapsae*, a microscopic wormlike organism that attacks cutworms and other insects that live in the soil. It won't harm beneficials or earthworms. Apply in the early spring around the base of your plants. You should see an effect within five days, but allow two months for maximum control. The nematodes will overwinter as far north as Minnesota.

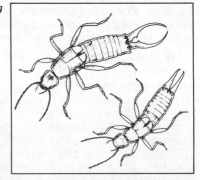

Earwig

Earwig: The Garden Roach

Q. In the middle of the night, something gnaws my seedlings down to stumps just as fast as I can set them out. What am I up against?

A. Probably earwigs. At night, earwigs come out, often in hundreds, and skeletonize plants (rather than chewing neat holes). But the best time to stop them is in the daytime, when they hide in moist, dark places. They congregate under bark, stones, or mulch and between boards. You can control them by making traps that provide dark crevices and cracks. Rolled newspapers or bamboo tubes make effective traps. You can also use old garden hose sections or a piece of black plastic about 2 feet square and folded twice. Place these traps throughout the garden and in the yard beneath shrubbery, under groundcover plants, and against fences. Pick up the traps every day or two and knock out the insects into detergent and water or crush them. Most earwigs are beneficial because they feed on insect pests such as aphids, but a few species like the European earwig (*Forficula auricularia*) also feed on stems, foliage, and fruit. They're distinguished by a pair of sharp pincers at the tail end, and they look a lot like cockroaches—hence their nickname, "the garden roach."

Put Out the Fire Ants

Q. Fire ants are all over my Fairhope, Alabama, yard and garden. Can you help me?

A. Biologists at Florida State University recommend pouring 3 gallons of hot tap water on the ant mound to kill the colony. Eight of the 14 colonies they treated this way were completely wiped out. If you still see ants after a few days, repeat the treatment. Hot water is most effective when the ants are near the surface. Douse the mounds on a cool, sunny day after the sun has warmed it.

Another approach to fire-ant control was developed by the U.S. Department of Agriculture (USDA). Researchers isolated a growth hormone that prevents the larvae from developing into worker ants. With fewer and fewer workers to gather food and maintain the mound, the colony eventually dies of starvation. Stauffer Chemical Company produces and markets Pro-Drone, s synthetic version of the hormone. This product contains the synthetic hormone mixed with a bait of corn grits and soybean oil. This material breaks down quickly in the environment, and according to tests is harmless to mammals, fish, birds, and beneficial insects. It will remain active for months in the stomach of a fire ant. Check with your state department of agriculture and local garden stores for availability of Pro-Drone.

Hot Compost Kills Flies

Q. I find a lot of fly larvae in my compost pile. What can I do to get rid of them?

A. Your pile isn't heating up enough to kill the larvae. If you do not turn the contents frequently to aerate it, that may be your problem. Turn the pile every three to five days and it should stay hot. If you do turn the pile and it still doesn't heat up, your compost may not have enough nitrogen. Mix fresh manure or grass clippings into the heap, and it should heat up. If adding nitrogen doesn't work, the pile is probably too wet or too dry. A good compost heap is moist but not soaking wet. It should be as wet as a wrung-out sponge. To dry a waterlogged pile, turn it every day. When it dries enough, it will start heating if there is sufficient nitrogen. Cover the pile with discarded plastic bags to keep out rain.

Drat the Gnats

Q. I sterilize garden soil in my oven to use for potting soil, but I still have a problem with fungus gnats. Is there a remedy?

A. Fungus gnat adults, actually a type of fly, don't hurt plants. Their maggots, however, can damage roots. The maggots live in manure and decaying vegetable matter, so potting soil rich in humus can harbor them. Soil pasteurization (140° to 180°F for 30 minutes) should take care of the problem, except during the summer. Since the flies are only $\frac{1}{10}$ to inch long, they can easily slip through screens and poorly sealed areas. If you see fungus gnats on your houseplants, kill the maggots by letting the soil dry out as much as possible without harming the plants. In a severe infestation, the plants won't grow well and the leaves will turn yellow. Give the soil a good soaking with a rotenone or pyrethrum solution.

Hunting for Hornworms

Q. I'm surprised that I didn't see the tomato hornworms in my garden until they were 4 inches long, with cocoons on their backs! Can you tell me more about their life cycle?

A. You can spot the well-camouflaged caterpillars earlier by looking for dark-colored droppings on the foliage. Some gardeners have found that spraying the plants with water causes the worms to thrash around and give away their locations. Adult hormworms are large, fast-flying, mottled gray or brown moths with five orange spots along each side of the body. Their long, narrow forewings span 4 to 5 inches, and they have two dark, diagonal zigzag lines on each hind wing. Watch for them at dusk, when they hover near tubular flowers like hummingbirds. The female moths lay round, greenish-yellow eggs singly on the undersides of leaves. The eggs hatch within a week, and the larvae grow to their full size—3 to 4 inches—in about a month. The caterpillars then burrow 3 to 4 inches underground and spend the winter as pupae in hard, brown, 2-inch-long spindle-shaped cases. These cases have a distinctive handlelike proboscis curving from the front. You may notice them when you work the soil in fall or spring.

June Bug:
Grub (top),
Adult (bottom)

June Bug Jitters

Q. Are June bugs harmful? I understand milky spore disease infects June bug grubs and is a good method of control.

A. Full-grown June bug beetles can damage plants, including fruit trees and blackberries, by feeding on foliage and flowers. However, more damage is caused by grubs, the immature form of many common large beetles. Grubs harm corn by feeding on roots. They may also feed on the roots of bluegrass, timothy, and soybeans, as well as decaying vegetation. Milky spore disease is effective against 41 types of white grub, including those of the June bug.

Leaf-Cutter Lowdown

Q. **Leaf-cutter ants are a terrible problem here in Athens, Texas. Every year they strip the leaves from my peach and plum trees and ornamentals. What can I do?**

A. A single leaf-cutter ant nest can be anywhere from 10 square feet to ¼ acre and 15 feet below ground, housing hundreds of thousands of ants, according to Dr. James Robinson of Texas A&M University. It can have as many as 100 entrances. Because of the number of ants and the difficulty of access to their nests, these pests are hard to control. However, there are steps you can take to protect your trees: Wrap several layers of cheesecloth around the base of each tree trunk, cover with paper, and coat with Tanglefoot; replace the paper when it is covered with ants. Dr. William Whitcomb of the University of Florida has studied leaf-cutter ants in South America, where in some places they are an area's worst agricultural pest. In almost every backyard he visited, trees were protected by shallow concrete "moats," 4 to 6 inches wide, filled with water. You could try this, or a trench lined with plastic, if you have only a few trees. In the United States, leaf-cutter ants live only in Louisiana, Texas, and Arizona.

Rooting Out Root Weevils

Q. **Strawberry root weevils are eating leaf margins of my rhododendrons and azaleas. My neighbor told me that they can kill the plants and that the only solution is to spray with Orthene. Is there an organic solution?**

A. Yes. Adult root weevils—including the strawberry root weevil and black vine weevil—are brown to black, ¼- to ½-inch-long, flightless beetles. They crawl up plant stems at night and feed by notching the leaf margins. This is seldom fatal, according to Dr. Arthur Antonelli, entomologist at Washington State University. However, the larvae—white grubs that hatch in summer—can kill plants by eating the roots and girdling the crowns. To deter weevils, coat stems with a band of Tanglefoot or other sticky material. Antonelli recommends applying a strip of plastic first to avoid injuring the stem. Make sure that overhanging branches or walls don't serve as bridges for the pests. Introducing insect-eating nematodes is even more effective. The nematodes seek out and kill larvae in the soil. Researchers recorded 64.6 percent larval mortality within ten days of application on a California farm.

Slowing Sow Bugs

Q. **Sow bugs are taking over my garden. How can I keep them under control?**

A. Sanitation is the first step. Sow bugs have seven pairs of legs on gray, oval-shaped, segmented bodies about ½ inch long. They prefer damp, cool hiding places. You can find them under boards and stones and in mulch and manure. Any cool crevice can harbor a sow bug. As much as possible, clear your garden area of any materials that will appeal to the bugs. The drier the area, the better. Since the bugs favor young, succulent growth, seedlings need protection. One Southern California gardener has had success protecting his seedlings with paper collars. He cuts off the points of cone-shaped paper cups and slips a cup over each plant. You can also trap the bugs. Put rolled-up corrugated cardboard or newspaper in your garden. At night, the bugs will crawl into these "logs" for shelter. In the morning, collect and dispose of the bugs. But since an adult female hatches 25 to 75 young in a brood (she retains the eggs in a body pouch until after they hatch), you'll have to trap quite a few to make a dent in the population.

Mist Those Spider Mites

Q. **My beans and melons were infested with spider mites last summer. What can I do this year?**

A. Spider mites can be a big problem in hot, dry weather. The reddish-brown, yellow, or green bugs (the color seems to vary with the plant they are eating) are so tiny they are almost invisible without a magnifying glass. Look for pale splotches on the leaves, then check for mites with a hand lens. In a bad infestation, the whole leaf may turn a light color, sometimes pockmarked with reddish-brown patches, before dying. Spider mites don't like high humidity and moist soil, so keep your plants well mulched and mist regularly to maintain the humidity. Bursts of water will also break apart the webs of established mite colonies. If your plants are badly infected, you should be able to control the mites with an insecticidal soap spray. The trick to using the spray is to realize that only the adult mites, not the eggs, are killed by the insecticidal soap. So you must spray at least three times at one-week intervals to kill the mites as they emerge from the eggs.

Stalking Stalk Borers

Q. A 1-inch-long, grayish worm tunnels into the stems of my
tomatoes, zinnias, and marigolds, causing them to wilt. I split
the stems and remove the worms, but this is very hard on the
plants. What is this pest, and is there a better way to control it?

A. The common stalk borer is the larva of a small, grayish-
brown moth. It often becomes a pest in gardens near weedy fields
and hedgerows where the female moths lay their eggs in late summer. The young borers are brown-and-white striped with a grayish-
purple band around the body. They become a dirty gray as they
grow. Borers attack many kinds of plants and are restless feeders,
moving from one plant to another. For control, keep weedy areas
near the garden mowed to discourage egg laying, and turn under,
compost, or burn all garden residues that might harbor eggs. As an
alternative to splitting stems, try injecting them with a *Bacillus
thuringiensis* (Bt) solution. If you cut back injured stems on zinnias and marigolds, they'll produce sideshoots that will flower later
in the summer.

Tripping Up Thrips

Q. Thrips have attacked my roses. What can I do?

A. The tiny, brownish-yellow, winged adult thrips are hard to
spot (they're only 1/20 inch long), but their damage to rose blossoms
is extensive. They are especially attracted to white flowers. The
damaged rosebuds either turn brown or open to reveal distorted,
brown petals. Thrips often lurk in the center of the open flower and
feed on the pollen. Thrips are difficult to control. Keeping the weeds
down and removing spent flowers will help reduce breeding
grounds. One clover head can support 30 to 40 flower thrips, and a
rose may contain as many as 200 thrips. Aluminum foil is one of
the few materials that repels thrips because the reflected light
confuses the pests. Protect prized roses with collars of aluminum
foil. You can also use the foil as a mulch. According to USDA researchers, the mulch should extend 1½ to 2 feet beyond the outer
edge of the plant. The foil mulch is not effective above 2 to 3 feet, so
for taller plants you may want to hang or stake aluminum-covered
boards. Researchers have found diatomaceous earth effective—
especially if it's mixed with pyrethrum or rotenone—against
greenhouse thrips on vegetables. It may also control the thrips on
your roses. Sprinkle it on the blossoms and on the ground to control

pupating thrips. The sharp particles will pierce the insects, dehydrating and killing them. Be careful not to inhale the dust, especially if it includes a botanical insecticide.

Pest Nests

Q. Last year we were plagued with wasps and yellow jackets in our yard. Can you tell me how to get rid of them?

A. Wasps and yellow jackets prey on garden pests. Unless they are a serious nuisance or a danger to hypersensitive people, you should probably leave them alone. To keep both types of wasps away from the house, make sure no food is left close by for them to eat. Cover trash cans with tight-fitting lids and clean up ripe fruit around the yard. Red or yellow clothing and some perfumes may attract the insects to you. Destroying nests hanging from trees or buildings can be dangerous. Wasps have barbless stingers, which permit them to repeatedly sting their victims. If you must approach a nest, warns Dr. Clarence Collison of Penn State University, do so only after dark and wear protective clothing. Spray aerial nests with a liquid or aerosol formulation of pyrethrum, rotenone, or a ready-mixed combination of the two.

Nests in the ground are slightly easier to deal with. Wear protective clothing and apply pyrethrum, rotenone, or both into the hole. Begin watching for wasp nests in spring. Because of their smaller size, the earlier you spot the nests, the less hazardous their removal will be. Wasps and yellow jackets die with the onset of winter, with the exception of the fertilized queens, which overwinter in bark and leaf litter. Each one killed eliminates one potential nest. You can lure the queens to a simple trap made from a mixture of sugar and soapy water in a pan. Commercial wasp traps are also available.

Control for Critters

Deterring Deer

Q. We had a terrible problem this year with deer eating fruit off our trees. Fencing is too expensive. Is there some way to repel them?

A. The only foolproof way to keep deer out of an orchard is fencing, but here are four repellents that in some situations have worked fairly well:

• Hang bars of deodorant soap in your trees; leave the wrappers on so they'll last longer.

• Mix 1 to 1½ dozen eggs in 5 gallons of water and spray on your trees. Reapply after each heavy rainfall.

• Hang a clump of human hair in a stocking from each tree. Cover with a plastic bag or weatherproof container, leaving an opening at the bottom. The hair should be replaced several times a season.

• Spray a solution of Tabasco sauce (2 tablespoons per gallon) on the foliage. Repeat every two weeks.

Shocking Treatment for 'Coons and 'Chucks

Q. **There is nothing more discouraging than finding that raccoons and groundhogs have invaded my gardens again. Is there any way to keep them out for good?**

A. Since both of these animals can either climb or burrow their way around obstacles and into your garden, take firm action by installing an electric fence. It may sound cruel, but it's the most effective way to stave off animal intruders. A little shock is just enough to frighten them without causing any physical harm. Some gardeners get by with one wire about 6 inches off the ground, but two wires, the second another 6 inches above the first, are better. Use steel or fiberglass posts if possible, since raccoons have been known to climb wooden posts over the fence to avoid coming in contact with the wire. Gardeners often assume that groundhogs (also called woodchucks) will burrow under a wire, but these rodents seldom do unless their dens are very close to the garden. Most of their digging is confined to den sites, and when they journey for a meal to your garden, they stay aboveground.

Gopher Grabber

Q. **How does the gopher plant keep away gophers and moles?**

A. Gopher plant or spurge (*Euphorbia lathyris*) has a poisonous milky juice in the roots and leaves. Gophers, notorious for eating anything, eat the roots and sicken or die. For best control, the plants, which grow to 4 feet tall, should be transplanted next to the gopher hole, spaced every 5 feet as a barrier. The gopher plant is an annual, but it seeds itself. If you save the seeds, sow in the fall for spring germination.

Serpentine Solution

Q. **Last spring, we found that snakes liked to crawl into the piles of mulch we raked to the side of the garden until the ground warmed. It made the material a problem to handle. Is there an organic way to repel snakes?**

A. Because snakes feast on garden problems like caterpillars and other slow-moving insects, you should not eliminate them completely from your area. We usually suggest removing all cover and hiding places and keeping grass and weedy areas trimmed. But snakes are known to enjoy the warmth of a compost pile or shelter of mulch. We're told snakes will hesitate to cross an area covered with ground limestone and that onions will drive them away temporarily. You could also whack the tip of the pile with a board or rake, chasing the snakes out before you handle the mulch materials.

Chapter 21

Rooting Out Weeds

Weed Worries

Chef's Best Weed Recipes

Q. My garden soil is very rich, so I use it in combination with other materials as a potting soil. How can I pasteurize my potting soil to get rid of weed and grass seeds?

A. There are two easy methods: Cook it in an oven or in a pressure cooker. For the oven method, fill a baking pan with 3 or 4 inches of soil and put a meat thermometer in the middle. Dampen the soil and put it in a preheated oven for 30 minutes, or until the temperature reaches 180°F. Don't let it get much hotter, or you will begin to destroy soil structure, organic matter, and all organisms in the soil. To prepare soil in a pressure cooker, cook for 20 or 30 minutes at 5 pounds pressure. Most weed seeds can be killed by a temperature of 175°F.

No to Herbicides

Q. **I have crabgrass in my gladiolus patch. What herbicide do you consider safe? I can keep the weeds under control by hoeing until the glads get large, but then it is hard to work close to the plants.**

A. The only two herbicides we can recommend are cultivation and mulching. Chemical herbicides have a detrimental effect on soil life and insect populations. By decreasing the number of soil microorganisms and insects, the chances for an insect imbalance or plant disease are greatly increased. You would be much better off to continue to hoe when the plants are young and then mulch heavily to restrict weed growth. If you don't have enough organic material for mulching, think about using something like newspapers to cover the ground. If your problem is severe, you may want to try a black plastic mulch with a small cut in it for each plant. Whatever you use as a mulch, don't use an herbicide. Any chemical combination designed to kill off plants will have an adverse effect on the biological systems of your garden.

Weedy Wildflowers

Q. **We tried to grow a wildflower meadow on the five acres in front of our home, but so many weeds grew up that they hid the wildflowers. Is there a way of controlling weeds in meadows without using herbicides?**

A. The best way to manage weeds in meadows is to try to keep them from sprouting in the first place. Some meadow gardeners have found that the most successful way to do this is to avoid disturbing the soil when preparing a seedbed for wildflowers. Tilling or digging turns up thousands of dormant weed seeds, which sprout faster than the wildflowers and choke them out. Instead, kill existing vegetation by covering the ground with black plastic for a month or more before planting. After you remove the plastic, mix wildflower seeds with damp sand, sawdust, or soil to get even distribution, then broadcast them on the bare ground and cover lightly with straw. Water regularly for good germination and growth. Since weeds are quick to colonize bare ground, some are bound to appear. Pull them before they go to seed. Adding a low-growing, fast-germinating bunch grass to the seed mix may help suppress weeds and hold the soil while the slower wildflowers become established. Suitable bunch grasses are sheep fescue, chewings fescue, red fescue, and annual rye. Using this method, a large site would have to be converted to meadow bit by bit over several years.

Variations on this method were successfully used to establish test plots for an ongoing observation of commercial wildflower seed mixes at the Rodale Research Center. The 4-by-20-foot plots were prepared either by tilling repeatedly, planting and turning under cover crops, covering the ground with black plastic, or covering with straw for the entire season before sowing the wildflowers. All plots were tilled shallowly before planting in spring. During the next summer, the plots that had been covered with plastic or straw had fewer weeds than the other plots. Eileen Weinsteiger, the gardener in charge of the project, thinks she could have obtained equally good results covering the plots for a much shorter time.

Weeds in Review

Besting Bermuda Grass

Q. How do I rid ¼ acre of Bermuda grass? I plan to start a strawberry patch and I want to do it organically.

A. Bermuda grass is an aggressive weed and one of the most difficult to control because it spreads by underground stems (rhizomes). Persistence is the key. Dr. James Miller, weed scientist at the University of Georgia, says that if you cultivate the infested area frequently for a full season, you should be able to reduce the amount of Bermuda grass by 90 percent or more. Winter tillage is especially effective in areas where temperatures fall to 25°F or below. Using a spring-tooth harrow or a metal rake, work the rhizomes to the surface after every freeze. (A rotary tiller isn't as effective because it tends to bury the grass.) Miller recommends continued cultivation throughout the summer, once a week and after every rain, as soon as the soil becomes workable. Chances are, you'll never eradicate the Bermuda grass, but if you plant strawberries in the fall and mulch heavily with straw or other suitable materials, you shouldn't have much of a problem.

Coming Up Clover

Q. **If I plant clover as a cover crop and till it under in the spring, what's to keep the clover from coming up in all my spring and summer vegetables?**

A. If you sow clover as a cover crop in fall, it will survive the winter as young plants. Though it begins growing in spring before the ground can be worked, it does not have time to seed before you turn it under. When thoroughly buried, it rots, roots and all, and helps loosen the soil. Two weeks after turning under a cover crop, you can prepare a seedbed. You'll find few traces of the clover in the soil, and it will not regrow.

Dandelion Day?

Q. **I am the pastor of a church in Iowa whose building and grounds committee wants to spray the 1-acre-plus lawn for dandelions. Is there a practical nonchemical alternative?**

A. Yes. Although you probably won't be able to eliminate every last dandelion, it is possible to reduce their numbers to a tolerable level. Eliot Roberts, director of the Lawn Institute in Pleasant Hill, Tennessee, suggests the following program: As soon as the blossoms begin to open in the spring, have the Sunday school class (or other willing volunteers) pick off the flowers. This will prevent seeds—and thousands of new dandelion plants—from forming. Have a group of older children or adults take a sharp knife or forked dandelion weeder and cut the long taproots as far down as possible. If the prospect of pulling weeds on such a large lawn seems a bit formidable, you may want to concentrate initially on the area around church buildings, where the visual impact of a healthy green lawn is most important. Since a lawn that is cut too short is weak and favors the growth of weeds, Roberts recommends mowing northern lawns at a height of 1½ to 2 inches. Also, applying a slow-release, organic fertilizer such as Erth-Rite or Fertrell, available at some garden centers, will make the lawn fill in with strong, vigorous grass, squeezing out weeds in the process.

Monitoring Mint

Q. I would like to grow mint, but I've heard it will take over my garden. Is there any way it can be contained?

A. Mint can be contained by sinking metal barriers, like lawn or garden edging, 12 to 18 inches into the ground around the plants. The rapid spread of the plant is due to underground stems, called stolons. The stems generally travel a few inches below the soil, but if they hit a barrier they will dig deeper. Cyrus Hyde of Well-Sweep Herb Farm recommends reworking your mint beds every three years to maintain their vitality. In the fall he digs and replants the beds with some of the younger plants saved before digging. Digging the beds will also reduce the likelihood of runners escaping into the garden.

Perpetual Poison Ivy

Q. Is there a way to get rid of a patch of poison ivy without using weed killers?

A. Poison ivy is a perennial, so it's hard to kill. The safest time to work among the vines is in winter when the leaves are gone. Keep your eye on the patch in fall and learn to identify the plant in its dormant stage. Be careful during any season. Bruised or broken stems and roots exude the same rash-causing oil as the leaves. And the oil can remain active for months on gloves, shoes, and clothing. The best approach is to clip vines and creepers to within 1 inch of the ground and never let them grow higher. Even though the plant is able to creep along by sending out long shoots, eventually the absence of aboveground foliage will affect the plant's reserves of strength. It also helps to cover the trimmed area with black plastic sheeting thoroughly anchored in place. On small patches, you can try pulling out the roots. It's best to do so in the early spring after the ground has thawed but while the plant is dormant. Never burn the vines, since the toxic oil that causes blisters will volatilize in the fire, and the smoke will contaminate you. Put on heavy clothes that cover as much of your body as possible, and wear cotton gloves that you can throw out when you're finished. Then put one hand inside a large trash bag so you can use the bag as an outer glove. As you gather roots and stems, fold the bag over them. You'll end up with a bagful of poison ivy without having to handle the mess twice, and very little will have touched your clothing.

Ducking Quack Grass

Q. I have battled quack grass for the last two years. I've tried thick straw and leaf mulches, but the quack grass either goes right underneath or comes up through the mulch. What more can I do?

A. Just keep pulling it. The trouble with quack grass is that its rhizomes—those long, ivory-white, spearlike stems underground—are so tenacious. Once established, this perennial grass spreads by both seeds and rhizomes. The seeds stay viable for four years or longer, and the rhizomes can shoot 2 feet underground (and through mulches) without surfacing. Quack grass is bad news for another reason—it excretes a toxin from its roots that inhibits the growth of some vegetables, especially corn. When you pull, try to get the main clump of roots beneath the leaves you're grabbing. Cutting the new topgrowth reduces the food reserves in the rhizomes, weakening them. Hoe or cultivate every week during the growing season. Spading late in the fall will kill many of the rhizomes by exposing them to drying and freezing. The thicker your mulch, the better. Heap on as many leaves, grass clippings, and straw as you can—at least a 6-inch layer. If that doesn't keep the rhizomes from branching out, spread a layer of black plastic over the mulch and anchor it securely. You can also sow an early-spring smother crop like buckwheat. This fast-growing, fibrous-rooted plant will establish itself in a month and shade out the quack grass. After two years of continuous cover-cropping, the quack grass should be gone.

Sedge Advice

Q. Nutsedge is a very tough and troublesome plant in my garden. I have been told that the roots are edible and commonly used in Europe. Can you tell me how to cook it?

A. There are a number of members of the sedge family that go under the name nutsedge. The member of this family most gardeners have come to know and loath is *Cyperus esculentus*, an edible perennial plant that reproduces by seeds and tubers. It inhabits cultivated fields and gardens. Like all sedges, it prefers wet soils and hates well-drained soil. Proper drainage is one way to control any member of the sedge family in your garden. The most practical way to control them in large areas is to allow the field to lie fallow for a year. Nutsedge's small tubers may be boiled, peeled, and seasoned, or even toasted and used as a substitute for coffee. In Europe, nutsedge tubers have been used for flour. Harvesting the tubers is also a good means of control.

Sumac Solution

Q. How can I stop my neighbor's sumac from invading my yard?

A. Although sumac plants are lovely to look at and are valued for their aromatic red autumn foliage and velvety red fruits, they tend to sprawl wherever they can. The shrubs multiply by sending out underground runners, which form a close mat beneath the soil. Although these shallow, spreading roots control erosion, they dominate other vegetation. To stop sumac from spreading, mow it every week during the summer months. Using a spade and pickaxe, dig out as many root runners as you can and compost them.

Thistle

Thistle Do It

Q. Can you tell me a way to get thistles out of my garden that really works? Years of chopping, tilling, and mulching have only made them worse. This summer I tried covering a 12-foot-square area with black plastic for three months, but shortly after I removed the plastic, the area was covered with thistle sprouts.

A. You're probably fighting the Canada thistle (*Cirsium arvense*). It's one of the most difficult perennial weeds to control because of its rhizomes (underground stems), which can travel 20 feet a season. That's why covering a small area with mulch won't work. However, a properly applied mulch is the best technique to use with thistles, according to Dr. Thomas Cordey of Delaware Valley College in Doylestown, Pennsylvania. Cordey, who has done extensive field studies on the performance of different materials, recommends a plastic mulch for warm-season crops and shredded paper for cool-season crops. Straw laid down at least 3 inches thick will also smother thistles. But he found that the weeds were able to come through a leaf mulch. Since Canada thistles are perennial, their rhizomes will lie dormant for three or four years, so your weed control program must be consistent. In addition to mulching, Cordey suggests plowing the garden deeply in fall to bring the rhizomes to the surface. Avoid rototilling the garden at any time. Tilling cuts the rhizomes, and each piece becomes a new plant. And any root pieces left on the tines can spread the weed problem to new areas of your garden. Cover-cropping isn't effective, either, says Cordey, because thistles can outcompete the cover.

Thistle vs. Lawn

Q. Is there any organic way to remove thistles from a lawn? I have tried digging them up with little success—there are far too many, and they seem to be too well established.

A. Unfortunately, short of large-scale mulching (see "Thistle Do It," above), or plowing the ground and starting over, digging thistles up is the best solution. The digging should be followed by repeated hoeings, for any piece of root left in the soil will produce new plants. Cut thistles whenever you can see them. Early in the season, this weed accumulates enormous food reserves in its roots. But as soon as the thistle matures and flowers, the reserves diminish. Weaken it by cutting at the base at the onset of flowering. If you can cut just before a rain, so much the better. The cut stem is hollow, and rainwater accumulates in it. If the temperature is sufficiently high, mold may result and hasten the destruction of the plant.

Index

A

Acer negundo. See Box elder

Acer nigrum. See Maple(s), black

Acer platanoides. See Maple(s), Norway

Acer rubrum. See Maple(s), red

Acer saccharinum. See Maple(s), silver

Acer saccharum. See Maple(s), sugar

Acid soil, 26–27, 84
    indicator plants for, 22

Actinidia arguta. See Kiwifruit

Actinidia chinensis. See Kiwifruit

Actinomycetes scabies. See Potato scab

Adobe soil, 23–24

Adzuki beans, 95

African violet, 260, 262–63

Agapanthus, 230

Ajuga, 232

Alder, 245

Alfalfa, 16, 22, 62, 66

Allium, 294

Allspice, Carolina, 256

Almonds, 208–9

Alternaria dauci. See Leaf blight

Alternaria leaf spot, 126

Aluminum, greensand content of, 34

Aluminum foil, as mulch, 285

Alyssum, sweet, 218

Amaranth, 152–53

Amaranthus caudatus. See Amaranth

Amaranthus cruentus. See Amaranth

Amaranthus hypochondriacus. See Amaranth

Amaranthus retroflexus. See Pigweed

Amaryllis, 230, 263–64

Anise, 233, 294

Annual flowers, 218–23

Ant(s), 52, 195, 248, 288
    aphids and, 293, 294–95
    fire, 297
    leaf-cutter, 300
    winged, 293

Anthracnose
    dogwood and, 247
    melons and, 109
    strawberries and, 172
    tomatoes and, 82–83
    walnuts and, 214

Sawdust
  as compost, 47–48
  as fertilizer, 24, 37–38
Sawflies, 282
  currant, 181
Scab, 195–96
  apple, 196
  potato, 133–34
Scale, 189, 248
Scarlet runner bean, 91
Sclerotinia sclerotiorum. See
  Stem rot
Sclerotium rolfsi. See Southern
  blight
Scorzonera, 164
Scotch heather, 253–54
Scrub oak, 22
Seaweed, 31–32, 261, 292
Seaweed extract, 55, 56
Secale cereale. See Rye, winter
Sedge broom, 22
Sedge peat, 33
Seed(s)
  certified, 7–8
  fungicide-coated, 7, 92, 281
  germination of, 5–6
    bottom heat for, 9
    soil temperature for, 8–9,
      72
  germination percentage of, 5–6
  germination test of, 5
  hybrid, 6
  old, 5
  from standard stock, 6
  storage of, 4–5
Seed-corn maggots, 150
Seedling(s)
  damping-off disease of, 11
  hardening-off of, 11–12
  light requirements of, 10
  potting mix for, 41
  transplantation of, 9, 16, 77,
    81, 218–19
Seed-weevils, 156
Seek, 123
Septic tank, 16
Septoria leaf spot, 81
Sewage, as garden contaminant,
  16
Sewage sludge
  as compost, 48–49, 51
  as fertilizer, 35–36
Shading
  of garden, 3
  of lawn, 239, 240, 241
Shasta daisy, 223
Sheep fescue, 307–8
Shrubs, 15, 251–57. *See also*
  names of individual shrubs

Shuckworms, hickory, 210, 211
Sicilian fennel, 161
Silkworms, cecropia, 293
Silt, 22
Silver maple, 215
Sitka spruce, 251
Skunk cabbage, 22
Slugs, 22, 98
Smudge pot, 199
Smut, corn, 151–52
Snails, 22
Snakes, 305
Snapdragon, 218
Snowberries, 256
Soap(s)
  biodegradable, 15
  insecticidal, 107, 196, 245,
    247, 251, 261–62, 294
  in washing-machine water, 15,
    16
Soil(s)
  acid, 26–27, 84
    indicator plants for, 22
  adobe, 23–24
  aeration of, 21, 23–24
  clay, 12–13, 23, 25
  clods in, 12–13
  color of, 23
  compaction of, 13, 24, 144
  loamy, 13, 22–23
  minerals in, 2, 21–22
  moisture content of, 12–13
  pH of, 25, 26–28
    hydrangea color and, 255
  for potting. *See* Potting soil
  preparation of, 12–14
    for orchard, 186
  salt content of, 25
  solarization of, 25
  testing of, 26–27
  wet, 21, 22
  working of, 12–14
Soil fungus, 283
Soil-heating cable, 9
Soil mix. *See* Potting soil
Soil testing, 26–27
Soil thermometer, 9
Soldier bug, 294
Sooty blotch, 196
Sooty mold, 196, 198
Sorrel, 22
Sour gum, 22
Southern blight, 224–25
Southernwood, 235
Southwest injury, 200
Sow bugs, 301
Sowing, 8, 9
Soybean(s), 91, 94, 186
  as deer repellent, 190

Rodale Press, Inc., publishes RODALE'S ORGANIC GARDENING®,
the all-time favorite gardening magazine.
For information on how to order your subscription,
write to RODALE'S ORGANIC GARDENING®, Emmaus, PA 18098.